D0269508

G.S.

11

011

4 3 3 9 5 0 1 0 0 3 0 9 8 4 4 2 7 7 2 6 0 1 2

The ANGEL of MONS

The ANGEL
Phantom Soldiers and Ghostly Guardians
of MONS

DAVID CLARKE

WILEY

Published in the UK in 2004 by   John Wiley & Sons Ltd, The Atrium, Southern Gate, Chichester, West Sussex PO19 8SQ, England
Telephone (+44) 1243 779777

Email (for orders and customer service enquiries): cs-books@wiley.co.uk
Visit our Home Page on www.wileyeurope.com or www.wiley.com

Copyright © 2004 David Clarke

All Rights Reserved. No part of this publication may be reproduced, stored in a retrieval system or transmitted in any form or by any means, electronic, mechanical, photocopying, recording, scanning or otherwise, except under the terms of the Copyright, Designs and Patents Act 1988 or under the terms of a licence issued by the Copyright Licensing Agency Ltd, 90 Tottenham Court Road, London W1T 4LP, UK, without the permission in writing of the Publisher. Requests to the Publisher should be addressed to the Permissions Department, John Wiley & Sons Ltd, The Atrium, Southern Gate, Chichester, West Sussex PO19 8SQ, England, or emailed to permreq@wiley.co.uk, or faxed to (+44) 1243 770571.

This publication is designed to provide accurate and authoritative information in regard to the subject matter covered. It is sold on the understanding that the Publisher is not engaged in rendering professional services. If professional advice or other expert assistance is required, the services of a competent professional should be sought.

David Clarke has asserted his right under the Copyright, Designs and Patents Act 1988, to be identified as the author of this work.

Other Wiley Editorial Offices

John Wiley & Sons Inc., 111 River Street, Hoboken, NJ 07030, USA

Jossey-Bass, 989 Market Street, San Francisco, CA 94103-1741, USA

Wiley-VCH Verlag GmbH, Boschstr. 12, D-69469 Weinheim, Germany

John Wiley & Sons Australia Ltd, 33 Park Road, Milton, Queensland 4064, Australia

John Wiley & Sons (Asia) Pte Ltd, 2 Clementi Loop #02-01, Jin Xing Distripark, Singapore 129809

John Wiley & Sons Canada Ltd, 22 Worcester Road, Etobicoke, Ontario, Canada M9W 1L1

British Library Cataloguing in Publication Data

A catalogue record for this book is available from the British Library

ISBN 0-470-86277-7

Typeset by Mathematical Composition Setters Ltd, Salisbury, Wiltshire
Printed and bound in Great Britain by T.J. International Ltd, Padstow, Cornwall
This book is printed on acid-free paper responsibly manufactured from sustainable forestry in which at least two trees are planted for each one used for paper production.

10 9 8 7 6 5 4 3 2 1

To my great-uncle, Sgt. Major John Charles Hibbert, 1896–1975, of the King's Own Scottish Borderers, awarded the Croix de Guerre for distinguished service, courage and self-sacrifice during the Flanders offensiv

PORTSMOUTH CITY COUNCIL	
C800173122	
H J	08/06/2004
133.1	£16.99
0470862777	

PORTSMOUTH
CENTRAL LIBRARY
TEL: 023 9281 9311

G.S.

Contents

Acknowledgements

Numerous individuals and organisations have provided assistance in the research and writing of this book. I owe my biggest debt of all to my family and friends who have supported and encouraged me throughout, particularly my partner Carolyn who edited the first draft and never gave up on the idea. Steve Payne was, as always, a constant source of information on the more obscure byways of the First World War and its battlefields. Vanessa Toulmin and Richard Jenkins were pillars of strength. Jane Waudby kindly conducted a search of German newspapers on my behalf.

I wish to thank my agent Chelsey Fox for persistence in finding a home for this project and to Sally Smith and everyone at Wiley for seeing it through to the end.

Of the organisations that provided material and permissions I wish to thank:

The British Academy for providing a research grant which made the original research possible.

The Imperial War Museum and specifically Alan Jeffries of the Department of Exhibits and Firearms for access to a range of material related to the Angel of Mons and other wartime legends.

The British Library at St Pancras and the Newspaper Library at Colindale.

The National Archives at Kew and the Bristol Record Office.

BBC Radio 4, particularly Chris Morris and Martin Kurzik.

The Liddell Hart Centre for Military Archives, King's College, University of London.

The Liverpool Scottish Museum Trust.

Ann Clayton and Dr A.J. Peacock of the Western Front Association.

The City of Mons Tourism Bureau: Fernand Martin and Michel Vasko.

The Friends of Arthur Machen and particularly Adrian Eckersley, Mark Valentine and Roger Dobson for access to John Gawsworth's unpublished manuscript, *The Life of Arthur Machen*.

For assistance with picture research, thanks to Jill Jeffries, Hilary Evans and the Mary Evans Picture Library, Janet Bord of the Fortean Picture Library and John Weeks who provided a copy of the original music for the 'Angel of Mons Waltz'.

Of the many friends, colleagues and fellow researchers who have provided material I wish to thank the following and apologize in advance to anyone who is missing from this list: Harold Holwell, Danny Sullivan, Nigel Watson, Granville Oldroyd, Andy Roberts, Kevin McClure, Emma Heathcote-James, Fay Weldon, John Harlow, Lyn Macdonald, Peter Hassall, Gillian Bennett, Ian Jones, Philip Haythornthwaite, David Sutton and *Fortean Times* and *This England* magazine.

The author wishes to acknowledge the permission of A.M. Heath & Co. Ltd. for permission to reproduce Arthur Machen's story, 'The Bowmen' (1914).

Introduction

The Angel of Mons is the most inspiring, most widely believed and influential legend to emerge from the First World War. Versions of the story have been translated into almost every language. Thousands have come to believe the appearance of angels at Mons is fact. The legend has continued to gain momentum, passed on by word of mouth, and has established itself in the history books. Today, almost a century later, versions continue to be circulated via modern media such as the Internet. But where did it all begin? And how did it come to take such a hold on our collective imagination?

The Battle of Mons was fought in the opening weeks of the conflict between a small British force and a huge German army advancing into Belgium. Within months of the battle, in August 1914, a story spread that British troops had escaped defeat because a supernatural vision appeared on the battlefield and brought the German attack to a sudden halt.

There were many different versions of the event but most agreed that at a critical moment when all seemed lost, the British soldiers saw a wonderful cloud or bright light in the sky. This was followed by the appearance of a knight in armour, mounted on a white horse, who the troops recognized as St George, leading them on against the enemy. One version claimed the saint was accompanied by a company of bowmen who showered the Germans with deadly arrows, while another described how a company of angels, robed in white, appeared to form a protective barrier between them and the enemy.

It was the *idea* of angels at Mons that quickly caught the imagination of the British public, who longed for a miracle to bring them a swift victory and an end to the war. The legend of the 'Angel of Mons', born a year after the battle, has since become familiar to millions around the world. Although in strictly military terms Mons was little more than a skirmish compared to the terrible losses suffered by the British Army at the Somme, belief in a miracle at Mons lived on as a symbol of hope for the remainder of the war. Across the British Empire many believed divine intervention in 1914 signified that Britain and her Allies, despite dreadful losses, would eventually prevail against the Germans.

Acres of newsprint and dozens of books, pamphlets and religious tracts were devoted to the Angel of Mons in English-speaking countries during the First World War. At the height of conflict, sceptics and believers fought their own pitched battles to prove and disprove the truth or otherwise of the evidence for the event. Journalist and author Arthur Machen maintained throughout his life that the legend arose entirely from a short story, called 'The Bowmen', that he wrote in the aftermath of the battle [see pp. 247–50]. But an opposing army of writers sought to persuade their readers that supernatural intervention really did occur at Mons and, furthermore, that soldiers continued to experience divine powers on the battlefield throughout the course of the war. It is virtually impossible to untangle this web of facts, fiction, fable and fantasy and discover the truth behind this intriguing phenomenon.

One of the believers was an occult writer, Rosa Stuart, who published a collection of supernatural experiences from the Western Front in *Dreams and Visions of the War* in 1917, the year in which the Third Battle of Ypres (Passchendaele) was fought. Her account provides an insight into the kind of testimony upon which the Angel of Mons legend was built and illustrates the problems faced by those who seek to find historical fact at its core.

In her book Stuart describes her chance meeting in a military hospital with a veteran who fought at Mons. The man, a sergeant, survived the battle and the subsequent retreat where thousands of his pals were killed and wounded, only to suffer a leg wound in a subsequent action in 1915, which meant a return to London for treatment. His face, she said, 'bore traces of the hard times he had witnessed, for there were tired lines at the corners of his mouth, and at times I saw a far-away expression in his eyes'.

His mother, who was visiting at the time, was overheard to ask: 'Is it true that when things looked black against you, St George appeared with a company of his bowmen, and led our troops to victory instead of defeat?'

Before he could answer the soldier in the next bed, a new recruit in Kitchener's New Army, interrupted, 'It isn't true,' he said. 'The whole story was invented by a journalist. He's written to the papers and told them so.'

The sergeant from Mons then turned to the soldier and said: 'I dunno about the story the writer chap said he made up but all I do know is I saw the vision with my own eyes, and that's how I can say it's true.'

There was a moment of silence as the man's mother gave a little shudder. A deep flush rose to the cheeks of the man from Mons as he saw what was expected of him. He spoke slowly as the whole ward listened in silence:

I'll never forget that sultry evening in August. We'd been marching for sixty hours on end, and scarce a taste of food had passed our lips ... On and on them Boches were coming, push, push, pushing us back. It looked as though they were going to close upon us, and all would be up. Many of the chaps grew so faint and heart-sick they didn't seem to care what happened, and I couldn't blame them, for though I tried to hearten them best as I could, I was feeling a bit that way myself. Weary and footsore, we'd just reached the outskirts of one of those quaint French villages, with the streets all narrow and cobbled, and the cottages roofed with thatch, when the alarm came that the Boches were once more upon us, crowds of 'em, giving battle all along the line, outnumbering us by seven to one at least. And where our lot was it was the most critical part of the line. We must hold it or be wiped out, not only ourselves, but most of the British Army too.

Could we hold it? It seemed hopeless. The enemy cannon were thundering, hundreds of men were dropping around like flies, and there wasn't many of us all told. Why hadn't we got guns like them? was the thought that kept coming into my head. 'It's hopeless,' gasped my pal Billy, 'it's ten to one against us, guns and men.'

It was one of those very dark nights of August. Somehow all of a sudden there was a stillness in the night for a few seconds. The guns stopped. I looked up, and saw the sky bright with a wonderful light, and then suddenly, well in advance of us all, I made out the figure of a man on a great white horse. There were two other figures there, one on each side of him; but it was only the face of the man in the centre that I remember. He was dressed like one of those pictures you see of old-time knights in armour, and he seemed to wave his hands, urging us on.

From that moment I knew we were going to hold our own in the fight. Bill, my pal, knew it too. He told me so afterwards, just before he died from a bullet wound in the lung. Poor Bill! Over half of us had gone under, but those that remained fought so well that they beat off every attack, and in another twenty-four hours the tables had turned. Instead of the Boches pushing us back, it was we and the French as was pushing back the Boches.[1]

This story is just one of hundreds of similar accounts that were circulated, published and believed at a dizzying rate during the 'war to end all wars'. In an era before radio and television when the content of newspapers was heavily censored, stories of angels and saints on the battlefield were as familiar to the masses as flying saucers and UFOs are to people today. The society that produced the Angel of Mons was the same one that experienced bravery, courage and terrible loss of life that would leave an indelible imprint upon future generations. As was the case with myths and legends that emerged during earlier conflicts, the true facts behind the Angel of Mons have become obscured by the fog of war.

This book will disentangle the many threads that make up the legend and answer the fundamental questions that remain almost a century after these events. Did all these stories evolve from an innocent tale of fiction that was meant to offer comfort to readers in England? Or were some of them based upon real experiences? If that was indeed the case, then what was the nature of those experiences? Did angels really appear at Mons and during other battles of the First World War, or is there another explanation that does not involve the supernatural? For instance, were angel stories deliberately fabricated by the authorities to cover up the terrible losses in the early days of the war? Or were they carefully used to encourage an army of new recruits to fight on in dreadful conditions, safe in the knowledge that God was on their side and victory was therefore certain?

The supernatural in war

Today wars are fought in a detached, virtual universe ruled by computers and satellites. As an audience of millions watch on television an armoury of hi-tech weapons are programmed to find their targets hundreds of miles away from command centres. Smart-bombs and Stealth aircraft have now largely replaced the recruits armed with rifles and bayonets who, almost a century ago, went 'over the top' into the killing fields of No Man's Land, or fought in the jungles of Asia and the deserts of North Africa.

While the technology by which wars are fought has changed beyond recognition, belief in divine and supernatural intervention on the battlefield remains. From the earliest times people have placed faith in miracles, signs and portents, and that tradition continues today in many forms. Some of the world's greatest generals and war leaders have sought divine guidance at times of great peril and have prayed for direct intervention in battle. Another aspect of war that remains unchanged is the human capacity to weave myths and legends around events that are perceived to be mysterious or miraculous. In this way mankind tries to establish a level of control over unpredictable events, the outcome of which appears to depend not on chance but upon the will of some higher power.

Two years after the attack upon the World Trade Centre on 11 September 2001 an opinion poll found that 48 per cent of Americans believed that the USA had special protection from God for most of its history.[2] In a speech to West Point graduates in 2002 the US President, George W. Bush, proclaimed that 'we are in a conflict between good and evil, and America will call evil by its name'. Bush turned to his evangelical beliefs in the aftermath of the crisis and came to believe God had called upon him to engage the forces of evil. Surveys have found that one in three Americans describe themselves as evangelical Christians. Furthermore a 2002 *Time*/CNN poll found that 59 per cent of Americans accept the literal truth of the 'end times' predicted in the book of Revelation, which they believe will end in a final battle with the antichrist during their lifetime.[3]

If these figures are accurate then millions of people will interpret the outcome of the War on Terror not as being decided through military might, but as being divinely ordained. Ironically, among some radical Muslims, the USA itself is portrayed as the antichrist and 'the great Satan'. These types of fundamentalist interpretations and misinterpretations of history are typical of times when threats against civilizations are perceived to be apocalyptic in nature. During the Second World War many people believed that Adolf Hitler was the incarnation of the antichrist, and the German kaiser was portrayed in a similar fashion a quarter of a century earlier. Furthermore, the revival of faith in miracles and prophecies as a reaction to a seemingly irreconcilable enemy is neither a new phenomenon nor is it confined to the West during the War on Terror.

Anxiety and uncertainty provide a fertile breeding ground for a range of fringe beliefs, conspiracy theories and ancient prophecies. One example is the contemporary obsession with finding significance and meaning in the prophecies of the

medieval mystic Nostradamus, which also found a new lease of life following the 11 September atrocities. Similarly, at the time of the English Civil War, apocalyptic predictions and stories of supernatural visions were common. These included claims that a phantom army had appeared in the sky following the Battle of Edgehill (see Chapter 1). This and other stories were widely published and interpreted by both sides as omens or messages sent directly by God.[4]

In both world wars of the twentieth century Great Britain and her Allies faced the prospect of defeat by an immensely strong and seemingly invincible foe. German militarism and fascism were eventually defeated through a combination of enormous sacrifice of life and overwhelming force. Yet stories such as the Angel of Mons have grown up that seek to persuade us to believe that civilization was saved not by human will and ingenuity, but by divine intervention. The 'miracle' at Mons now forms part of a semi-official mythology that provides a deep well of reassurance for the British nation at times of crisis. For many in Britain divine intervention on the battlefields of Europe in 1914 is not a myth but an article of faith that underpins and shadows the 'accepted history', both on an individual and wider level.

Meanwhile, even those who profess not to hold religious faith cannot escape the pervasive influence of the supernatural in war. As a microcosm of beliefs held by nations or religions, soldiers have always been careful to acknowledge the role of spiritual forces in battle. The folklore of all armed forces are replete with stories that attempt to explain the supernatural and uncanny. Every war has stories of phantom soldiers appearing on the battlefields, of superstitions concerning lucky and unlucky objects and people, and miraculous escapes attributed to the intervention of guardian angels. These individual narratives and traditions have become such an accepted part of the folklore of war they have been adapted into the plots of numerous movies and TV programmes.

Individual soldiers continue to place their trust in a variety of charms and amulets which they believe will protect them in battle. During the Iraq War of 2003, pilots of US Black Hawk helicopters – the most sophisticated fighting machines in existence – insisted on carrying lucky charms. Copies of Psalm 91, 'the psalm of protection', remain popular, and were also carried into battle during the First World War. Indeed, some military personnel have come to rely so much upon the protection provided by charms of this kind that they are willing to risk both official reprimands and the ridicule of their peers.[5]

The most impressive collection of such charms dates from the First World War, when superstition was widespread among rank-and-file soldiers. The Imperial War Museum has preserved many amulets and talismans that were carried to the Western Front by soldiers of both Allied and Central powers in the 1914–18 war.[6] The motley collection includes religious medals of St Christopher, St George and the Virgin in addition to 'lucky' stones and horseshoes that were part of a far older folk tradition. These objects represent a curious mixture of Christian and pagan beliefs and at first sight they appear to be more representative of the material culture of a medieval army than one drawn from a twentieth-century society. Whatever the source of their power, the continuing use of these charms indicates the survival of belief and superstition in modern armies that has its roots in the medieval mind.

Traditional historians may scoff at the suggestion that occult forces and magical spells could have played any role in the outcome of military campaigns in modern times. We learn the accepted view of history from books that assure us that wars are fought and won purely by military might, by belligerents who control the greater resources, or have access to the latest technological developments. But is this really the whole story, or have the magical spells of the past simply been replaced with a range of superstitions more suitable for a modern hi-tech society? The intention is often the same: an appeal for divine protection in battle. There is a considerable body of evidence to suggest that in times of great peril and crisis even the most rational war leaders will turn to their god or gods for support. There are many stories

and anecdotes of this kind from the medieval era and others from recent times. For example, in the reign of Queen Elizabeth I the destruction of the Spanish Armada in an Atlantic storm was widely attributed in England to divine intervention. The victory was celebrated in England by the striking of a special medal containing the words: 'God blew and they were scattered.' In Spain the defeat was attributed to black magic employed by Sir Francis Drake. His name was easily latinized into Draco (the dragon) and it was widely believed that his power 'to garner winds and to loose or bind them at his will' was the result of a diabolical pact.[7]

This is not the only account that attributes military victory against overwhelming odds not to military might, but to dramatic and unexpected changes in the weather, as if some unseen force or power was working behind the scenes to influence the outcome. Even when viewed purely in tactical terms, the weather can often prove decisive in battle, particularly in terms of the effects of rain or storm upon a battlefield or marine landings.

Consider the story that grew out of a crucial point in the invasion of Nazi-occupied Europe. In December 1944 the Allied armies were spread out and pushing towards the borders of Germany at Arnhem when a weak point in the front line opened up. On 16 December, while heavy rain, thick fog and mist grounded the Allied air force, the Nazis took advantage of the situation to launch a surprise attack in the Ardennes. For several days, the fate of the Allied forces hung in the balance. Everything depended upon a break in the weather. It was at this point that the US General George Patton, a devout Christian, telephoned the Third Army Chaplain and said: 'Do you have a good prayer for weather? We must do something about those rains if we are to win this war.' The Chief Chaplain at the time, Mgr James H. O'Neill typed up an improvised prayer on a piece of card, which read:

Almighty and most merciful Father, we humbly beseech Thee, of Thy great goodness, to restrain these immoderate rains with which we have had to contend. Grant us fair weather for Battle. Graciously hearken to us as soldiers who call upon Thee that, armed with Thy power, we may advance from victory to victory, and crush the oppression and wickedness of our enemies and establish Thy justice among men and nations.[8]

Patton ordered 250 000 copies of the prayer to be printed on a special Christmas greeting card to be distributed among his troops, personally signed by the General. In written instructions to his chaplains, Patton ordered them to urge all his fighting men to pray hard as 'this Army needs assurance and the faith that God is with us. With prayer, we cannot fail.' On 20 December, to the consternation of the Germans, the weather broke and Allied planes were able to attack the massed Panzer divisions in the Ardennes. The Nazi offensive was halted.

Was the change in the weather at the crucial point in the battle purely a result of chance? Did God answer Patton's Prayer, or was some other mysterious force at work to influence the weather at the crucial moment? Perhaps better questions would be: Are any of these stories factual? Or are they just another example of propaganda designed to encourage and reassure soldiers that God is on their side and victory is near?

Myths and legends in war

The First World War was the first conflict that fully harnessed the inventions developed during the Industrial Revolution for destructive purposes. For four years millions of troops were thrown into battle against massed artillery bombardment, machine guns, tanks and poison gas. Between 1914 and 1918 Britain and her Allies lost a staggering 5 100 000 soldiers; Germany and the Central powers a further 3 500 000.[9] Many millions more were maimed for life, physically and psychologically, by their experiences. For the first time in history, civilians hundreds of miles behind the lines were exposed to indiscriminate attack from the air, and at sea submarine warfare had been developed. Never before had the boundary between the worlds of the living and the dead become so thin and close both for civilians and those trapped in the hellish trenches. These factors seem to underpin the widespread revival of supernatural belief that grew and spread to all levels of society.

It is hardly surprising that out of the unspeakable terror of trench warfare there emerged among soldiers what the social historian Paul Fussell described as 'a world of reinvigorated myth'.[10] Myth is defined by the *Oxford English Dictionary* as 'a traditional narrative sometimes popularly regarded as historical but unauthenticated'.[11] Other examples include the Greek myths, the creation stories found in ancient Babylonia and the book of Genesis. Myths have always been created and spread by human beings in order to explain and make sense of the great mysteries of life, death and the origins of the universe. In our modern, logical, secular age the term 'myth' has become synonymous with falsity and its very use places an immediate value judgement on whether a story is 'true' or 'false' when in fact no such easy distinction can necessarily be made. This new definition of myth is a by-product of the mechanistic, scientific view of the universe that is characteristic of the modern world. In this book I will employ the term not as an explanation in itself but as it was defined by Bronislaw Malinowski in 1926:

[a] Myth fulfils ... an indispensable function: it expresses, enhances, and codifies belief; it safeguards and enhances morality; it vouches for the efficiency of ritual and contains practical rules for the guidance of man. Myth is thus a vital ingredient of human civilisation; it is not an idle tale, but a hard-worked active force.[12]

The function of myth, according to Malinowski, is to 'strengthen tradition and endow it with a greater value and prestige by

11

tracing it back to a higher, better, more supernatural reality of initial events'.

Starved of real news and increasingly sceptical of the written word, many soldiers of the First World War turned to the pre-industrial world of myth in order to find meaning and order in the chaos of trench warfare. Marc Bloch was a French infantryman during the war and in the trenches he discovered 'a prodigious renewal of oral tradition, the ancient mother of myths and legends'. In the midst of the destruction and death, rumours and myths spread like wildfire from the trenches to the Home Front and back again. 'That such a myth-ridden world could take shape in the midst of a war representing a triumph of modern industrialism, materialism, and mechanism is an anomaly worth considering,' Fussell wrote in *The Great War in Modern Memory*. One outcome of the reversion to a medieval mindset was 'a plethora of very un-modern superstitions, talismans, wonders, miracles, relics, legends and rumours'.[13]

A legend is a story set in the modern world, which is presented as miraculous, uncanny or bizarre and which is 'told as if it were true'. For the British soldiers, and to some extent the Allies as a whole, the Angel of Mons was the most widespread of all the legends of the First World War. While many other stories and rumours were short-lived, the idea of angels protecting the British Army against the brutal Germans endured longer than any other and attained a level of immortality. The Angel of Mons is frequently portrayed in popular history books and newspaper stories as an icon that provided hope and faith in the dark years of 1914 to 1918. These more superficial accounts fail to provide any really satisfying explanation of the origins of the story, or the level of importance that was attached to belief in supernatural intervention at Mons that persisted in England until the end of the conflict. Likewise, historians of the war have tended to portray the Angel of Mons either as a quaint historical footnote, or the most influential of the preposterous stories spawned by a mixture of wishful thinking and grief.

Earlier surveys of the myths and legends of the war that have included the Angel of Mons in their lists have relied upon earlier, second-hand and often poorly researched accounts for their source material. Few have used primary sources from the war itself as their starting point and until now no comprehensive account of the legend and its evolution has been published. In this book I use the phrase 'Angel of Mons' to refer not just to a single vision or sighting during the battle itself but to define the wider phenomenon, including the revival of interest in the legend during the present day. The phrase incorporates a host of other visions and incidents that took place during retreat from Mons, the Battle of the Marne and other actions during the First World War. This includes stories describing not only traditional angels but also visions of angels as archers, cavalry, bowmen, St George, Joan of Arc and other supernatural personages. Readers will also find frequent references to 'angels' or 'Angels of Mons' in the plural throughout the chapters that follow, where the context refers to experiences with more than one supernatural entity.

This book is not only an inquiry into the facts surrounding what Kevin McClure has described as 'the single most influential paranormal event in British history'.[14] It is also the story of my personal quest for the truth, as far as truth can be reliably ascertained, behind a fascinating moment in history. The Angel of Mons is a mystery that would have tested the detective skills of Sherlock Holmes, whose creator Arthur Conan Doyle was one of the leading figures in the spiritual revival that followed the First World War. My aim is to prune away the many layers of belief and interpretation that have clouded the events at Mons, and to employ the maxim of Holmes, who claimed that 'when you have eliminated the impossible, whatever remains, however improbable, must be the truth'.[15]

In writing and researching this book, I was to discover that to divine the 'truth' behind myths and legends is never a straightforward process. I began to sympathize with Gustav

Davidson who wrote in the introduction to his *Dictionary of Angels* (1969) that:

> At this stage of the quest I was literally bedevilled by angels. They stalked and leaguered me, by night and day. I could not tell the evil from the good ... I moved, indeed, in a twilight zone of tall presences ... I passed from terror to trance, from intimations of realms unguessed at to the conviction that, beyond the reach of our senses, beyond the arch of all our experience sacred and profound, there was only – to use an expression of Paul's in I Timothy 4 – 'fable and endless genealogy.'[16]

In my earlier books and articles I have combined the techniques of the investigative journalist with a penchant for historical detective work to scrutinize the facts that lie behind other modern 'mysteries'. This methodology has worked well when employed to examine more recent claims where key documents could be examined and living witnesses or participants in events could be traced and interviewed. But with the Angel of Mons I was separated from the events that were the subject of my inquiry by almost a century. To add to the problems, all the major participants were beyond reach and what documentation that did exist was largely misleading.

When historian Michael Wood set out to find the 'real Shakespeare' he described the process as 'a historical detective story, an Elizabethan whodunit' and that was how I approached the unravelling of the facts of the Angel of Mons.[17] Wood was following a well-trodden path into 400-year-old tax records and property purchases to reconstruct the life of a man whose work is familiar to millions around the world. My quest for the truth behind the Angel of Mons followed a similar route, but this one was lacking any of the clear or established signposts traditionally used by historians for navigation. Shakespeare's life and death are matters of historical fact, and experts will continue to argue about their precise interpretation, but no one seriously doubts Shakespeare existed. How does one apply the same historical

methodology to reconstruct the birth, evolution and future trajectory of a legend?

The most effective approach to the investigation of supernatural belief is to approach the evidence with an open mind. Folklorist David Hufford has appealed to researchers who collect supernatural experiences not to disbelieve or reject the stories of informants on the basis of their own beliefs and prejudices. Earlier last century Charles Fort, the eccentric American collector of anomalies and oddities, ridiculed attempts by scientists to reject and ignore inconvenient data that could not be explained in terms of current knowledge of the workings of the universe. In *New Lands* (1924) he wrote:

> There's small chance of such phenomena being understood ... because everybody's a logician. Almost everybody reasons: 'There are not supernatural occurrences: therefore these alleged phenomena did not occur.'[18]

Fort believed all phenomena defined as 'supernatural' existed in a transient state between extremes and in examining them he employed the dictum that 'one measures a circle beginning anywhere'. Following his advice, I decided to open my inquiry into the Angel of Mons, not in 1914, but in the days when the intervention of angels and demons in human history were accepted as fact.

CHAPTER ONE

The unseen host

Now and then the western clouds after sunset assume a shape resembling that of a vast extended wing, as of a gigantic bird in full flight – the extreme tip nearly reaching the zenith, the body of the bird just below the horizon. The resemblance is sometimes so perfect that the layers of feathers are traceable by an imaginative eye. This, the old folk say, is the wing of the Archangel Michael, and it bodes no good to the evil ones among the nations, for he is on his way to execute a dread command.

Richard Jefferies, *Wild Life in a Southern County*, 1879[1]

From the beginning of recorded history there are stories of spectral armies seen in the sky and of visions appearing before war leaders on the eve of battle. The idea of divine intervention at the Battle of Mons in 1914 is only the most recent and best-known example of a tradition of belief in supernatural intervention that has become a fundamental element in world mythology. These traditions have very deep roots indeed.

In the ancient world the gods had an intimate and often stormy relationship with the world of humans. For instance, in the myths and legends of ancient Greece, the vengeful gods frequently intervened in earthly battles to provide assistance to the warriors whom they favoured, or to send plague and storm against those who had offended them. In early Hebrew tradition, the God Yahveh behaves in a very similar manner. He appears, speaks directly to individuals, and sends storms and thunder to punish both individuals and nations. Job, for instance, loses his sheep, his servants and ten of his children to storms and calls out, 'Why is there evil in the world?' The voice of Yahveh speaks to him from the midst of a whirlwind, explaining that he has ultimate control over nature, and that humans cannot understand the divine plan but should place their trust in his ultimate purpose.

These stories suggest that in the ancient world divine intervention occurred regularly, in a seemingly partisan manner that can appear arbitrary, cruel and even incomprehensible today. In the Old Testament, God exerts his power on the world by the use of the weather, sending storms, floods and earthquakes. The myth of a universal deluge is the most persistent and widespread of these early myths. In many early traditions, the flood marks the end of the age where gods directly interfered in human affairs and the beginning of a new era in which God became more distant and merciful.

The age of the angels

With the separation of the sacred from the profane, angels were necessary to act as messengers between humans and the distant God. The word 'angel' is derived from the Greek *aggelos* and is translated from the Hebrew *mal'akh*, which means 'messenger'. The role played by angels in the cosmic scheme has been the subject of dramatic changes in the transition from the ancient to the modern world.

Angels are closely associated with the monotheistic religions and first appear as supernatural entities in the early Zoroastrian cosmos, which exerted a heavy influence upon the evolution of Judaism. Zoroaster was born in Persia (Iran) around the beginning of the first millennium BC and the religion he founded was based around a cosmic battle between good and evil that was fought by angels and demons. Similar beliefs are found in Judaism, where the Old Testament God was portrayed as the 'Lord of Hosts' whose angel warriors fight against the forces of evil led by Satan. All these elements were eventually adopted and modified by Christianity and Islam, where angels are portrayed as benevolent and righteous. They are in effect the powers that oppose Satan, the 'fallen angel' and his demons, who symbolize the destructive power of the old gods. Judaism also adopted the Zoroastrian division of the universe into three realms, with heaven as the upper celestial region inhabited by Yahveh and his angels. Hell is the subterranean world of chaos and darkness that was the abode of Satan. The world inhabited by humans was positioned between the two, forming the battleground between the forces of good and evil.[2]

In the Old Testament, angels could be malevolent and murderous when they acted to enforce divine law or punish the wicked. In the early eighth century BC, Sennacherib, the King of Assyria, besieged and captured the fortified cities of Judah, demanding the payment of a huge tribute in gold and precious stones. As the Assyrian army rested overnight in their camp they were visited by an angel who killed 'every valiant warrior, leader and commander'.[3] The Israelites were frequently assisted by angel hosts particularly when the odds were heavily stacked against them. The second book of Kings describes how the prophet Elisha was surrounded by the armies of Assyria at Dothan. During the siege Elisha turned to his terrified servant and said: 'They that be with us are more than they that be with them', and prayed that his eyes be opened. At that moment the servant saw 'the mountain was full of horses and chariots of fire around Elisha' protecting them from the enemy forces.[4]

Another story describes how in the second century BC more divine horsemen appeared as Judas Maccabeus led his army in an uprising against Roman oppression. The army of Judas fought on against overwhelming odds and at the height of the battle the Romans saw 'five magnificent figures' in the sky, riding horses with golden bridles. The divine horsemen placed themselves at the head of the Jews and formed a protective circle around their leader. According to the Hebrew account, 'they launched arrows and thunderbolts at the enemy, who, confused and blinded, broke up in complete disorder.' Later in the same campaign and in the midst of a bitter siege of Jerusalem, a horseman appeared among them, 'arrayed in white, brandishing his golden weapons', and led them to victory.[5]

These Old Testament stories have become familiar precisely because of their biblical source, which has ensured their survival. What is less well known is that pagan nations had their own traditions of supernatural intervention in battle, which are less likely to have been preserved by the Christian scribes. The Romans had a tradition that attributed the outcome of the battle of Lake Regillus in 496 BC to appearance of the divine twins, Castor and Pollux, in the guise of phantom horsemen. In the *Lays of Ancient Rome* Lord Macaulay portrays the gods as armed and mounted on magnificent white steeds riding at the head of the legions. After the victory the twins carry the news of the victory with supernatural speed to Rome. A mark resembling a horse's hoof was later identified in the volcanic rock of the lake and it was believed this had been left by one of the celestial chargers.[6]

The angel hierarchy grew ever more complex in the first four centuries of the Christian era and on occasions the church had to move to end the worship of angels by some early sects. During this period angelology – the study of angels – was influenced by older pagan traditions and by the teachings of a sect known as the Gnostics, whose name means 'the knowing ones'. The Gnostics shared the old view of the universe as a battleground between good and evil forces and believed that angels controlled the movements of the stars and the four elements. A hierarchy of angels had emerged who were able to assume human form and, by their actions as God's messengers, bridge the boundary between heaven and earth.

The Bible identifies the three most important archangels as Michael, Gabriel and Raphael. St Michael is the warrior angel who leads the heavenly hosts in their war with Satan. He is often depicted in Christian art wearing elaborate armour and wielding a sword as he stamps on the defeated armies of evil. Beneath the archangels were lesser orders of angels, including the cherubim and the seraphim who surrounded the divine throne. The cherubim were described by the prophet Ezekiel as bizarre creatures with four wings and four faces (lion, ox, eagle and man) that travelled on fiery wheels surrounded by eyes. In the twentieth century, Ezekiel's vision of angels has been portrayed by some as a description of extraterrestrial beings visiting the earth in a fleet of flying saucers.[7]

This modern interpretation is the latest example of the way depictions of angels have reflected the culture and beliefs of the society that portrays them. Originally angels were depicted as androgynous youths or children, as it was believed they were created directly by God and could not reproduce. However, Renaissance art represented them as adolescent males and indeed the original Greek word *aggelos* is a masculine noun. By the late Gothic period a further change had occurred, with increasing emphasis being placed in Christian art upon the beauty and compassion of angels. This led to the development of the familiar image of the female guardian angel wearing white robes and bathed in radiant light that became very popular during the Victorian era in England. Out of this complex cultural background a concept emerged that portrayed angels as God's messengers and ministers. They ministered and guided Christians towards salvation, and adopted the older role of guardian spirits to the individual.

Supernatural intervention in wars continued to occur as the ancient world gave way to the modern. In early Christian times, stories of vengeful pagan gods were still widely believed, but were slowly integrated into the new religion. Across Europe, the saints and angels adopted the role in battle formerly occupied by the gods of war. In Irish tradition, saints were able to summon magical reinforcements or send magic mists to conceal Christian armies from their enemies. Newly Christianized kings and emperors were encouraged to forsake the war gods that had once been called upon by their ancestors, for the protection of patron saints. During the Middle Ages, this tradition continued with victories against pagans and heretics attributed by the church to the direct intervention of God via his agents on earth. Meanwhile newly Christianized warriors inherited some of the roles of the angels as supernatural protectors of territory and the patrons of kings and soldiers.

St George

Many nations and peoples have traditions of supernatural protectors that emerge at times of great danger and national emergency. The foundation for a British tradition of divine intervention emerged during the early medieval period. At that time the Christian church preferred magic to be worked in the name of the one true God via the saints. In early medieval England, armies relied upon a variety of competing patron saints for supernatural protection, but by the time of the Crusades the church was keen to promote a single supernatural personage as protector of soldiers preparing for campaigns in the Holy Land.

These qualities were all found in St George, whose cult is similar if not identical to that of St Michael. Both the saint and the angel are depicted by artists as warriors who overcome the forces of evil, which are depicted symbolically in the form of a dragon. St George's elevation as patron saint and supernatural protector of English armies can be traced to the eleventh century at the time of the First Crusade. Although the warrior saint is one of the most famous Christian icons, little is known of his life, and contemporary evidence is so poor that some historians doubt that a real historical person of that name ever existed. Early hagiographers claimed that George was a soldier martyred in what is present-day Syria during the reign of Diocletian in late third or early fourth century AD. One version claims he held the rank of tribune in the Roman army and was beheaded by the emperor for protesting against the persecution of Christians. His bravery in defending the poor and defenceless quickly led to veneration, and by the sixth century his cult had spread to western Europe, with churches and convents dedicated to him across Christendom, including several in England.

St George's connection with England was popularized in the early histories of the saints that appeared during the eighth century AD. The apocryphal *Acts of St George* describes his visits to the Roman city of Caerleon and to Glastonbury, and these stories were translated into Anglo-Saxon. Later, the *Legenda Aurea* (*The Golden Legend*) popularized the story of 'St George and the Dragon', which had a particular appeal to the Anglo-Saxons who had their own traditions of struggles between warriors and monsters. While it is unlikely that the real St George – if he did indeed exist – ever visited the British Isles, these legends were encouraged by the church as they cemented his role as a patron and protector of the English in battle. The seal was placed upon this role by the Crusades, which gave impetus to the veneration of St George by Christian armies, and by the English in particular.

The enthusiasm of the Crusaders for the soldier–martyr continued to grow and eventually became a military cult. The invocation of his name as a rallying cry in battle raised the popularity of St George among the nobility in England, Aragon (part of Spain) and Portugal who adopted him as their patron. When in 1095 Pope Urban II announced a crusade to reconquer the Holy Land from the Muslims, he declared that God alone would lead the Christian army to victory. But feuds between the Crusaders split the army into two forces and they entered Asia Minor with little knowledge of the terrain or the enemy they faced. Despite the famine and hardships endured by the Crusaders, they initially enjoyed success against the Muslims who were also divided by their own internal rivalries.

Christian chroniclers such as William of Malmesbury were quick to attribute the early success of the Crusaders to divine intervention. In his account, it was during the Battle of Antioch in 1098 that the visions of saints George and Demetrios appeared in the nick of time to save the besieged Crusader army, which had become trapped by hordes of advancing Saracens. He claimed they saw a mighty host charging down the hillside to their aid, 'with banner flying and horse hoofs thundering', the sight of which rallied the Crusaders and led them to overcome the fearsome odds and achieve victory. He also claimed that a phantom horseman, presumably St George, appeared to rally the Crusaders who captured Jerusalem from the Muslim forces on 15 July 1099.[8] This story was probably influenced by the biblical story of the angel horsemen who appeared at Jerusalem during the Maccabean wars. From that point the legend of St George and the stories of warrior angels described in the Old Testament became interchangeable in the medieval mind.

Knights and troubadours returned from campaigns in the Holy Land and began to spread stories of these miracles across western Europe. They were so influential that in 1191–92, during the Third Crusade, when King Richard I of England was campaigning in Palestine, he placed his entire army under the protection of St George. When his rearguard force was attacked by Saracens during his march along the coast road to Acre in 1191 one of the knights called out to the warrior saint for help. Although St George did not appear on this occasion, the mere mention of his name helped to rally the defenders who were able to mount two charges against the Saracens and drive them off. The invocation of the warrior saint at a moment of great peril became a lasting tradition among Christian soldiers. It was also during the reign of King Richard I that the banner of St George – the red cross on a white background – was adopted for the uniform of English soldiers, and later became the flag of England and the white ensign of the Royal Navy.[9]

By the time of the Hundred Years War, St George was widely accepted as the sole protector of English soldiers in battle. In 1348 King Edward III founded St George's Chapel at Windsor and with it the Order of the Garter, the oldest ancient order of chivalry, with the saint as its principal patron. According to Thomas of Walsingham, when in the following year the king laid siege to Calais he was moved to draw his sword and cry: 'Ha! Saint Edward! Ha! Saint George!'[10] The words inspired his soldiers to attack and they routed the French armies. Thereafter, the cult of St George was skilfully exploited by English kings to provide both protection and justification for their military adventures abroad. By the fifteenth century, St George interceded on the side of the English not only in campaigns against the Saracens but also against the armies of other Christian nations, further cementing his identification as a supernatural protector of English troops. When Richard II invaded Scotland in 1385 his men were ordered to wear a 'a signe of the arms of St George' on their uniforms. Folklorist Christina Hole wrote that:

> in many medieval battles, from the days of Richard I onwards, his aid was invoked, and his name shouted by English men-at-arms and their leaders as the attack was launched, or in moments of special peril ... Tales of victory or last-minute deliverance told by returning soldiers carried the saint's fame into townships and villages all over the country and, for some simple folk at least, it seemed that so close a friend must be not only for England but of it.[11]

The most famous invocation of St George in battle was that by Henry V at Agincourt in 1415. Henry was a pious warrior who believed it was his destiny to assert his divine right over French territory. The *Gesta Henrici Quinti*, written after his campaign by a member of his private chapel, emphasized the message that Henry and his army were protected throughout by divine power and compared the English people with the Israelites in the Old Testament. During Henry's campaign in France, appeals were made to the Virgin Mary, St George and other patron saints for direct assistance in time of need. The banner of St George, as England's military patron and favourite symbol, was carried alongside those of the Virgin and the royal standard onto the field at Agincourt. The Middle English *Brut* account of the battle, which dates from 1377 to 1419, describes how the king addressed his men with these words:

'Now is a good time for all England is praying for us. Therefore be of good cheer, let us go into battle.' Then he said in a high voice 'In the name of almighty God and St George, advance banner. St George, give us this day your help.'

As the enemy knights advanced into a wall of arrows from the longbows of the English archers, the chronicle tells how the Frenchmen:

saw St George in the air over the host of the English fighting against the Frenchmen ... thus almighty God and St George brought our enemy to the ground and gave us victory that day.[12]

At Agincourt, Henry's army consisted of a mere 2,500 men-at-arms and 8,000 archers. This small army faced a heavily armoured French host that is thought to have been 50 000 strong. Yet a combination of luck, skilful tactics and the advantages of geography and weather resulted in victory for Henry, and disaster for the French who suffered 11 000 killed and many more taken prisoner.[13] At the time tactics and weapons were believed to be of little advantage if God was fighting on the side of the righteous, and thus the English victory was attributed to divine intervention. Five centuries later another heavily outnumbered British army faced overwhelming forces in a confrontation that took place on French soil in a new world ruled not by miracles, but by scientific progress. How prophetic the words attributed to Henry V must have sounded to those who came to believe that St George and his angel bowmen would answer the call for help one more time.

Something in the air

Historians tend to regard 'divine intervention' in history as a device used by church and state to justify wars, and to provide legitimacy for campaigns against other nations and peoples.

Certainly, medieval adventurers who set out to make their fortunes in the Holy Land, and to impose their religion upon the inhabitants of the New World, attempted to justify their actions by attributing their apparent success to the saints who they believed fought on their side. By doing so they established a deep well of tradition of belief that could be drawn upon in the event of future crisis.

There is another form of divine intervention that can be traced from the very earliest period. It took the form of visions of phantom armies and signs in the sky that have appeared both to individuals and, on occasions to large groups of people. Mystical visions such as those experienced by biblical figures such as Ezekiel and St Paul were frequent in the ancient world and often took the form of blinding lights from the sky. In more recent times, visions that were once described as miraculous have been reinterpreted as celestial phenomena such as comets and eclipses of the sun and moon, when they have coincided with significant events on Earth.

One of the most detailed stories of a vision pre-empting the outcome of an important battle occurred in the fourth century AD and led a Roman emperor to abandon pagan gods and convert to Christianity. The new religion was forbidden by law across the Roman Empire when Constantine was proclaimed caesar at York in 306 AD. At that time it was ruled by two emperors known as Augustus of the West and Augustus of the East and two junior caesars, with Constantine holding sway over much of Gaul and Britain. By all accounts Constantine was a cruel and superstitious man and his decision to unite the whole empire under his sole rule was entirely in keeping with politics in pagan Rome. That Constantine emerged victorious against the odds stacked against him would have far-reaching effects for the future of western Europe and Christianity.

His army moved into Italy to unseat his rival Maxentius in October 312 and the two forces met ten miles outside Rome at a place called Milvian Bridge. Constantine's army was heavily outnumbered and militarily it appeared that Maxentius had the advantage. But as the armies prepared themselves for battle, Constantine saw a vision of a cross in the sky as he looked toward the sun. The cross was accompanied by the Greek letters 'Chi-Ro' (Christ), and an inscription which read: 'By this sign, you will conquer.' Constantine, a pagan, had the symbol of the cross placed on the shields of his soldiers and the next day they went into battle under the protection of the Christian god. In the slaughter that followed, Constantine's army was victorious and Maxentius was killed. The medieval historian R.H.C. Davis writes that although the traditional account of the events is suspect, the victory had great symbolic significance. Constantine was proclaimed sole ruler of the western half of the empire and he was later to become sole ruler of the entire empire:

> Late in his life he even became convinced that the only reason why he had won the battle of the Milvian Bridge ... was the effect of divine intervention. He thought that he had been commanded by Christ to make a banner modelled on the Christian monogram which he had seen in the sky; and he was convinced that this banner, the *labarum*, had given him victory.[14]

Constantine came to believe his vision was a sign from heaven, but at the time it occurred he was a pagan and his actual baptism into the Christian faith came later in his life. At the time of Milvian Bridge, the appearance of visions and spectral armies in the sky at a critical moment in battle was fully in keeping with pagan mythology. In the British Isles, the Irish and the Anglo-Saxon records frequently mention signs and prodigies appearing in the sky before battles and depredations of the Vikings. The *Anglo-Saxon Chronicle*, in a famous entry dated 793 AD, tells how:

> terrible portents appeared in Northumbria, and miserably inflicted the inhabitants; these were exceptional flashes of lightning, and fiery dragons were seen flying in the air, and soon followed a great famine, and after that in the

same year the harrying of the heathen miserably destroyed God's church in Lindisfarne by rapine and slaughter.[15]

Similarly in April 1066, the arrival of Halley's Comet, known at that time as the 'long-eared star', was widely believed to be an evil portent. Again, the connection of signs in the heaven with a momentous event on earth was confirmed when on 14 October that year King Harold was killed at the Battle of Hastings and Anglo-Saxon England was swept away by the Norman invaders led by William the Conqueror.

Fairy cavalcades and phantom armies

Elsewhere in the folklore of northern Europe the appearance of the Wild Hunt and the fairy cavalcade was widely seen as a portent of war. In Germany and Scandinavia, the Wild Hunt was led by the war god Odin, seated upon his eight-legged horse Sleipnir. In Devonshire, the leader of the spectral host was believed to be the Elizabethan hero Francis Drake. Historian Jennifer Westwood links the numerous early modern stories of 'spectral armies' seen in the sky directly with the older tradition of the Wild Hunt.[16] One of the earliest written accounts is an entry in the *Anglo-Saxon Chronicle* from 1127, which portrays the apparition as an evil portent of the arrival in England of an unpopular abbot, Henry of Anjou, who set about the systematic plunder of the monastery at Peterborough. The *Chronicle* notes how:

> it was general knowledge throughout the whole country that immediately after his arrival ... many men both saw and heard a great number of huntsmen hunting. The huntsmen were black, huge, and hideous, and rode on black horses and on black he-goats, and their hounds were jet black, with eyes like saucers, and horrible. This was seen in the very deer park of the town of Peterborough, and in all

the woods that stretch from that same town to Stamford, and in the night the monks heard them sounding and winding their horns.[17]

Unearthly battles in the sky and visions of spectral armies were frequently reported during the sixteenth and seventeenth centuries. The chronicles and histories of the time frequently refer to them as portents of battles to come, or as signs of God's displeasure at wars and social upheaval. For instance, the outbreak of the conflict between King Charles I and his parliament was accompanied by a host of signs and portents both on earth and in the skies. Stories and rumours of prodigies were popularized by seers and millenarian preachers and news could now spread more quickly and effectively than in past centuries with the invention of the printing press. The most popular were the sensational pamphlets and broadsheets that both sides lost no time in employing for propaganda purposes.

The most spectacular supernatural vision of the Civil War was the phantom army that was said to have appeared in the sky two months after the Battle of Edgehill in October 1642. The visions at Edgehill in present-day Warwickshire became such an enduring part of English folklore that three centuries later they were compared to the visions allegedly seen by British soldiers at the Battle of Mons. The Edgehill spectral army is described in a contemporary pamphlet entitled *A great Wonder in heaven, shewing the late Apparitions and Prodogious Noyse of War and Battels, seene on Edge-Hill, neere Keinton, in Northamptonshire, 1642*. It describes how:

> between twelve and one o'clock of the morning was heard by some shepherds, and other countrey-men, and travellers, first the soyund of drummes afar off, and the noyse of soulders, as it were, giving out their last groanes; at which they were much amazed, and amazed stood still, till it seemed, by the neereness of the noyse, to approach them; at which too much affrighted, they sought to withdraw as

fast as possibly they could; but then, on the sudden, wilest they were in these cogitations, appeared in the ayre the same incorporeall souldiers that made those clamours, and immediately, with Ensignes display'd, Drummes beating, Musquests going off, Cannons discharged, Horses neighing, which also to these men were visible, the alarum, or entrance to this game of death was strucke up, one Army, which gave the first charge, having the King's colours, and the other the Parliaments, in their head or front of the battells, and so pell mell to it they went ...[18]

The spectators were frozen in fear while the spectral battle ran its course over three hours, whereupon the king's soldiers fled and those of parliament 'stayed a good space triumphing, and expressing all the signes of joy and conquest, and then, with all their Drummes, Trumpets, Ordnance, and Souldiers, vanished'. Immediately the men went to Keinton where they awoke the incredulous Justice of the Peace and the minister and 'averred it upon their oaths to be true'. The following night, a Sunday which fell upon Christmas, they returned with a larger group of villagers to the spot where the phantoms had first appeared. Again the phantom re-enactment of the battle was seen and heard, leaving 'the Gentlemen and all the spectatours, much terrified with these visions of horrour, withdrew themselves to their houses, beseeching God to defend them from those hellish and prodigious enemies'. So disturbed were some that they moved out of their homes, but the minister stayed and witnessed further, increasingly noisy appearances. Eventually the story reached King Charles at Oxford, and he sent six of his most trusted officers to Keinton to investigate. They too saw the phantoms and recognized the faces of some of the soldiers that were slain.

Rumours of the events at Edgehill spread rapidly and appear to have inspired further reports of phantom armies seen at other places. The news from England caused great excitement in Scotland, where similar visions and prodigies were reported early in 1643. Propaganda was widely circulated by both sides during the Civil War, which makes it a difficult task to determine if any of these stories were 'real' accounts of mystical visions or entirely fictional stories invented by those who wished to maintain the divine right of King Charles to rule England. The writer of the account of the Edgehill battle ended his story by asking 'what this doth portend, God only knoweth, and time perhaps will discover' and to many readers there would have been no doubt that it was a sign of God's displeasure. The phantom armies were a sign, many believed 'of his wrath against this Land, for these civill wars, which He in his good time finish, and send a sudden peace between his Majestie and Parliament'.

The age of the Enlightenment saw the end of the religious interpretations of visions and portents that had been automatic during the Middle Ages. After the religious wars, belief in signs from God was losing ground to rationalism, and across Europe there was growing scepticism of the supernatural among the educated classes. The eighteenth and nineteenth centuries saw a rise in the popularity of natural phenomena as a standard explanation for a range of apparitions that were seen as miraculous in what was now regarded as a more superstitious, credulous past. As a result, many early scientists decided that meteorological phenomena such as mirages and optical illusions could account for all reports of 'phantom armies'. Others could be explained as psychological projections, or the product of mass hysteria at times of tension and war. But while mirages could account for a range of static visions in the sky, it is more difficult to apply the same explanation to cases where movement and action was apparently observed over a long period of time.

Rational explanations are reduced to guesswork in cases such as the 'spectral horsemen' seen on a mountain called Souter Fell in Cumbria during the summer of 1744. Around 7 p.m. one evening Daniel Stricket, a servant at Wilton Hall, saw a troop of men on horseback riding briskly along the steep mountainside.

After first doubting his senses, he fetched his master who also saw the vision, followed by the rest of his family. An account of 1854 describes how:

> There were many troops, and they seemed to come from the lower part of the fell, becoming first visible at a place called Knott; they then moved in regular order in a curvilinear path along the side of the fell, until they came opposite to Blakehills, when they went over the mountain and disappeared. The last, or last but one, in every troop, galloped to the front, and then took the swift walking pace of the rest.[19]

The vision lasted for two and a half hours, and during the time was seen by 'every person at every cottage within a mile' of the place. Some 27 people saw the phantom soldiers and a number swore their testimony before a magistrate. Nevertheless, scientific commentators, such as Sir David Brewster, stated categorically that the vision *must* have been an optical illusion, possibly of British troops drilling in secrecy on the other side of the mountain in preparation for the Jacobite rebellion of the following year. The fact that no soldiers were present in the area at the time did not alter his opinion. Another writer in *Lonsdale Magazine* stated equally categorically that the phantom soldiers were 'rebels exercising on the western coast of Scotland', whose movements had been reflected by some fine transparent vapour similar to the *Fata Morgana*.[20]

There are many other similar instances where groups of people have observed a vision of a phantom army simultaneously in circumstances which throw doubt upon straightforward rational explanations. As Charles Fort observed, 'There has never been an explanation that did not itself have to be explained.' This was the case with the phantom soldiers seen by one of Britain's most illustrious military legends, Field Marshal Lord Roberts of Kandahar, during the Indian Mutiny. In *Forty-One Years in India* (1897), Lord Roberts describes a 'curious adventure' he had in the company of the future General

Sir John Watson, VC, during the movement of the English army to Mohan on 25 February 1858. During the march Roberts and Watson had left the main camp on horseback to pursue an antelope when:

> all at once, we beheld moving towards us from our right front a body of the enemy's Cavalry. We were in an awkward position; our horses were very nearly dead beat, and we could hardly hope to get away if pursued. We pulled up, turned round, and trotted back, very quietly at first, that our horses might recover their breath before the enemy got to closer quarters and we should have to ride for our lives. Every now and then we looked back to see whether they were gaining on us, and at last we distinctly saw them open out and make as if to charge down upon us. We thought our last hour was come. We bade each other good-bye, agreeing that each must do his best to escape, and that neither was to wait for the other, when lo!, as suddenly as they had appeared, the horsemen vanished, as though the ground had opened up and swallowed them; there was nothing to be seen but the open plain, where a second before there had been a crowd of mounted men. We could hardly believe our eyes, or comprehend at first that what we had seen was simply a mirage, but so like reality that anyone must have been deceived.[21]

Lord Roberts described how relieved the two men were when it became apparent they had been scared by a phantom enemy, which he later came to believe was a protective force. The vision, he wrote, had

> the good effect of making us realize the folly of having allowed ourselves to be tempted so far away from our camp without escort of any kind in an enemy's country, and we determined not to risk it again.

The eve of war and the mighty sword

During the Franco-Prussian War there was a striking example of a miraculous vision that would become a precedent for apparitions in the approaching world war. The conflict of 1870–71 is viewed by military historians as the watershed between the Napoleonic wars and the widescale destruction of 1914–18. In 1870 the German nation-states were on the verge of unification under a belligerent Prussia when Napoleon III of France was drawn into a pre-emptive strike against his enemy. Within months the French army suffered humiliating defeat. Prussian troops bit deep into French territory then went on to lay siege to Paris. By January 1871 the French armies had suffered severe losses and morale was at its lowest ebb. Prussian troops were close to the town of Pontmain, near Laval and the German border, where it was claimed that a remarkable apparition appeared in the sky.

There are few reliable contemporary accounts of what happened at Pontmain, but in a 1985 study Kevin McClure found the earliest was the testimony gathered by L'Abbé Richard in August, 1871.[22] This described how, as the crisis escalated, two peasant children, Joseph and Eugene Barbadette, aged ten and 12, were working with their father in a barn at five-thirty on the afternoon of 17 January. Snow lay on the ground, and spirits were lifted when news arrived that the children's half-brother, who was serving in the French army, was safe. Eugene went to the door of the barn to look at the sky, and within minutes saw a vision of a woman 'of extraordinary beauty'. The figure was tall and young, with a golden crown, and she wore a dark blue dress decorated with stars. The vision hovered some 20 feet away above the roof of a nearby house. For some minutes Eugene said nothing but when the village undertaker approached he asked her if she could see anything. Neither she nor Eugene's father could see the vision, but Joseph said: 'Yes, I can see a beautiful lady.' From that point the excitement spread and a crowd of villagers began to gather inside the barn. Two more youngsters, both girls, claimed they too could see the vision.

When one of the nuns who ran the village school exclaimed, 'The children can see the Blessed Virgin', the identity of the vision was cemented. As the village priest began to recite a Marian devotion the children said the figure seemed to increase in size and brilliant 'stars' began to arrange themselves beneath her feet. Writing appeared on a banner that appeared below the vision which read: 'But pray, my children' and 'God will soon answer your prayers.' A third and final message, 'My son allows himself to be moved', was spelled out before a red crucifix appeared, a white veil slowly rose and the figure disappeared.

News of the approach of Prussian troops arrived in the middle of the excitement but then, according to the legend, unexpectedly the German army halted its advance. One of the versions of the story claims the commander received his orders to pull back from Laval that very evening, and another attributes to him the statement: 'We cannot go farther. Yonder, in the direction of Brittany, there is an invisible Madonna barring the way.'[23]

The vision at Pontmain is significant because of the time and place at which it occurred. Within ten days, the crisis ended with an armistice that imposed humiliating conditions on the French. The loss of the provinces of Alsace and Lorraine in particular led to simmering resentment that would resurface before the outbreak of the First World War. By that time, the Blessed Virgin was replaced by Joan of Arc as the supernatural figurehead who would help the French gain deliverance from the German invader.

As war clouds gathered over Europe in the summer of 1914, people in all nations were dreaming dreams and seeing visions as they had in earlier ages as the cataclysm approached. Nurse Vera Brittain recalled seeing lurid sunsets over England before the outbreak of the First World War and how many religious people came to believe they had seen blood upon the sun and the moon.[24] In 1917 an artist, S. Ruth Canton, sent an account to the spiritualist magazine *Light* of 'an extraordinary sky' she saw in August 1914. The magazine felt her story was one John Ruskin would have enjoyed, 'for he was a seer who found marks of spiritual significance in the clouds.' Mrs Canton said it impressed her so strongly that she could paint it, even after three years, from memory. She explained:

> I went to Falmouth three days after war was declared. One evening, when returning from a walk, I was greatly struck with the wonderful effect of a sunset. The sky was a greenish blue, and large masses of rounded clouds appeared just above the hills. Towards the north all was grey and amorphous. Out of this grey came more or less straight streaks of grey cloud across the sky; but one of these streaks was shaped exactly like a huge, straight sword-blade coming to a sharp point, which point was drenched in sunlight, and small spots of similarly sunlighted clouds dropped, as it were, from the point, just as would drops of blood from a sword-point. The sides of the 'blade' were as straight and unbroken as if they had been ruled. It was so striking that I received an instantaneous impression that it portended a war much greater than we at that time realised. The mighty sword swept right across the heavens.[25]

By August 1914, two thousand years of stories and beliefs concerning visions, saints, the return of heroic leaders and the intervention of divine forces came to a head as the 'war to end all wars' began. With the world in crisis once more, it is no surprise that angels were once again about to appear on Earth.

CHAPTER TWO

The Battle of Mons

The First World War had been expected for many years. The alliances that spread across Europe in the wake of the Franco-Prussian War had bound the most powerful nations into a web of interlocking treaties from which none could escape. Britain, France and Russia formed one alliance, while Germany and Austria-Hungary formed another. If any of the opposing nations or their client states made an aggressive move against another, a cascade of treaty obligations would set off a chain reaction. The spark that finally ignited the war came from the Balkans, a region whose instability would remain a thorn in the side of the European powers. The assassination on 28 June 1914 of Archduke Franz Ferdinand, the heir to the throne of the Austro-Hungarian Empire, during a visit to the Bosnian capital of Sarajevo set off a domino effect, which could not be reversed. The Austrians blamed the Serbs for the outrage and were determined to teach their small and troublesome neighbour a lesson. The Serbs in turn appealed for help from their Slavonic ally, Russia. Alarmed by the Russian mobilization, the Germans declared war on 1 August. Within two days Germany and France were at war and the conflict was unstoppable.

The Kaiser's generals wanted to avoid having to fight simultaneously on two fronts and turned to a plan drawn up by Count von Schlieffen. His strategy was to capture Paris and defeat the French armies in one quick, decisive blow before Russia had time to attack from the east. Unfortunately for them, the French had heavily fortified their border with a line of defences that made a direct assault a slow and bloody process. To overcome this problem, Von Schlieffen envisaged a great wheeling movement through neutral Belgium into northern France to surround Paris. A German request for Belgium to allow its troops free passage through its territory was rejected, and Britain made it clear that it would enter the war if she was invaded. It appears the Germans believed this was a bluff and her armies crossed the Belgian border. On 4 August the British Cabinet was told that Belgian neutrality had been violated and war was declared on Germany.

Out of all the countries caught up in the rush to war, Britain was the only one that did not have a system of universal conscription. In 1914 the British army was a small, well-trained regular force that had learned lessons from its colonial wars and developed tactics and arms that made it a force to be reckoned with. At the outbreak of the First World War the British Expeditionary Force (BEF) consisted of four infantry divisions and one large cavalry division. The assertion, wrongly attributed to the Kaiser, that the British were 'a contemptible little army' was wildly inaccurate, as the battles of August and September 1914 would prove.

While the BEF was numerically weak compared with the Germans, it was armed with a weapon that would prove decisive in the forthcoming battles. British infantry were trained to use the lightweight and reliable .303 Short Magazine Lee Enfield, which one expert described as 'one of the most efficient rifles ever to be put into the hands of a fighting soldier'. The tough regular soldiers of the BEF, many of whom were veterans of the Boer War, were accomplished marksmen who could hit a target 300 yards (273 metres) away 15 times in one minute. Most could double this speed without losing accuracy. This made them a force to be reckoned with on the battlefield.

The BEF were mobilized on 4 August 1914 and the first troops safely crossed the English Channel without knowledge of their movements reaching the Germans. The main force arrived in France by 17 August and was quickly moved by train to concentrate around an agreed position to the left of the French

Fifth Army commanded by General Lanrezac. The British Secretary of State for War, Field Marshal Lord Kitchener, appointed Sir John French, a veteran of the Sudan campaign and the Boer War, as Commander-in-Chief. At this point the strength of the BEF consisted of two corps, each made up of two divisions. I Corps was commanded by a Scot, Sir Douglas Haig. II Corps was commanded by the portly Sir James Grierson, but he died from a heart attack on a train before he saw any action. Kitchener replaced him with General Sir Horace Smith-Dorrien, whom Haig detested.

The BEF went to war with 100 000 professional soldiers. They would face General Alexander von Kluck's German First Army, which numbered some 240 000 troops. Ironically, the last time the British army had fought against such odds on mainland Europe was at the Battle of Waterloo in 1815 in alliance with the Prussians against the French. The countryside through which the German and British armies marched was littered with reminders of those earlier campaigns. Although the BEF was heavily outnumbered by a ratio of more than three to one, its commanders were unaware of the full strength of the German armies until it was too late. The Kaiser's Generals believed the overwhelming force of their armies could brush aside the small BEF and outflank the larger French armies rushing to the defence of Paris. In fact, neither side had accurate intelligence on the size or movements of the opposing forces, which was fortunate for the smaller British army.

The Allied plan was for the BEF to join Lanrezac's French Fifth Army in an offensive against the Germans. Long before any offensive could be contemplated, Von Kluck's army had steam-rollered through Belgium, captured Liège and Brussels and breached the defences at the River Sambre. The planned French offensive ended in disarray as its armies were devastated by German howitzers and machine guns. Lanrezac decided to abandon the offensive and ordered his army to retreat towards Paris, leaving the British suddenly exposed on both sides. With the French pulling back, the BEF continued to march northwards, unaware they risked being surrounded.

Saturday 22 August 1914

After a long march along cobbled roads in oppressive summer heat, the first British soldiers reached the line of the Mons-Conde Canal in Belgium. During the night their commanders received news of the French withdrawal and Sir John French agreed to hold the line of the canal for 24 hours to allow Lanrezac time to regroup. The landscape where the BEF collided with the German army was a 'close, blind country' and not the most ideal location for a small force to make a stand against a large advancing army. The only barrier was the man-made line formed by the Mons-Conde Canal north of the town. The canal was 64 feet wide and 7 feet deep in places but was crossed by 18 road and railway bridges as well as lock gates that would prove difficult to defend. It was here that French decided to deploy his II Corps on the evening of 22 August, with I Corps on its right, defending the town of Meubeuge.

During the Middle Ages, Mons was famous for its textiles. In 1914 the city lay at the centre of the Belgian coalfield and the canals, pitheads and spoil tips were a legacy of the Industrial Revolution. Adding to these obstacles, the battlefield was swampy in places and its watercourses and osier beds were intersected by canals, cobbled roads, old pitheads, deep ditches and slag heaps that rose up to 100 feet in height. These obstacles restricted some lines of fire and the loop in the canal between Nimy and Obourg northwest of Mons left the defending soldiers exposed on three sides.

That morning British cavalry scouts spotted German *uhlans* (mounted lancers) at Casteau on the Mons-Brussels Road and a squadron led by Captain Hornby drew their swords and charged. In the melee that followed, several Germans were killed and others captured before the cavalry pulled back. Meanwhile in Mons itself advance soldiers from the Fourth Royal Fusiliers had begun to arrive in the city centre and paused to rest their sore feet on the cobblestones of the Grand Place. They were unaware that five miles to the north the opening shots of the war for Britain had already been fired. Within 24 hours many of the soldiers captured in the photograph taken that day [see plate 10] would be killed or wounded.[1]

St George and Mons

The idea of supernatural intervention in the war was expected by the people of Belgium because they believed St George slew the dragon in Mons. The dragon represented the forces of evil that in 1914 were fully identified with the Kaiser and the German armies.

The city of Mons was established around a monastery founded by St Waudru in the seventh century on the prominent hilltop from which it takes its name ('Mons' meaning 'mountain'). Mons is the capital of the Belgian province of Hainault, and its proximity to the French border made it strategically important. During the Middle Ages, the region was fought over and occupied by troops from many nations including English, French, Dutch and Spaniards. During the twentieth century, the district became the focus of important battles in both world wars. For the British, Mons was important symbolically as the place where the First World War began and ended. Although the battle that took place there was minor in comparison to what was to come, the stand made by the BEF was tactically crucial and it would become an enduring part of British mythology. The graves of the first and last Allied soldiers killed in the war can be found today side by side with those of German soldiers in the peaceful military cemetery at St Symphorien, southwest of the city centre.

The trauma of being a battleground in both world wars and its continual occupation by foreign powers may explain the origin and continuing popularity in Mons of the ancient tradition known as *Lumecon* whose origins lay in the late Middle Ages. In 1380 the brotherhood of 'God and Monseigneur Saint Georges' was founded in Mons to maintain the worship of the warrior saint who was venerated throughout Christendom but was particularly favoured by the English who controlled the textile trade in Flanders. The earliest references to 'the game of St Georges' date from 1440 and at that time it may have been part of a Trinity Sunday procession in which the shrine of St Waudru is paraded in a golden coach through the narrow streets. A figure on horseback, representing St George, accompanied the procession and fought a battle against a dragon and his imps, which represented the forces of evil.

At some stage the procession became separated from the combat. Today both continue to thrive, but the *Lumecon* has retained its pagan overtones and the annual event has grown to elaborate proportions and is attended by thousands of onlookers. The spectacle reaches its climax in the Grand Place where St George battles against a giant dragon constructed from wickerwork and canvas, decorated with ribbons and lucky charms. As crowds surge forward to snatch lucky charms from the tail of the monster, the dragon is slain and St George rescues the town from the forces of evil for another year.[2] Here we have one of the odd coincidences that occur throughout this story. The tradition of St George as a supernatural personage who protects the city from the forces of evil was an ancient tradition in Mons centuries before the events of 1914. One wonders if the Belgian villagers who left for church on that Sunday morning in August were praying earnestly for their patron saint to intervene in the approaching battle.

Sunday 23 August 1914

As morning broke, infantry battalions from II Corps were deployed along a thin 20-mile front along the canal from Conde in the west to Obourg station in the east. The most exposed section was the bend in the canal between Nimy and Obourg that was defended by the Eighth Infantry Brigade. The weather was misty with drizzle clearing by ten o'clock, when the first sunlight broke through the clouds. Unaware of the hellish battle that was about to begin, villagers spilled out into the streets on their way to church. Some were killed in the crossfire and others taken hostage by the Germans as they forced their way into the city centre. Hidden along the canal towpath, hundreds of British soldiers waited expectantly behind the makeshift barricades they had thrown up. Then as the mist lifted they saw for the first time, moving towards them from the north, the advance elements of Von Kluck's First Army. The British Eighth Infantry Brigade were made up of the Fourth Middlesex who defended the railway station, supported by the Second Royal Irish, Second Royal Scots and the First Gordon Highlanders. Further to the west, the Royal Fusiliers held the bridges at Nimy to the left of their position on the canal bend.

The German attack opened up with artillery barrages from guns positioned on high ground to the north of the canal. These were quickly followed up by dense lines of infantry moving towards crossing points at the bridges and locks. The British troops put up a brave defence, cutting down wave after wave with devastating rifle and machine-gun fire. The Middlesex men suffered heavy casualties and as the Germans began to cross the canal men from the Second Royal Irish regiment were moved up in support. One of them was Corporal John Lucy who, in his autobiography *There's a Devil in the Drum*, described the devastating effects of the British rifle fire:

A great roar of musketry rent the air ... For us the battle took the form of well ordered, rapid rifle-fire at close range as the field grey human targets appeared, or were struck down, to be replaced by further waves of German infantry who shared the same fate ... Such tactics amazed us, and after the first shock of seeing men slowly and helplessly falling down as they were hit [it] gave us a great sense of power and pleasure. It was all so easy.[3]

43

The German advance continued into the afternoon and despite heavy losses they managed to cross the canal along unguarded bridges and work their way behind Obourg station. As the battle intensified, they pressed on with their attack on the bridges at Nimy where they came up against the Royal Fusiliers' machine guns. These were placed in an exposed position on the abutment of a railway bridge, and their crews were killed one after the other. The guns were commanded by Lieutenant Maurice Dease who was himself wounded five times as he tried to keep them firing. Finally he was taken to a dressing station where he died. His place was taken by Private Sid Godley who continued firing despite suffering serious wounds. As the enemy surrounded him, Godley smashed his gun and threw it into the canal before he was captured. Both men received the first two Victoria Crosses awarded in the war, but in Dease's case the award was posthumous. He was laid to rest in the military cemetery alongside many other officers and men from his battalion. During this battle a German soldier swam the canal and managed to operate the machinery that closed the swing bridge before he was killed. His action allowed the Germans to cross the canal and move towards the town centre.

Meanwhile the German Captain Walter Bloem, commander of the Twelfth Brandenburg Grenadiers, prepared to lead an assault on the canal bank at Tertre, west of Mons. Bloem was a reservist when he was called up at the age of 46 to lead his company into battle. His dramatic account of the slaughter is described in his book *Vormarsch* (1916). As his company lay down to recover, a corporal produced a bottle of champagne and Bloem shared a glass with Lieutenant Graser. It was to be his final toast. As they rose:

> the enemy must have been waiting for this moment to get us all together at close range for immediately the line rose it was as if the hounds of hell had been loosed at us, yelling, barking, hammering as a mass of lead swept in amongst us ... 'Graser!' I called out. 'Where is Lieutenant Graser?'

And then from the cries and groans all around came a low-voiced reply: 'Lieutenant Graser is dead, sir, just this moment. Shot through the head and heart as he fell.'[4]

After the battle Captain Bloem was horrified to find that 25 officers and more than 500 men from the regiment were dead and his proud battalion had been 'shot down, smashed up – only a handful left'. His account helps to explain one part of the myth of the Angel of Mons. This was that the German troops believed they were facing huge numbers of British troops when in fact they were opposed only by a thin line of men. In fact, the Germans faced such rapid and sustained fire they came to believe they were facing a wall of machine guns, when the British had in fact just two guns per battalion. Bloem spoke on behalf of all his men when he wrote: 'Our first battle is a heavy, unheard of heavy, defeat, against the English, the English we laughed at.'

As the day wore on the German advance began to spread to the west to outflank the troops defending the canal bridges, and the British feared they would soon be surrounded. According to the official guidebook to the Mons battlefield produced by the Belgian Tourist Office, the Angel of Mons appeared near midnight at the point in the battle when Germans had outflanked the BEF to the east, occupied the town and threatened the British lines of retreat. Simultaneously, on the right the British faced the Seventy-fifth German Infantry Regiment from Bremen which had occupied Spiennes and for a few hours there was a grave danger they would be encircled and unable to retreat. According to the legend:

It was at this moment ... that angels descended from heaven dressed as archers stopping the Germans in their tracks. The British, under their protection, were able to retreat in the darkness, thereby saving the brigade from annihilation.[5]

There is not a single account from the veterans of the battle to support such a sensational claim. I have found just three accounts that appear to describe supernatural incidents on the first day of the battle and only one of these refers specifically to angels. The first comes from the early morning at the opening of hostilities. Its source was a BEF veteran, Harold Malpas, whose letter describing the event was published by the *Daily Mirror* in 1954:

> In the morning ... about eight or nine o'clock, as far as my memory recalls, there appeared in the sky a large white light, brighter than daylight. It stayed for two or three minutes. At the same time there was a lull in the battle, and a sudden hush of silence settled over the battlefield. My own experience was an uncanny feeling of awe. The men about me felt the same way. As to what it was I cannot express any opinion, but it certainly was *not* angels.[6]

A second, heavily romanticized account came from Private J. East of the Lincolnshire Regiment, which fought the Germans in the streets of Mons. Pte. East's story appeared in the London *Evening News* in October 1915. He claimed to have been part of a rearguard left behind to allow the Third Division to retreat. As the Germans advanced on their position he saw:

> not two hundred yards in front of us ... a long line of white forms, stretching from house to house. They were making mysterious motions with their arms. 'Good lor'!' said one man, 'what is it?' But no man answered. Yet every man felt in his own heart that the white barricade had been sent by some unseen power to protect that small body of English. We retired. No one spoke until we were well clear of Mons. I said they were angels, and not a man contradicted me.[7]

The third story appeared in the spiritualist newspaper, the *Two Worlds* and was reprinted by the *Daily Express* in April 1915. Although it was second-hand it has a ring of authenticity that is lacking in the other stories. It came from a correspondent who had spoken to two soldiers who were wounded on the first day of the battle. They claimed that during the action:

> they kept seeing the figure of woman in a queer poke bonnet
> and bright blue skirt, who repeatedly got in their line of fire.
> 'At first we thought she was a Belgian farm woman,' they
> said, 'but when she continued to move about under a
> constant hail of bullets, some of which must have hit her,
> we realised she was nothing human. We commented on
> her presence, and a sergeant who overheard us exclaimed,
> 'So you see her, too, boys. It's my old woman, who died
> twelve years ago, in her eighty-second year. I believe she's
> come for me.' And he spoke the truth, for directly he had
> finished speaking a shrapnel burst almost on top of us, and
> literally blew him to pieces. We lay wounded there for some
> hours, but the old woman did not appear again.[8]

When a ceasefire was called at nightfall on Sunday, a number of
German regiments were utterly devastated. There had been 1,600
casualties among the BEF, but the full German losses were never
disclosed. They are generally agreed to have been at least 5,000
and possibly as high as 10 000. By that evening the British
commanders realized the enormity of the odds stacked against
them. Not wishing to lose contact with the French army, Sir
John French ordered a complete withdrawal.

The 25-mile retreat from Mons to Le Cateau had begun.

Monday 24/Tuesday 25 August 1914

The BEF withdrew from Mons skilfully but the rank-and-file
soldiers were puzzled and made unhappy by their orders. They
believed they had fought and won a famous victory, and could
not understand why they were not allowed to stand and fight.
General von Kluck's army had received a bloody nose and their
advance – relentless until that point – had slowed and stalled
the German drive through Belgium, allowing the French time to

recover. Nevertheless, on the morning of 24 August the BEF faced a relentless pursuit by superior forces. Sir John French issued orders to both Corps commanders to withdraw to a line running east-west through the town of Bavay. A rearguard was left to hold back the Germans while the main force slipped away south to regroup at Le Cateau. Haig's I Corps pulled away without problems, but the left flank of II Corps were left exposed. A small force was left behind to defend the ridge between Audregnies and Elouges, south of Mons. This consisted of two infantry battalions of Norfolks and Cheshires supported by a battery from the Royal Field Artillery. It was their task to hold back the Germans and Major-General Allenby's cavalry division were to provide support.

Facing the small force was the entire German IV Corps, who outnumbered them six to one. Despite the odds, the British soldiers demonstrated remarkable discipline and bravery, and the accuracy of their rifle fire once again proved crucial. In the midst of the carnage, the Norfolks managed to break away and rejoin the retreating BEF, but the orders to retire never reached the Cheshires. They stood and fought on as the German infantry overwhelmed them, fighting hand to hand with rifles and fixed bayonets. At a roll-call later that night, only 200 of the 1,000 battalion were left alive. In all the British suffered almost 2,600 casualties on 24 August, far greater than at the Battle of Mons itself, but in total still fewer than those suffered at Waterloo in 1815.

The main British force that fell back from Mons regrouped in Bavay, and prepared itself for a further gruelling 20-mile march towards Le Cateau. At this stage the troops left the industrial region of Belgium behind and entered the rolling countryside of northern France. South of Bavay their movement was blocked by the dense Forest of Mormal. Roads on either side were choked with groups of fleeing Belgian civilians and the remnants of French reserve divisions. Fearing ambush if they marched through the forest, the British force were split in two and passed on either side of it. The BEF's commanders now realized the force was at its most vulnerable position. II Corps took the western route around the forest while I Corps followed the more difficult eastern route, that involved three separate crossings of the River Sambre. The plan was for both to join up that evening at Le Cateau, but the forced march put a ten-mile gap between them. They would not regroup for eight days.

The march south was hellish. Men went without food and sleep for 36 hours and endured sweltering heat. Each soldier carried an 80-pound kit, which included a loaded pack, rifle, ammunition, bayonet and entrenching tool. The cobbled roads were a nightmare for the reservists who had been issued with new boots that had not yet been broken in. Footsore and exhausted, a number of soldiers and officers began to slip into a dreamlike state. Some fell asleep as they walked or simply collapsed by the side of the road. From this period there emerged nightmarish accounts of visual and auditory hallucinations experienced by officers and men alike. When the exhausted men of the Middlesex Regiment reached the crossroads at Bavay they were:

> stumbling along more like ghosts than living soldiers, unconscious of everything about them, but still moving under the magic impulse of discipline and regimental pride. Marching, they were hardly awake; halted, whether sitting or standing, they were instantly asleep.[9]

Likewise, the Northumberland Fusiliers were like 'a column of automatons that dragged along through the darkness of the night'. They began to see visions in the sky:

> To one there gleamed a bright light a mile ahead and another a mile to the rear, while the road seemed flanked on either side by a sheet of water, beyond which other troops, mounted and dismounted, appeared to be moving. In the dreams of another, every group of trees was presented as a village. A third, who was mounted, recalls how he spent the night in ducking his head to escape imaginary arches that spanned the road.[10]

Private Frank Richards, a reservist with the Second Battalion Royal Welsh Fusiliers, was among the infantrymen who slogged along the cobbled roads of northern France toward Le Cateau. In his autobiography, *Old Soldiers Never Die* (1964), he describes the hallucinations experienced by his mates Billy and Stevens as the group passed through the Forest of Mormal:

> We retired all night with fixed bayonets, many sleeping as they were marching along. If any angels were seen on the Retirement, as the newspapers accounts said they were, they were seen that night. March, march, for hour after hour, without no halt: we were now breaking into the fifth day of continuous marching with practically no sleep in between ... Stevens said: 'There's a fine castle there, see?' pointing to one side of the road. But there was nothing there. Very nearly everyone were seeing things, we were all so dead beat.[11]

Moving lights, imaginary arches and fine castles were soon joined, in the retelling, by visions of angels, which appeared in the sky to hold back the advancing Germans. One of the more apocryphal stories came from the men of the Fourth Royal Fusiliers who had so heroically defended the bridge at Nimy during the Battle of Mons. During a brief halt in the retreat, a group of fusiliers collapsed in exhaustion by the side of the road. According to Tim Carew's account in *Wipers* (1976):

> Waking suddenly from a drugged sleep, they saw angels standing over them, young women of startling and ethereal beauty, and accoutred with actual wings. To the soldiers they spoke words of a wondrous comfort; God was with them on this fearful march and would see them through safely.[12]

Exhaustion also took its toll on the pursuing Germans, who had been marching constantly for three weeks. Captain Arthur Osborn of the British Fourth Dragoon Guards spent most of 24 August intercepting German cavalry and guns that were pursuing the left flank of the BEF. As the light faded, Osborn's men fell in with three other cavalry brigades, formed into squadrons, and clashed with the German horse artillery as it tried to drive them back. In his memoir he refers to the ominous black thunderclouds that hovered above the battlefield:

> Over the brown masses of surging horsemen charging across that rather dreary plain beneath a lowering sky on that sultry afternoon came white feathery bursts of shrapnel. The threatening sky, the restless symmetrical movements, the whole scene reminded me in some strange way of Milton's description of the legions of dark angels practising for giant warfare with St. Michael on the plains of hell. Anyway, the German Michael, for all his 'shining armour', did not like the look of things. By three o'clock his contemplated flank attack on our infantry had faded out.[13]

Also watching the skies was the Reverend Canon W.M. Lummis with the regimental transport of the Eleventh Hussars, First Cavalry Brigade. In 1982 he wrote:

> As we rested in bivouac that night I was fascinated by the lighting up of the sky. It was no wonder that men considered the clouds as angels. In my opinion the effect was caused by searchlights from both our army and that of the enemy.[14]

The ominous skies seemed to reflect the growing mood of the opposing armies. On the evening of 25 August the summer heatwave was reaching its height and a violent thunderstorm broke, soaking them to the bone. The little town of Solesmes was at the centre of the storm. It was also a bottleneck for the retreating II Corps. The three roads that ran into it had been blocked off to allow French cavalry to pass through, causing a traffic jam full of shuffling, exhausted soldiers, horses and desperate refugees.

Approaching Solesmes from the north were the German cavalry, now within a whisker of the British rearguard. Waiting nervously on the high ground behind the town was General Snow, commander of the newly arrived British Fourth Division. His orders were to stay until all the retreating troops had passed through the town, and only then give the order for his men to join them. The plan had not taken into account the chaos on the roads, the hold-ups and the three-hour delay caused by the bottleneck, and Snow messaged GHQ to say, 'The situation is becoming serious.' The German cavalry were almost upon them. Lyn Macdonald writes how:

> it was their biggest chance of the day – but they missed it. If the Germans had realised the situation, if they had guessed that Solesmes was filled with British troops, helpless to escape, they might have scored a pretty victory ... but they did not know ... They stopped. They hesitated. They made up their minds to wait for their artillery to come up ... but the sky was closing in ... and then it erupted in a great rolling peal of thunder and the heavens opened.[15]

Among General Snow's division was a battalion of Ulstermen from the Second Battalion of the Royal Inniskilling Fusiliers. One of these soldiers was a 35-year-old private from County Tyrone, John Ewings. In 1980, shortly after his 101st birthday, Ewings gave an interview to the BBC in which he described the vision that appeared from out the clouds at the height of the battle:

> We were surrounded by Germans at the time and we were out to the last round. We had only one round left in our rifles. I got down on my knees, I had the rifle ready to blow my own brains out. And, I'm shaking, my whole nerves are shaking just thinking about it. And I got down on my knees and I looked up to the sky, you know what you do when you are going to pray there ... and there was like what we thought a [clap] of thunder. I just looked up and the clouds parted – this big cloud parted – and this man came out with a flaming sword.[16]

Ewings said the figure 'was like a man [but] at that time I couldn't say that he had wings on him. But the Germans, some of them let a yell at him and they turned and they fled, and one of them said in English, 'The world's at an end.' According to his story, none of the other soldiers saw the figure as they were too busy firing and praying. Afterwards Ewings found no one would believe him. Years later he came to believe the 'angel' had saved them from the Germans and prevented him from using the rifle on himself. When the BBC interviewer asked what he thought he saw, he replied:

> Well now, what I thought I saw was an angel. But it was a man, that I could make out, that he was a man. And somehow or other, you know ... it was the first time I think that I was afraid in my life during the war.

Torrential rain poured from the sky for over an hour, drenching the Germans, who suddenly and, it seemed, inexplicably gave up and turned around to find billets for the night. Writing in 1915, a soldier with the Third Division Gordon Highlanders described how this extraordinary downpour seemed to them 'a definite instance of divine intervention' in that it coincided with the sudden halt of the German advance. The soldier, who declined to give his name, said the remainder of his brigade, along with stragglers from the Royal Irish Regiment and the Argyles, were drawn up on a hillside as artillery shells sought them out.

> The Brigadier ordered his signaller to call in the cavalry and guns, and we thought that as far as [we] were concerned we were at our own funeral. Just then the heavens opened, and rain such as most of us never witnessed, even when the Indian monsoons burst, fell. The dry state of the ground caused the white mist so common to the Tropics to arise, and through that we marched towards the Germans, through a sort of chalk pit, through a village, and to our left, where we had the advantage of somewhat hilly, wooded land between ourselves and the enemy.[17]

These stories suggest that among the thousands of British soldiers trapped in the path of the advancing Germans there were a few individuals who came to believe they had been saved by a miracle. The clap of thunder and torrential rain to them coincided with a sudden halt in the movement of the enemy cavalry that were pressing down upon them. Was it divine intervention or just coincidence?

The angels in the forest

Separated from their comrades by ten miles of dense French forest, General Douglas Haig's I Corps were having problems of their own. It was during this part of the retreat that a company of Coldstream Guards, who were among the last to be withdrawn, lost contact with the main body of their division. Unable to find their mates, the men dug in and waited for daylight. In 1964 Arch Whitehouse, a former soldier who had fought in the war, described the Coldstream Guards' 'astonishing encounter with the Angel of Mons' in his book *Heroes and Legends of World War One*.

'Who's that messin' about out there, carrying a light, the damn fool?' one of them exclaimed as the company dug makeshift defences with their entrenching tools. The light moved closer and resolved itself into the dim outline of a female figure. The men decided it was an angel:

> It looked exactly like any angel they had ever seen in a regimental chapel: tall, slim, and wearing a white flowing gown. She had a gold band around her hair and Eastern sandals on her feet, a pair of white wings were folded against her slim back.[18]

The figure beckoned the men to follow her, and although initially reluctant to leave the safety of their trenches, one by one the soldiers began to follow her across the open field. Eventually they

54

came to halt on the upper rim of a sunken road that did not appear on the maps. The vision continued to lead the men until they reached the end of the road, 'then she floated up the bank and pointed towards a covering copse a few dozen yards away', smiled and vanished. According to Whitehouse, soon after the men escaped from their exposed position and rejoined their regiment, but were never able to find the sunken road on a map. Within a few days their story had spread along the front, 'and for a time the Angel of Mons was accepted as a friendly token of the Almighty.'

This apocryphal account, recounted in verbatim style by Whitehouse, does not contain the names of any real soldiers. Neither does this story, like any of the others, appear in the regimental histories of the campaign, but Whitehouse is not the least bit concerned. 'Members of the present-day regiment no doubt scoff at the legend and argue that those were weary, battle-tortured men whose minds were fertile soil for any kind of hallucination,' he wrote, 'but those same Coldstream Guards went from Mons to a very exposed position outside Ypres ... and held it, unrelieved, for three weeks.'

Wednesday 26 August 1914

Wednesday 26 August was the 568th anniversary of the Battle of Crecy won by English bowmen during the Hundred Years War against the French. It was at Le Cateau, after two days of unrelenting marching, that General Smith-Dorrien decided it was time to stand and fight. The Battle of Le Cateau was to be a 'stopping blow' against the Germans, but it was a risky decision to take because what remained of II Corps, separated from the rest of the British force, would have to stand alone.

The battle was bigger in scale and far more costly to the British in terms of casualties than Mons. Both flanks of II Corps suffered heavy casualties, with 7,800 men killed, wounded and missing.

Unlike Mons, the landscape around Le Cateau was more suited for a pitched battle, although the rolling plains gave little cover against the German howitzers and machine guns. The British heavy guns were brought forward to the front line so that the gunners were fighting side by side with the infantry in the way they had done a century before at Waterloo. It was to be the last battle fought in the old medieval style. When the time came to withdraw the guns, the teams and their horses were brought down one after the other as shells burst around them. There were many feats of heroism and three VCs were won that day. In all 38 guns were lost, but Smith-Dorrien's gamble had paid off and the German pursuit was checked more permanently than at Mons.

Once again the British army was in retreat, with scattered battalions fighting rearguard actions as they fell back towards Paris. Military historian Richard Holmes remarks upon the odd coincidence that as Smith-Dorrien's men retreated they crossed the River Somme at Voyennes at exactly the same spot that Henry V had passed on his march to Agincourt almost 500 years before.[19] The symbolism of the BEF marching in the footsteps of Henry's bowmen to face a much larger force appealed to those in England who saw medieval imagery in every aspect of the war fought in a new industrial age.

The Battle of Le Cateau left the Germans exhausted and gave the BEF time to regroup with their French allies beyond the River Marne. Among the columns of British troops moving towards the Marne was 'a distinguished Lieutenant-Colonel'. In a letter published by the London *Evening News* in September 1915 he described how his division came into action at dawn and fought until dusk, under constant shelling from German artillery until the order came to withdraw from Le Cateau.

[We] retired in good order [and] were on the march all the night of the 26th and on the 27th with only about two hours' rest ... by the night of the 27th we were all absolutely worn out with fatigue – both bodily and mental fatigue. No doubt we also suffered to a certain extent from shock; but the retirement still continued in excellent order, and I feel sure that our mental faculties were still quite sound and in good working condition. On the night of the 27th I was riding along in the column with two other officers. We had been talking and doing our best to keep from falling asleep on our horses. As we rode along I became conscious of the fact that, in the fields on both sides of the road along which we were marching, I could see a very large body of horsemen. These horsemen had the appearance of squadrons of cavalry, and they seemed to be riding across the fields and going in the same direction as we were going, and keeping level with us. The night was not very dark, and I fancied that I could see squadron upon squadron of these cavalrymen quite distinctly. I did not say a word about it at first, but I watched them for about twenty minutes. The other two officers had stopped talking. At last one of them asked me if I saw anything in the fields. I then told them what I had seen. The third officer then confessed that he too had been watching these horsemen for the past twenty minutes. So convinced were we that they were really cavalry that, at the next halt, one of the officers took a party of men out to reconnoitre, and found no one there. The night then grew darker, and we saw no more. The same phenomenon was seen by many men in our column. Of course we were all dog tired and overtaxed, but it is an extraordinary thing that the same phenomenon should be witnessed by so many different people. I myself am absolutely convinced that I saw these horsemen; and I feel sure that they did not exist only in my imagination. I do not attempt to explain the mystery – I only state facts.[20]

His story did not mention angels. It referred to a squadron of phantom cavalry that appeared to protect his exhausted men. General Sordet's French cavalry corps were moving towards Le Cateau to support the British at this time, and it is possible this is what the officer and his men saw. Later in 1915 Lance Corporal A. Johnstone, of the Royal Engineers, wrote to the London *Evening News* to describe more phantom horsemen seen during the retreat that were distinctly hallucinatory rather than real. He said:

> We had almost reached the end of the retreat, and, after marching a whole day and night with but one half-hour's rest in between, we found ourselves on the outskirts of Langy, near Paris, just at dawn, and as the day broke we saw in front of us large bodies of cavalry all formed up in squadrons – fine, big men, on massive chargers. I remember turning to my chums in the ranks and saying 'Thank God! We are not far off Paris now. Look at the French cavalry!' They, too, saw them quite plainly, but on getting closer, to our surprise the horsemen vanished and gave place to banks of white mist, with clumps of trees and bushes dimly showing through them! Quite a simple illusion, yet at the time we actually picked out the lines of man and horse as plainly as possible, and almost imagined we heard the champing of the horses' bits! When I tell you that hardened soldiers who had been through many a campaign were marching quite mechanically along the road and babbling all sorts of nonsense in sheer delirium, you can well believe we were in a fit state to take a row of beanstalks for all the saints in the calendar.[21]

A vision of angels

The 'Old Contemptibles' who had fought at Mons and Le Cateau no longer formed a regular army by the end of 1914. The BEF had suffered nearly 90 per cent casualties, killed and wounded. Of the thousand-strong battalions that defended Mons, on average there remained just one officer and 30 men alive. Many of the survivors from the retreat lay in field hospitals recuperating from injuries that would eventually take their lives. In August 1915 a Lance Corporal lay in Netley Hospital near Southampton. While 'going over again in his mind what happened during the great retreat', he mentioned a strange incident to a nurse, which he later repeated to the Red Cross superintendent at the hospital, Miss M. Courtenay Wilson. She told a reporter from the London *Daily Mail*:

> I took it down verbatim as he spoke it in order that my memory should not play me false. I have known him for some time in hospital and he is not at all imaginative or highly strung. He is a decent, plain-speaking fellow and a married man with a family. So satisfied am I of the value of his story to those who are discussing the vision of angels that I wish his words to be made public just as they were uttered, without the slightest idea that he was dealing with a topic which now excited newspaper discussion.[22]

The soldier was subsequently interviewed by Harold Begbie for his book, *On the Side of the Angels*. He said the soldier was a 'slow speaking and deliberate mannered man, the last person in the world you would suspect of hysteria or nervous ideas' who had clearly been deeply affected by his experiences in France. The Lance Corporal's battalion was one of those caught up in the retreat of II Corps from Mons to Le Cateau. Two days later, with the German cavalry in pursuit, his unit were waiting to fire and scatter them to allow General Sordet's cavalry, who were on their right, to make a charge. This never happened as their positions were discovered by German aeroplanes and the Lance Corporal's men stayed where they were.

> The weather was very hot and clear ... when at nine o'clock in the evening I was standing with a party of nine other men on duty, and some distance on either side there were parties of ten on guard. Immediately behind us half of my battalion was on the edge of a wood retreating. An officer suddenly came up to us in a state of great anxiety and asked us if we

had seen anything startling. He hurried away from my party of ten to the next party of ten. When he had got out of sight I, who was the non-commissioned officer in charge, ordered two men to go forward out of the way of the trees in order to find out what the officer meant. The two men returned reporting that they could see no sign of any Germans; at that time we thought that the officer must be expecting a surprise attack.

Immediately afterwards [he] came back, and taking me and some others a few yards away showed us the sky. I could see quite plainly in mid air a strange light which seemed to be quite distinctly outlined and was not a reflection of the moon, nor were there any clouds in the neighbourhood. The light became brighter and I could see quite distinctly three shapes, one in the centre having what looked like outspread wings, the other two were not so large, but were quite plainly distinct from the centre one. They appeared to have a long, loose-hanging garment of a golden tint, and they were above the German line facing us.

The soldier watched the strange shapes hovering in mid-air for 35 minutes. They kept growing brighter, and the central figure appeared to be much taller than the lesser figures on either side. Under the feet of the three was a bright star, which remained when the figures disappeared. Later he discovered this was the morning star, Venus.

All the men with me saw them, and other men came up from other groups who also told us that they had seen the same thing. I am not a believer in such things, but I have not the slightest doubt that we really did see what I now tell you. I remember the day because it was a day of terrible anxiety for us. That morning the Munsters had a bad time on our right, and so had the Scots Guards. We managed to get to the wood and there we barricaded the roads and remained in the formation I have told you. Later on the Uhlans attacked us and we drove them back with heavy loss. It was after this engagement when we were dog-tired that the vision appeared to us.

I shall never forget it as long as I live. I lie awake in bed and picture it all as I saw it that night. Of my battalion there are now only five men alive besides myself, and I have no hope of ever getting back to the front. I have a record of fifteen years' good service, and I should be very sorry to make a fool of myself by telling a story merely to please anyone.[23]

When Begbie asked the soldier what effect the vision had on the men his response was revealing:

Well, it was very funny. We came over quiet and still. It took us that way. We didn't know what to make of it. And there we all were, looking up at those three figures, saying nothing, just wondering, when one of the chaps called out, 'God's with us!' – and that kind of loosened us. Then when we were falling in for the march, the captain said to us, 'Well, men, we can cheer up now; we've got Something with us.' As I tell you, we marched thirty-two miles that night, and the Germans didn't fire either rifle or cannon the whole way.

After the Lance Corporal's story was published, a letter arrived from a French officer in Paris who said he recognized his description as typical of the 'Northern Lights', which he had seen on a number of occasions in August, particularly after hot days with a cloudless sky. He wrote:

I read out the description in the *Daily Mail* to a party of French officers who spontaneously, and without any comment on my part, pronounced the vision as the *aurora borealis* which they had often seen at the Camp de Chalons.[24]

The miracle on the Marne

On 2 September the German armies had advanced to within 30 miles of the French capital and began to slow as they approached the River Marne. Around a third of the inhabitants of Paris fled along with the Government as the French armies rallied for what they knew would be a decisive battle. As the Germans moved to surround the city a dangerous gap opened up between their first and second armies into which the Allied forces struck. The Battle of the Marne began on 5 September, lasted three days and was fought along a 300-mile front. The French armies had by now lost a quarter of a million men. The Germans had lost a similar number but their advance had outstripped their ability to supply their armies. Any chance they had to win a decisive victory was now lost, and for good reason the French referred to the victory as 'the miracle on the Marne'. The battle also ended the 'war of movement' in which opposing armies advanced and retreated over many miles of territory. In October the Germans retreated to high ground beyond the River Aisne and dug deep trenches that would come to characterize the long static phase of the war that continued until 1918.

Brigadier-General John Charteris followed the BEF to France and in December 1914, when his friend Douglas Haig was made Commander-in-Chief, he became Chief Intelligence Officer at GHQ. In the first month of the war, he was present as the BEF retreated from Mons to the Marne and despite the chaotic conditions he managed to write detailed and colourful accounts of the campaign. Charteris was a keen writer and sent more than 1,200 letters, sometimes several in one day, to his wife Noel. After the war this collection of letters, postcards and other notes were gathered together by Noel and in 1931 they were published in a memoir, *At GHQ*. Under the date 5 September 1914 is a letter that describes the end of the retreat from Mons and the preparations for the imminent Battle of the Marne. One section deals with the rumours that were allegedly circulating among the men of the BEF at this point. In it Charteris wrote of:

the story of the 'Angel of Mons' going strong through the II Corps of how the angel of the Lord on the traditional white horse, and clad all in white with flaming sword, faced the advancing Germans at Mons and forbade their further progress. Men's nerves and imagination play weird pranks these strenuous times. All the same the angel at Mons interests me. I cannot find out how the legend arose.[25]

As Chief Intelligence Officer, Charteris would be expected to be one of the first to hear about any unusual incidents during the British campaign. His note suggests that he was puzzled and fascinated by the story. However, despite his senior post and closeness to the events in time and space, even he was unable to discover how it began life. That does not bode well for those who have attempted to track down the source of the stories decades later, but one fact shines out like a beacon from his testimony.

If the date Charteris gave in 1931 for this letter was correct, it suggests that rumours of supernatural intervention were circulating among the soldiers of the BEF in August and September 1914, just days after the Battle of Mons. This was three weeks before Arthur Machen published his story, 'The Bowmen', in a London newspaper. Was the date provided by Charteris' memoir the critical piece of evidence that proved Machen's story was not the genesis of the legend? Or was it just a red herring?

Visions on the Eastern Front

Apart from the letters written by Brigadier-General Charteris there was even stronger evidence that Russian troops fighting on the Eastern Front had independently reported supernatural visions during the first two months of the war. At the outbreak of war the German High Command was taken by surprise when the Russians struck first in the east. On 17 August 1914 two huge Russian armies advanced deep into East Prussia and threatened the capital, Konigsberg, but their success was short-lived. By the end of the month, at the Battle of Tannenberg, the Germans turned the tables. More than 30 000 Russian troops were killed, 92 000 were captured and thousands more were in retreat. Among the dead was the Russian First Army Commander, General Alexander Samsonov, who became lost in a forest as he tried to rally his troops and shot himself, shocked by the disastrous defeat.

Although they had suffered a punishing setback, the Russians continued to attack and a second army led by General Rennenkampf pushed deep into Austrian territory. It was against this background that rumours began circulating of supernatural intervention on the side of the Russians. Ralph Shirley, editor of the *Occult Review*, claimed that stories were 'widely current' at this time among the Russian army that troops had seen 'the famous ghost of General Skobeleff in white uniform and riding his white charger'. Skobeleff had become a folk hero following the Russo-Turkish War of 1877–78. His legend was such that within two decades of his triumph, a story arose that his ghost would appear whenever the Czar's armies were in danger.[26]

Shirley was also the source for a more specific account of a vision, attributed to a 'Russian general', who was leading the army that invaded German East Prussia:

> While our troops were in the region of Suwalki, the captain of one of my regiments witnessed a marvellous revelation. It was eleven o'clock at night, and the troops were in bivouac. Suddenly a soldier from one of our outposts, wearing a startled look, rushed in and called the captain. The latter went with the soldier to the outskirts of the camp and witnessed an amazing apparition in the sky. It was that of the Virgin Mary, with the Infant Christ on one hand, the other hand pointing to the west. Our soldiers knelt on the ground and gazed fervently at the vision. After a time the apparition faded, and in its place came a great image of the Cross, shining against the dark night sky. Slowly it faded away. On the following day our army advanced westward to the victorious Battle of Augustovo.[27]

The Battle of Augustovo began on 1 October 1914 and lasted nine days, placing the appearance of the vision on the night of 30 September. On 11 October the Johannesburg *Star* printed an account of 'a wonderful vision in the sky', which it said had been described in a letter written home by a Russian general.[28] Another account was attributed to a Russian princess who told of a vision of St Michael seen during the battles on the Eastern Front in a letter to friends in the English Red Cross. It was claimed that her letter had arrived in the last mail from Russia on 14 September 1914. Occult writer Harold Begbie referred to the princess as 'a voluntary nurse' and claimed her letter spoke of wounded soldiers who testified to seeing visions. ' "Strange things", she wrote, "are happening in the trenches." '[29]

Confirmation of this story is provided by Major-General Sir John Hanbury-Williams, who was a British military attaché to Russia from 1914 to 1917. In a diary entry dated 24 November 1916 he wrote:

> Discussing the 'Angels at Mons' story, he [Czar Nicholas] said that one of his daughters was talking to a wounded Russian soldier at about the same time as the Mons episode and that he told her during the debacle in the beginning of the war, after the advance in East Prussia, they had seen the Virgin Mary.[30]

Czar Nicholas II and the Empress Alexandra, a German princess, had four daughters and a son, Alexis. On the outbreak of hostilities the two eldest daughters, Grand Duchess Olga, age 19, and Tatiana, 17, volunteered to work as nurses in field hospitals. It was possibly the Grand Duchess Olga, noted for being 'sensitive and spiritual', who wrote to friends in the British Red Cross with her story of visions seen by soldiers. Displayed at this time within the bedrooms at the Alexander Palace was a religious icon that was much venerated by the empress and the two eldest girls. The icon of Our Lady of Tsarskoe Selo, a variation of the Virgin of the Sign, depicted the Virgin and the infant Jesus Christ. It is curious that the form taken by the visions reported by the Russian General took a similar appearance.

The intervention of the Virgin Mary, St Michael and General Skobeleff had little effect on the progress of the war in the East. The Russian army's initial success was followed by crushing defeats and stalemate. That the source of some of the earliest rumours of supernatural intervention in the war was a Russian princess underlines how endemic supernatural beliefs were at all levels of society. It is curious that the Russian stories spoke of a vision of the Blessed Virgin similar to that described at Pontmain in 1871, rather than the elaborate angelic visions that were described in later years. Although these accounts originated in battles on the distant Eastern Front, it appears the news had reached England and possibly France within a month of the outbreak of war. The scene was set.

CHAPTER THREE

Rumours of war

Enter Rumour painted full of Tongues:

Open your eares; for which of you will stop
The vent of hearing, when loud Rumor speaks?

Shakespeare, *Henry IV, Part 2*

At the outbreak of war in 1914 there was no television or radio to keep the public updated about the progress of the campaign on the Western Front, and even less was known about events in the East. Newspapers and magazines were the main force for mass communication. Many new magazines such as the *Illustrated War News* emerged, but real news was in short supply. In Britain, France and Germany, restrictions were placed by the official censor on information that could be published, and for a time editors were forced to rely upon rumour and gossip rather than real 'news'. The movements of journalists were restricted and they were unable to report objectively upon the campaign in France. Hungry for news, families of soldiers and sailors had to rely upon the contents of their censored letters.

Within days of the declaration of war in August 1914, rumours spread of a battle between British and German warships in the North Sea. The story diffused through the towns and cities on the east coast of England after newspapers published anecdotal tales from the crews of trawlers and merchant ships. They had reported seeing flashes in the sky, the sound of shells exploding and what appeared to be an exchange of fire between cruisers.

On 7 August the *Inverness Courier* was 'reliably informed' by telegram that seven German ships had been sunk and two captured in a battle near the Orkneys, while a British vessel in Wick Bay was signalling, 'Prepare to receive wounded.' It went on to report that a hospital train from Aberdeen had reached Inverness in the early hours of the morning carrying two doctors and around 40 nurses, and motor cars had been gathered together in Wick to collect the wounded. The following morning a special edition of the London *Daily Mail* joined the fray with a claim that there had been a great naval battle off the coast of Holland. Later that day the First Lord of the Admiralty, Winston Churchill, moved to quash the stories in the Commons. They were, he said, 'untrue in every detail' but this was just the beginning.[1]

The most dramatic account of all came from Captain Peterson of the Danish steamer *Hilda Maersk*, which arrived at Hull on 13 August. He stated that on the previous afternoon, when 15 miles off Spurn Head, the crew had distinctly seen a number of ships' masts rising out of the water at the mouth of the Humber. Six of these were flying the German flag and he decided they were remains of enemy warships sunk in a battle with British cruisers. The steamer's first officer confirmed his account, and said the ship had passed among the submerged masts, which he said protruded two fathoms above the surface of the water.[2]

The day after the steamer's report the official Press Bureau issued a statement that warned the public 'against placing the slightest reliance on the many rumours that are current' regarding victories or defeats and the arrival of wounded men or disabled ships. It assured them that 'the public may be confident that any news of successes or reverses to the British arms will be communicated officially without delay'.

Stories of phantom naval battles were taken seriously because this was a precarious time for Britain. Virtually the entire regular army was deployed in France, leaving only reserve and territorial regiments to guard the east coast, which had long been suspected as the target for a German invasion force. In order to land in England the Germans would have to avoid the Royal Navy, which was waiting for their fleet to leave port. On 28 August at the naval Battle of Heligoland Bight, three German cruisers were destroyed and three others damaged by the Royal Navy. After this the real possibility of an invasion began to recede, but speculation continued.

What emerges from this early period is the fact that rumours, particularly when they are given a level of credibility by the media, produce eyewitness accounts of events that never took place. Even when the source of the rumour is traced, or the ambiguity is removed, versions of the story continue to circulate and are widely believed. The early months of the First World War were a fertile breeding ground for bizarre rumours of every kind and could perhaps have contributed to the 'eyewitness' accounts that seemed to be leaking back to Britain from Mons. As we shall see, at this point in the war, the rumours that took hold were quickly regarded as having indisputable veracity. The most prevalent, both in Britain and Germany, was the belief that spies were constantly active to undermine the war effort. These stories became so widespread that even senior military officials became caught up in what became known as the 'spy mania'. It was a period when many otherwise sensible people in England came to believe that a vast network of German spies existed who used carrier pigeons, radio messages and signalling apparatus to send messages to the enemy. In addition to the 'spy scare' there were two other rumours that were so widespread they became belief-legends in their own right.

The phantom menace

By 1914 great advances in technology and communications brought about by the Industrial Revolution allowed war to be fought simultaneously on a global scale by land, sea and, for the first time, from the air. At the turn of the century Count von Zeppelin launched the first of his huge airships into the sky over

Germany and in 1903 on the other side of the world the Wright brothers took to the air in the first successful flight in a heavier-than-air machine.

Long before the Wright brothers' achievement, mankind had conquered the sky, and visited other worlds in our imagination. During the nineteenth century, early science fiction writers drew upon new possibilities opened up by scientific progress to conjure up visions of the future, visions that often blurred the boundary between fact and fiction. Some of the more perceptive writers quickly realized that technology could be utilized for good as well as evil. When in the 1880s there was widespread speculation about the existence of canals on the planet Mars, H.G. Wells wrote in *The War of the Worlds* (1898) of a technologically superior but militaristic Martian civilization landing in Sussex as the spearhead for an invasion of Earth. A decade later in his *The War in the Air* Wells visualized an equally devastating future war in which cities were destroyed and civilians terrorized by bombs dropped by fleets of airships and aeroplanes.

The imaginings of writers such as Wells and Jules Verne, combined with underlying political and social tensions, triggered off sightings of 'phantom airships' in different parts of the world. The best known began in California in 1896 when thousands of people claimed to have seen mysterious lights in the sky attached to an airship with wings and sails similar to the ones imagined by Jules Verne. The craze for seeing airships spread across midwest America in 1897, when thousands of people reported seeing lights and objects in the sky, in what has been described by sociologist Bob Bartholomew as a case of mass wish-fulfilment.[3] While these nineteenth-century UFOs reported in America were viewed by many people as the product of a secret inventor, phantom airships sighted over towns and cities in the British Isles during 1909 and 1913 were widely interpreted in a more sinister light. As the First World War approached, patriotic British newspapers seized upon the rumours of these airships' nocturnal visits to the east coast to whip up a national panic, and openly accused Germany of spying on the countryside in preparation for an invasion. Politicians and newspaper editors played a major role in exaggerating the capabilities of Germany's fleet of airships, and in 1912 claims that one of the craft had paid a secret visit to the English coast caused a sensation.

On 13 October the powerful naval airship *L1* left her shed at Friedrichshafen for an endurance cruise over northern Germany with Count von Zeppelin in command of 20 crew members. The airship reached an altitude of 5,000 feet and remained aloft for 36 hours in a voyage that covered 900 miles. The flight was hailed as a great achievement in Germany, but in Britain many believed it marked the end of the protective barrier that had been provided by the English Channel for generations. The flight also coincided with reports in English newspapers that an aircraft had been heard, and lights seen in the sky above the dockyard at Sheerness in Kent on the evening of 14 October. The 'airship rumours' led to questions in the House of Commons where the First Lord of the Admiralty, Winston Churchill, was asked if he could confirm that a Zeppelin had indeed passed over England. Churchill replied that:

> I caused enquiries to be made and have ascertained that an unknown aircraft was heard over Sheerness about 7 p.m. on the evening of 14th October. Flares were lighted at Eastchurch, but the aircraft did not make a landing. There is nothing in the evidence to indicate the nationality of the aircraft.[4]

When quizzed as to the whereabouts of British airships on the night in question, Churchill replied, 'I know it was not one of our airships.' Hundreds of similar sightings followed in 1913 and led Count von Zeppelin to send a telegram to the editor of the *Daily Mail* which read: 'None of my airships have approached the English coast.' Official denials, particularly when their source is mistrusted, can often have the opposite effect of encouraging belief and, as historian Douglas Robinson observed,

> The reports of 'phantom airships' over England persisted in the manner of the 'flying saucer' craze of our own day, and

level-headed people, who did not believe that the German naval airship had flown over England, feared for the future when they realised that she could easily have done so.[5]

By the outbreak of war, the feared Zeppelin was widely portrayed by the British media as a national bogey, as Napoleon's invasion barges had been to a previous generation. Anxious citizens, primed by the stories in newspapers, began to report any odd light or unfamiliar object in the sky as enemy aircraft.[6] In recent years, believers in flying saucers and UFOs have reinterpreted the phantom airship stories within a new context, as observations of alien craft from another world. It is far more likely that they were Rorschach-ink-blot-style projections onto the night sky of a nation's fear and anxiety at the possibility for the time of an attack from the air. Despite the hype that the mighty Zeppelin threat received in the press prior to the war, the size and strength of the German airship fleet was unimpressive. At the outbreak of war, Germany had one naval Zeppelin and five army airships in service. Within the first few months of hostilities most of these were destroyed or disabled during action over the Western Front, leaving none available for raids against Britain until 1915. At this time aeroplanes were primitive and had a limited range of 50 miles, so that few were capable of crossing the North Sea to raid England until later in the war.

Nevertheless, fears of invasion from the air spiralled out of control following Britain's declaration of war with Germany. Encouraged by the scare stories spread prior to the war, many people anticipated that Zeppelin raids upon British cities would begin almost immediately. From the outbreak of war, rumours describing mysterious airships and aeroplanes flying secret night-time missions began to pour into police stations and newspapers from places as widely diverse as the Scottish borders and southern Ireland. Most described moving and flashing lights in the sky at night that were believed to be the headlamps of German aircraft on reconnaissance missions. In other cases, mysterious lights seen in remote areas were believed to be evidence of signalling apparatus used by German agents to contact ships or aircraft out at sea.[7]

The first real airship raid against England took place over East Anglia on 19 January 1915 and was followed by a further rash of rumours. During the raid the German Zeppelin *L4* crossed the coastline south of Mundesley at 7.44 p.m. and set a course to attack King's Lynn, while its sister ship the Zeppelin *L3* bombed Great Yarmouth, killing two people and injuring several others. No German seaplanes, or defending aircraft, were airborne during the raid. However, police officers and residents said they had clearly identified the raiders as being heavier-than-air machines with rudders and wings. Stranger still, the MP for King's Lynn, Mr Holcombe-Ingleby, claimed the raiding aircraft had followed the movements of two mysterious motor cars whose occupants used searchlights to help them locate their targets. The occupants of these cars, according to the MP, 'occasionally sent upwards double flashes and on one occasion these flashes lit up a church on which the Zeppelin attempted to drop a bomb'. It was further claimed that in King's Lynn one of these cars directed powerful lights upon the grammar school.

> The car then stopped in the town and attention was called to the lights as a breach of the regulations. Having put them out, the driver turned his car quickly round and made off at a rapid pace for the open country.[8]

Investigations by the War Office revealed that these claims, which were widely published and believed, had no basis in reality. An official history of the air raids completed in 1918 found nothing to support the belief that spies had used motor cars to help the Zeppelins navigate over England. In the Commons, the War Office minister Harold McKenna said:

> The allegations have been carefully investigated by the Norfolk constabulary who have traced eight cars which were on the roads about the times and places of the Zeppelins passing. The cars have been identified and in each

case their movements have been satisfactorily explained. Their occupants were all persons against whom there is no possible ground of suspicion.[9]

But how could the witnesses who claimed to have seen these events described by the MP be so mistaken? This question must have occupied the minds of military intelligence who were kept busy throughout the early part of the war investigating 'false reports' of air raids. The official investigations that were launched into reports of phantom aircraft and flashing signal lights wasted manpower and added to the burden of providing an effective air defence for the exposed British coastline. Rumours and false reports of air raids on British cities reached such a level in February 1916 that communications were disrupted, blackouts were imposed and munitions factories in towns and cities across the Midlands lost valuable production. Records show that the War Office concluded that the vast majority of the reported sightings of enemy aircraft and lights in the sky were 'false rumours' spread by what it described as 'irresponsible persons'.[10]

In May 1916 the General Headquarters of the Home Forces issued a confidential intelligence briefing, which summarized the findings of its inquiries into reports of enemy signalling activity during the first two years of the war. Under the section 'Moving lights in the air', the briefing said such reports 'are often difficult to explain satisfactorily' but noted that 'planets and very bright stars, searchlights and optical illusions' all played a role in deceiving observers. The briefing concluded that 89 per cent of the reports made to the War Office in 1914–15 could be explained and 'there is no evidence on which to base a suspicion that this class of enemy activity ever existed.' It identified newspapers as the main source for the publication and spread of false rumours, and action was swiftly taken to restrict what information could be published about the location of air raids. By the end of the war, censorship was so strict that the official censor would not allow newspapers to publish the names of towns and cities that suffered damage in air raids.[11]

In March 1916 the General Headquarters of the War Office went further, issuing an order which attacked what it called 'the groundless rumours regarding the presence of hostile airships over Great Britain [which] have of late become very frequent'. The Government imposed severe measures to combat the 'irresponsible people' who it said had assisted in spreading disruptive rumours, ordering that 'persons originating such reports or assisting to circulate the same should be dealt with under the Defence of the Realm Regulations'.

'Snow on their boots ... '

Belief in visits by phantom German airships was just one of a series of rumours and panics which spread rapidly through Britain during the opening months of the Great War. The most persistent and widely believed of all was the 'Russian rumour' that began to circulate during the last week of August and quickly spread throughout the British Isles. On 8 September 1914 Michael McDonagh of *The Times* noted the rumour in his diary:

> There is being circulated everywhere a story that an immense force of Russian soldiers – little short of a million it is said – have passed, or are still passing, through England on their way to France. They are being brought from Archangel – just in time before that port was closed by ice – landed at Leith, and carried at night in hundreds of trains straight to ports on the south coast. This great news is vouched by people likely to be well informed, but it is being kept secret by the authorities – not a word about it is allowed in the newspapers – until all the Russians have arrived at the Western Front. It is said in confirmation that belated way-farers at railway stations throughout the country saw long train after long train running through with blinds down, but still allowing glimpses of carriages

packed with fierce-looking bearded fellows in fur hats. What a surprise is in store for the Germans when they find themselves faced on the west with hordes of Russians, while other hordes are pressing upon them from the east![12]

Although it was 'just a rumour', many witnesses came forward to claim they had seen the railway carriages containing the Russians, some of whom still had 'snow on their boots'. Again newspapers played the lead role in spreading the stories across Britain and the world. On 28 August the *Bradford Telegraph* in Yorkshire published what may have been the first written reference to it. The newspaper reported that many people in Bradford and Shipley said they had seen troop trains passing through railway stations. The most popular theory was that the trains were carrying Russian troops destined for the Western Front. When quizzed by reporters, officials denied that any troop trains loaded with Russians had passed through Shipley 'as yet'.

On 31 August 1914 the *Lancashire Daily Post* repeated the rumour that Russian or other foreign troops had spoken to drivers, and had been offered cigarettes at railway stations during their trek southwards. When enquiries were made it was found that no one appeared to have first-hand knowledge of the event. The paper then consulted the Government's official Press Bureau, who said: 'there is no truth at all in the rumour', and that they 'are quite puzzled as to its origin'. Given the secrecy which surrounded the war preparations, the *Manchester Guardian* decided to keep an open mind. Their London correspondent asserted that 'it would be unwise – indeed it would be foolish – to assume that the unlikely is not happening'.[13]

Initially, newspapers tended to suspend disbelief because it was known that 100 000 troops of the BEF had been safely shipped across the English Channel in great secrecy early in August. In fact, the trigger for the Russian rumour can be traced to a lengthy hold-up of railway movements that occurred on 24 August. This was imposed to allow reservists to move from their barracks to embarkation points on the south coast. One of the battalions involved were the Gaelic-speaking Fourth Seaforth Highlanders who travelled by train from the north of Scotland. Roland Bottomley, a Londoner who had arrived in Boston on the steamship *Arabic* on 4 September told the *New York Times* that

> there was a seventeen hour period in which all train service from Scotland was suspended. People who had expected to make Liverpool were very angry at the delay, being unable to account for it, but it became an open secret that 70 000 Russians were using the trains.[14]

In the USA, news about the war was not subject to censorship restrictions, and so the story about the Russians travelling through Britain was described in great detail. On 4 September the *New York Times*, in an article titled 'Russian Army now in Belgium?', claimed that 72 000 Russians arrived at Aberdeen on the night of 27 August and were then transported by train to Grimsby, Harwich and Dover. From there they were shipped to Ostend. Altogether it took 17 hours for this troop movement to take place, during which time all other train services were suspended on the east coast lines. The source for this information was the passengers and crew of the Cunard liner *Mauretania*, which had docked at New York on 3 September. More details emerged on 5 September when the liner *Philadelphia* docked at New York. One passenger, Mr Parker Sloan, said that on 28 August he was travelling by train to Liverpool when it was sidetracked and delayed for three hours. He told the *New York Times* this 'was to allow trains containing 50 000 Russian soldiers to pass from the north on their way to Belgium'.

In the early hours of the same day, Mr G.R. Gifford claimed he saw 10 000 Russians marching along the Embankment in London. They boarded a train at London Bridge destined for Dover where ships had arranged to meet them and transfer them to Ostend. Meanwhile, a porter at a station in Durham found an automatic chocolate machine was jammed by a rouble. In Malvern it was claimed a Russian jumped off a train and ordered 300 'lunchsky baskets'. A woman near Stafford said she saw hundreds of men in long grey overcoats stretching their legs next to their waiting train, while one night 250 000 men wearing astrakhan tunics were said to have marched through a town in North Wales.[15]

These fantastic stories were quickly spread to soldiers on the Western Front in letters from home. Brigadier-General John Charteris wrote that one of his fellow officers was 'full of stories of Russians passing through London: says his sister saw them, and when I said I didn't believe it, retorted, 'Do you mean to say my sister is a liar!' So that ended that discussion.' Charteris said he made inquiries at GHQ and was told the story was rubbish as 'they could not get there and would have nowhere to go, if they did.'[16] Nevertheless, many soldiers heard the Russian rumour and came to believe it was true, as in 1915 they would believe newspaper stories concerning the Angel of Mons.

By 7 September many who doubted these tales were convinced by what was regarded the strongest evidence for the existence of the Russians. The great cloud of speculation and rumour was given credence by a telegram from Rome, which was transmitted by the Central News Agency. It was published by the British press and read:

> The *Tribuna* publishes a telegram from Berlin, stating that the Kaiser has left French territory with the headquarters staff for Metz. The *Tribuna* attributes this retreat to 'the official news of the concentration of 250,000 Russian troops in France'.[17]

The news seemed to provide the reason why the German army had veered south-eastwards as it neared Paris and explained why the battered Allies had been successful in checking and forcing them back beyond the Marne. Up to this point the German army had appeared invincible in its march towards Paris and the idea that the Russians had played a part in the 'miracle on the Marne' was believed by senior figures such as Lord Lester Wemyss, the Rear-Admiral commanding the Twelfth Cruiser Squadron in the England Channel. Wemyss said his information came from a senior official at the Admiralty.[18] The Rome telegram was followed up by a dispatch from Percy J. Philip, a special correspondent for the London *Daily News and Leader*, who wrote from Ghent in Belgium on 12 September:

> Tonight in an evening paper I find the statement 'de bonne source' that the German Army in Belgium has been cut at Courtenberg between Brussels and Louvain by the Belgian Army, reinforced by Russian troops. The last phrase unseals my pen. For two days I have been on a long trek looking for the Russians and I have found them – where and how many it would not be discreet to tell – but the published statement that they are here is sufficient, and of my knowledge I can answer for their presence.[19]

Philip's circumstantial report gave credence to a sensational story told by a Cardiff mining engineer, Mr W.H. Champion. He told the *South Wales Echo* that on the declaration of war he had been working for the Russia-Asiatic Mining Corporation in Siberia and with five other Englishmen made his way to Warsaw, where he found he was unable to return to England via Berlin. Mr Champion then travelled to St Petersburg where the English Ambassador advised him to try to reach home via Archangel. From there he booked a steamer to Newcastle where he met 2,500 Cossacks en route to France. Two members of the Russian Duma travelling on the steamer told him:

> They were the last lot of 72 000 Cossacks who were going through to France, and that in addition to them 130 000 other troops had also been dispatched to the seat of the war in the west. They were landed at Leith, Peterhead and Newcastle and hurried down to the south coast in special trains.

Mr Champion arrived in England on 29 August and claimed to have travelled on the 192nd train loaded with Russian troops that had passed through York on its way to the south coast. Along the way he saw crowds of people waving Union Jacks cheering them on. He added:

> It is true that they were ordered to travel with the blinds down, but this condition did not prevent the Russians from pulling up the blinds in order to have a peep at England, a country for whose people they expressed the greatest admiration ... The Russians did not know in the least where they were going to land on the Continent of Europe. Even the superior officers were, I believe, quite ignorant of their exact destination. They were quite content to leave that to England ... The Cossacks travelling through England were a fine body of men. There was not a single man under 5 ft 10 in., and the majority were over 6 ft in height.[20]

The Russians told him they planned to march into Berlin by 28 September. Champion also claimed that he had taken several photographs of the Cossacks, which he gave to the Cardiff *Evening Express*, but the newspaper were prevented from publishing them by the press censor.

Mr Champion's and Mr Philip's stories were published on 14 September in the aftermath of victory at the Battle of the Marne. Prior to that point the British Government's official Press Bureau had held back from issuing an official statement about the Russian rumour. On that day they announced:

> There is no truth whatever in the rumours that Russian soldiers have landed or passed through Great Britain on their way to France or Belgium. The statement that Russian troops are on Belgian or French soil should be discredited.[21]

The denial led many newspapers to declare the whole story was a delusion, but in other quarters it had the opposite effect. Michael McDonagh noted that there were people whose faith in the story was strengthened rather than shaken by the official denial.

> 'Believe you me,' they say with a delightful air of confidence, 'the contradiction is meant to deceive the Germans. The Russian Army is on the Western Front all right.'[22]

After the 'Miracle on the Marne', enthusiasm for the Russian rumour began to wane and newspaper references to the sensation were relegated to the inside pages. On 23 September the London *Times* noted that the Berlin newspapers believed the rumour was deliberately circulated in order to confuse the Germans. If this was a correct reflection of the German High Command's opinion, it suggests the story was taken seriously in Berlin. If British Intelligence were responsible for seeding the rumour on the Continent they certainly did an effective job because the story seemed to puzzle as many people in Britain as it did in Germany. It was not until May 1915 that possibly the best explanation for the origin of rumour appeared. This was provided by the Honorary Secretary of the Press Representatives Committee at the Press Bureau, Mr H.B. Steele. He also explained why the story was not comprehensively suppressed:

> Important military movements at the time rendered difficult the scotching of what will go down as 'the Russian troops myth.' The facts regarding this famous story are simple. A large number of Russian officers visited this country to buy munitions of war or to join as attaches to the staffs of various commands then leaving for the front. Accompanying them was a number of soldier servants, and the bulk travelled from Archangel to the Scottish ports. These officers and men were undoubtedly seen by reliable witnesses. The same weekend the War Office decided to change the location of camps of the Territorials, then in training. To secure this end the trains were handsignalled and moved at night with blinds drawn. The engine drivers knew nothing of the loads they pulled. Meanwhile, however, some Scottish railway officials had corresponded with Southern friends and talked of having a lot of Russians travelling on their line.[23]

Steele's statement ties in with the known movements by rail of the Seaforth Highlanders and other Scottish battalions. A version of this story attributed the origins of the rumour to a rather amusing embellishment of the story already mentioned regarding the dispatch of a company of Gaelic-speaking Highland soldiers, and their arrival at a railway station somewhere in the English Midlands. A village porter asked them: 'Where are you from?' and the reply in broken English was, 'From Ross-shire.' To the English questioner this sounded like *'from Russia.'*

After the war more ingenious explanations for the Russian rumour were put forward by a variety of highly placed officials. One of the most intriguing originated from Professor R.V. Jones, who was head of Scientific Intelligence at the Air Ministry during the Second World War. He described how before the war there used to be a large consignment of eggs imported from Russia, and one of the ports at which they were landed was Aberdeen. An agent there sent a telegram to his headquarters in London warning them that the eggs had been landed and were on the train. 'With telegraphic economy he sent a signal such as '100,000 Russians now on way from Aberdeen to London' and inadvertently started the legend.'[24]

James Hayward notes that MI5 files from the period released at the Public Record Office in 1997 reveal that 'eggs' was a code-word for troops used by German spies before the war.[25] Jones said his source for the story was Major-General Sir Stewart Menzies, who was Chief of Intelligence at MI6 from 1939 to 1952. The involvement of the secret services in the spread of the rumour is a theme that recurs frequently in various accounts published after the war.

The Russian rumour reached its height at the end of August 1914 when Winston Churchill sent 3,000 troops from the Royal Marine Brigade to Ostend to help the Belgian Army hold back the German offensive. Among the brigade was a Colonel named George Aston who said the marines 'might easily be taken for Russians by German spies' and it is possible this was precisely the impression the Admiralty wished to cultivate.[26]

At the same time British Intelligence encouraged a hapless spy, Carl Lody, to feed the Russian rumour back to his masters in Berlin. Lody was arrested in Ireland in October but long before then his letters and telegrams to his handler had been intercepted by MI5. According to Basil Thomson, the wartime head of CID at Scotland Yard, the only report they allowed to pass to Berlin 'was the famous story of the Russian troops passing through England'. At his trial in London, Lody said he heard the rumour while lodging in Edinburgh where 'everybody was speaking about it'.[27]

In 1948 Bernard Newman, a former British Intelligence officer and prolific author of spy novels, claimed the Russian troop rumour was deliberately planted to confuse the German High Command. Newman said a German agent, presumably Lody, picked up the yarn and fed it back to Berlin where senior generals believed it was true. He wrote:

> They [German High Command] detached two divisions to guard the Belgian coast against the expected invasion – two weeks before the Battle of the Marne began. These two additional divisions might have turned the battle in the Germans favour – and, with it, the whole course of the war.[28]

Journalist Arthur Machen, writing in the *Evening News* in September 1914, described the rumour as 'one of the most remarkable delusions that the world has ever harboured ... a monumental instance to the museum of human delusions'. As if to pre-empt the future controversy that was very soon to dominate a large portion of his life, he added that during the height of this delusion:

> There was always this suspicious circumstance: you never met a man who had seen the Russians ... You met a man who knew a man who had seen the Russians, and this should have 'aroused our suspicions. We should have remembered the immortal ruling delivered in the Court of Common Pleas many years ago – Starleigh, J. – '*You mustn't tell us what the soldier said, it isn't evidence.*'[29]

Machen was one of the few commentators to appreciate that the expectant and anxious atmosphere which gripped the population of England in 1914 was ripe for the re-creation of old myths and the creation of new ones. Until the end of August 1914, because of reporting restrictions, the British public knew little about the true progress of the war in Europe, or the fate of the Expeditionary Force. In the absence of fact, wild stories like those of the phantom Russians spread like wildfire. It is impossible to discover just how far the British Government quietly encouraged these rumours, or sought to manipulate them for military advantage. The War Propaganda Bureau was not fully established in 1914 and directed propaganda would not be targeted against the Germans until the end of the war. But even at this early stage, the Government recognized how useful the media could be if manipulated in the correct way. In the case of the Russians, the War Office did nothing direct to counter the widespread rumour. While it circulated unchallenged, the story inflated the imagined size of the forces on the Western Front and confused the enemy at a crucial moment before the decisive battle.

The War Office was more directly implicated in the circumstances by which the Home Front came to learn about the Expeditionary Force's 'miraculous' escape from disaster at Mons. This story was carefully constructed by the War Office and the Secretary of State for War, Lord Kitchener, whose primary aim was to encourage the widespread recruitment he knew was necessary if Britain was to win the war.

Throughout the conflict the War Office and the French Ministry of War treated journalists with contempt. Their movements in France were hampered to the extent that Fleet Street's finest were held under arrest and prevented from approaching the Front. According to Lyn Macdonald, 'any suggestion that they should be allowed to travel on troop trains, enter the war zone, or even get within striking distance of the Army still in barracks, was treated with disdain and stamped on hard.'[30] When editors complained at the lack of news from the front, Kitchener appointed an army officer to write officially approved reports on the progress of the war that could be published under the by-line 'Eyewitness'. Nothing could have been further from the truth, and by the time of the first hostilities, newspapers were complaining bitterly that the flow of news had dried to a trickle.

Those reports that did get through were subject to the draconian hand of the press censor. Anything that did not reflect the optimistic, uplifting images of gallant British Tommies fighting bravely, as opposed to fleeing from the Hun, fell victim to the censor. Disaster, defeat and retreat were words that were inconceivable for an audience who believed the British Army was invincible. Arthur Ponsonby, author of *Falsehood in Wartime*, famously wrote that the war was the most 'discreditable period in the history of journalism'. It was not until a later stage that cynical troops began to question what they read in the newspapers. War correspondent Philip Gibbs said the fourth estate was as hungry for news as was the great British public, 'whose little professional army had disappeared behind a deathlike silence'. The outcome of this situation was that newspapers:

> printed any scrap of description, any glimmer of truth, any wild statement, rumour, fairy tale or deliberate lie, which reached them from France and Belgium; and it must be admitted that the liars had a great time.[31]

The Amiens dispatch

It was a full week after the Battle of Mons before the first accounts of the action were brought directly home to the public. Paradoxically, it was with the blessing of the head of the official Press Bureau that the 'facts' emerged in a most dramatic fashion. The war correspondents of *The Times* and *Daily Mail* had been detained on arrival in France, but gained their freedom and drove from Boulogne towards the Front, where they came upon British soldiers retreating from the battlefield at Le Cateau. Henry Hamilton Fyfe of the *Daily Mail* and Arthur Moore of *The Times* pressed on to Amiens where they could hear the sound of distant guns. Fyfe wrote:

> We drove about all that day seeking for news and realising
> every hour more and more clearly the disaster that had
> happened. We saw no organised bodies of troops, but we
> met and talked to many fugitives in twos and threes, who
> had lost their units in disorderly retreat and for the most
> part had no idea where they were.[32]

On Friday 28 August, the two exhausted newsmen arrived at
Dieppe where they placed their copy on a boat that left for
England. Moore's dispatch reached the editor of *The Times*, Henry
Wickham Steed, by special courier on Saturday night, and the
extreme gravity of its contents was immediately apparent. He
agreed that the story must be submitted to the press censor,
though Steed believed, 'It was highly improbable, on the
assumption that the news was true, that the authorities would
allow it to be published except in the form of an official
announcement.' When nothing was heard from the censor for
two hours, preparations were underway to put the paper to
bed without it when at midnight a messenger returned from
Whitehall holding an edited version. Certain passages from the
original had been cut out and others which Steed had crossed
out as 'undesirable' were marked *stet* for publication. Even more
astonishing, fresh sentences 'summarising the effect of the news
and pointing its moral', had been inserted. The new version was
accompanied by a signed memorandum from the press censor,
F.C. Green MP, which Steed said:

> ... begged us to publish it in the form in which he returned
> it ... with this document before us we could no longer hope
> that our correspondent had been misled, and we published it
> in accordance with the official request.[33]

By tradition, during its entire history the front page of *The Times*
had been filled with advertisements. Steed's staff produced a
special Sunday War Edition on 30 August 1914, with the front
page filled with dramatic news from the front. Taking prime

position was a report 'from our special correspondent' Arthur
Moore. The headlines screamed:

HEAVY LOSSES OF BRITISH TROOPS – Mons and Cambrai
– Fight Against Severe Odds – Need for Reinforcements.

This story was the first to break the 'patriotic reticence' observed
by the gentlemen of the press. The Amiens dispatch opened as
follows:

> I read this afternoon in Amiens this morning's Paris paper.
> To me, knowing some portion of the truth, it seemed
> incredible that a great people should be kept in ignorance
> of the situation which it had to face. It is important that
> the nation should know and realise certain things. Bitter
> truths, but we can face them. We have to cut our losses, to
> take stock of the situation ... Since Monday morning last
> [24 August] the German advance has been one of almost
> incredible rapidity. The British Force fought a terrible fight
> which may be called the action of Mons, though it covered
> a big front, on Sunday. The German attack was withstood to
> the utmost limit, and a whole division was flung into the
> fight at the end of a long march and had not even time to
> dig trenches.

The report told how the promised French support had failed to
materialize, the fortified city of Namur had fallen and General
Joffre's armies had fallen into full retreat along their whole
length. The BEF were described as a 'broken army' and Moore
revealed British losses 'are very great ... I have seen the broken
bits of many regiments ... with some divisions losing nearly
all their officers.' The remainder of the army 'fought its way
desperately with many stands, forced backwards and ever backwards by the sheer unconquerable mass of numbers'. Moore
painted a vivid picture of an outnumbered BEF whose artillery
had cut down line after line of German infantry to no avail. 'So
great was their superiority in numbers that they could no more
be stopped than the waves of the sea.' The final paragraph of the

dispatch was rewritten by the government censor and carried the cross head: 'MEN IMPERATIVELY NEEDED.' It read:

> To sum up, the first great German effort has succeeded. We have to face the fact that the British Expeditionary Force, which bore the great weight of the blow, has suffered terrible losses and requires immediate and immense rein-forcement. The [BEF] has won indeed imperishable glory, but it needs men, men, and yet more men.

Green, later Lord Birkenhead, had taken Moore's honest impression of disaster and used it to rouse a complacent nation to a sense of the need for greater effort. His intervention gave the impression, in Fyfe's words, 'that the truth was far worse than the public could be allowed to know'. The Amiens dispatch had the desired effect, but Green did not survive the storm he had invited.

The Times splash was read with incredulity and disbelief at breakfast tables across the British Empire. Furious questions were asked in the Commons. To cheers in the Commons, the Prime Minister, Herbert Asquith, said it was 'impossible too highly to commend the patriotic reticence of the Press as a whole from the beginning of the war up to the present moment. [*The Times*] appears to be a very regrettable exception.'[34] While his masters were pontificating in public, Green's plan had produced the results he had envisaged. Lord Kitchener published his first appeal for 100 000 new recruits early in August, but it was not until the publication of the Amiens dispatch that the floodgates really opened. During the first two days of September a tidal wave of men enlisted in the British Army. On 3 September alone 330 204 had taken the king's shilling, the highest figure achieved on a single day. So many turned up at the recruiting office in Scotland Yard that it was overwhelmed and a new office was opened in Trafalgar Square. Within eight weeks 761 000 men had joined up and by the end of the year the number was approaching one million.

On 5 September as French armies, reinforced with the help of Paris taxicabs, halted the German advance on the banks of the Marne, London magazines published a recruiting poster that would become an icon of the war. Lord Kitchener's stern, unblinking visage glowered from billboards on every street corner, his finger pointing at every British man of service age:

YOUR COUNTRY NEEDS YOU
God Save the King.

Until they awoke to read *The Times* that Sunday morning, the lives of the majority of people at home in England had been hardly touched by the outbreak of war. They were confident that the BEF would win the day as they had done a hundred years before at Waterloo. The shock when it came was palpable. Moore's description of the fate of British troops during the retreat had two immediate results that would have enormous impact upon the public perception of the events. The newspaper accounts shocked their English audience and, more importantly for the seeding of rumour, predisposed sections of society towards a belief that the BEF had only survived defeat *as a result of a miracle*.

Out of the background of censorship and rumour emerged a powerful myth actively promoted by the War Office: that the tiny British Army had single-handedly born the weight of the German blow at the Battle of Mons, and had escaped by 'a miracle' to fight another day. The contribution of the French armies to the victory at the Marne was overlooked in the move to plant within the British mind the idea that the BEF had saved Western civilization from the German hordes.

Soon, and apparently by accident, this idea would combine with another describing how ghostly bowmen had intervened at a vital moment to save the British Army from destruction. In those testing days, many wanted to believe and prayed for a miracle. As summer turned to autumn, one man emerges from the great mass of people as the conduit for the creation of new myths and legends around the momentous events unfolding in Europe ...

CHAPTER FOUR

The sinister genius

Long after the war is over, and the facts of it have been recorded in histories, one of the most widely known events will be the appearance of St George and his angel-warriors in the defence of the British during the retreat from Mons. We say 'known'; because posterity will 'know' that the Saint came down. People 'know' it already. The papers are full of the occurrence, and the testimony pours in from all sides. And here is Mr Arthur Machen roundly declaring that none of the testimony yet given is worth a rap; that the whole thing arose out a story which he himself made up, out of his head, in church, and sent to the *Evening News* ...

Times Literary Supplement, 19 August 1915

Arthur Machen is remembered as a master of a genre of horror fiction known as 'mystery and the imagination'. Although his stories and novels were admired by his contemporaries, Machen never found the critical acclaim he sought until late in his life. It is only in recent years that a Machen revival has led admirers from a new generation to recognize him as a truly canonical writer. While his best-known work was produced in the last decade of the nineteenth century, Machen's connection with the Angel of Mons came about during his career as a wartime journalist. It was during this period that a rival author, Harold Begbie, attacked his 'rather sinister genius' in claiming credit for the origin of the legend.

He was 51 when Britain declared war on Germany, and too old to add his name to the list of those determined to 'do their bit' for king and country. What was unrecognized, even by his peers, was the contribution he could make to the war effort if his fertile imagination was channelled through the pages of a mass circulation newspaper.

Born in the old Roman town of Caerleon, South Wales, to middle-class parents in 1863, he was the son of an Anglican vicar, John Edward Jones. Machen was his mother's maiden name. During his classical education at Hereford Cathedral School, a talent for writing and a passion for literature and history emerged. From an early age his imagination was captured and inspired by the numinous landscapes that surrounded his childhood home in Gwent. Caerleon was a place of magic and mystery framed by the Black Mountains, the ancient forest of Wentwood and the Severn Valley. In Machen's youth archaeologists were digging in the ruins of the Roman fort at Caerleon which Geoffrey of Monmouth in his twelfth-century *History of the Kings of Britain* claimed was the court or round table of King Arthur. This was the environment in which Machen grew up and his fascination with Britain's Celtic past, particularly the legends of Arthur and the quest for the Holy Grail, stayed with him and influenced much of his literary output.

In the 1880s, Machen left his beloved Wales to pursue a career as a journalist in the city of London. He soon came to appreciate his fellow mystic William Blake's observation that the career of the writer was accompanied by poverty and obscurity. He worked hard in a variety of temporary jobs in the heart of the city that was the bustling capital of the British Empire. He was determined to pursue his passion for writing, but it was not until the final decade of the nineteenth century that he produced some of the finest examples of the highly crafted imaginative fiction that would become his trademark. His first major work in the horror genre, *The Great God Pan* (1890) established his style of blending subtle, transcendental horror with supernatural themes. During the 1890s Machen became one of the movers and shakers among the fashionable and decadent group of London writers and artists who surrounded Oscar Wilde, but he was careful to distance himself from the trials and disgrace of Wilde.

In 1899, following the death of his first wife, Amy, Machen was devastated and suffered a near breakdown. During this period he experienced a series of mystical experiences that were to have a profound influence upon his writings. Machen was reluctant to fully describe the nature of these visions, but said they led to 'a singular rearrangement of [his] world'.[1] He recovered from this personal crisis with the help of his closest friend, the occult writer A.E. Waite. It was Waite who invited him to join the Order of the Golden Dawn, founded in 1888. For a time the order counted among its members such names as William Butler Yeats and Aleister Crowley, but Machen was not impressed by Crowley and developed a negative impression of occultists. Their attitude, he wrote, could be summed up thus: 'If the tale has anything of the supernatural it is true, and the less evidence the better.'

Machen remained a fringe member of the order, but by this time he had begun to turn away from what he saw as the dark pagan themes that characterized his earlier work. He was beginning to formulate his own individual brand of mysticism with its foundations firmly rooted in the Celtic Christianity of his home-land. To Machen, the act of writing was to induce a state of self-revelation, or ecstasy, that lifted the curtain and allowed him to look upon another world that co-existed alongside our own. Like Yeats, he became a passionate believer in mystic and spiritual values as a reaction against the evils of materialism and science.

Nevertheless the occult influences from the early period remained at the forefront of what became the most productive period of his life. His literary output during the 1890s concentrated upon what were very racy subjects at that time: paganism, sexuality, transcendental horror and the supernatural. For inspiration Machen drew upon his own experiences of 'waking visions' and the folk traditions he absorbed from his native Gwent. The depth of this weirdness is exemplified by his short story, 'The White People' (1899), an eerie account of a young girl's encounters with primeval forces. This contained, said Machen, 'some of the most curious work that I have ever done, or ever will do ... it goes ... into very strange psychological regions.' The intermingling of this world and the 'otherworld' was a recurring theme in his work. In Welsh folklore this otherworld was the domain of the *Tylwyth Teg* or fairy folk, and traffic with them was chancy and fraught with danger. The fairies of Machen's stories are not the tiny, benevolent creatures depicted in Victorian children's fiction, but malevolent, elemental forces who haunt and abduct humans who fall under their spell.

Machen's better-known works, and the novel regarded as his masterpiece, *The Hill of Dreams*, did not find publishers until the first decade of the twentieth century. By this time he had largely given up writing and in the year of Queen Victoria's death he joined a touring repertory theatre group.

In 1903 he met and married an actress who shared his Bohemian tastes, Dorothie Purefoy Hudleston. The couple had two children. Machen had by now distanced himself from the decadence of the 1890s and became a vocal apologist for Anglo-Catholicism. As the First World War approached he refined his idiosyncratic, opinionated brand of mysticism in preparation for his return to writing for a living. For the first time in his life he could see his work in print as soon as it was completed.

The cauldron of war

In 1910 Machen decided to take a full-time paid job as a journalist. The opportunity came when Alfred Turner, the editor of the London *Evening News*, offered him a position on his reporting staff. Machen accepted and quickly found his niche as a specialist writer in the arts and religion. His eccentric and erudite style proved immensely popular with its readers and he provided the paper – part of the Northcliffe empire that included the *Daily Mail* – with a steady flow of what today's news editors would recognize as 'colour pieces'. Although the newspaper treated him well and paid a good salary, he regarded the 11 years he spent there as a form of living hell.

But one story he wrote for the *Evening News* in 1914 was to become his single most successful piece of writing. Its runaway success was to Machen the source of both consternation and pride, and the storm it created continued to haunt him for the rest of his life. Even today, 'The Bowmen' and the legend of the Angel of Mons that appeared in its wake have become synonymous with his name. Much to his annoyance this story, which he had dismissed as 'an indifferent piece of work', finally brought him the recognition and respect he craved and made him a household name. It became what Peter Buitenhuis calls 'one of the most successful propaganda myths of the war'.[2] But unlike the atrocity stories concocted by British Intelligence, this was a fantasy created innocently and, initially at least, without direct official encouragement.

Looking back upon his wartime career, Machen recalled the shock that was felt in 1914 by many ordinary people who had grown complacent in the shadow of the British Empire. Setbacks against the Boers had been an unpleasant surprise, but it was widely held that when war with Germany finally arrived, 'It would be all right on the night.' The fourth estate was better informed about the realities of war than the mass of their readership. At the offices of the *Evening News*, rumours and gossip arrived daily along with privileged information suppressed by the authorities. The war was brought home to London on 6 August when the British cruiser HMS *Amphion* sank at the mouth of the Thames after striking a mine laid by the crew of a German ship it had just captured. Within days the Kaiser's armies were sweeping through Belgium. Liège fell on 16 August and was soon followed by Brussels. By 30 August 1914 the German tidal wave seemed unstoppable. Meanwhile, the Russian invasion of East Prussia was turned to defeat at the Battle of Tannenburg, and in the west the German advance led French generals to warn their Government to abandon Paris. Quite clearly, it 'wasn't going to be all right on the night'.

In the midst of this crisis Arthur Machen awoke at his London home in Lisson Grove and looked out of his window to see newspaper bills papering the front of the little shop across the way. The headlines he saw were from the *Weekly Dispatch*:

THE TRUTH FROM THE BRITISH ARMY – Tidal Wave of German Troops – Need for the Country to Grasp the Danger – British Wall of Steel Remains Unbroken – Infantry's 'Withering Fire'.

These lines made his heart sink, almost to the point of despair. They told of the British Army in full, desperate retreat, on Paris: 'The correspondent of the newspaper rather pictured an army broken to fragments and the fragments scattered abroad in confusion,' he wrote. 'It was hardly an army any more; it was a mob of shattered men.' Long afterwards Machen came to realize the newspapers had exaggerated the crisis facing the BEF. Nevertheless, the headlines had a shattering effect – 'I know what we read, and how we were sick at heart' – and it was while in this state of mind that he set about writing something that might comfort himself and the whole nation:

I seemed to see a furnace of torment and death and agony and terror seven times heated, and in the midst of the burning was the British Army. In the midst of the flame, consumed by it and yet aureoled in it, scattered like ashes and yet triumphant, martyred and for ever glorious ... so I saw our men with a shining about them.[3]

Machen took these thoughts to mass at St Mark's in Marylebone and, while the priest sang and the incense drifted above his Gospel book, he sat making up a story in his head. The image he conjured up was of dead soldiers rising through flames and being welcomed into a British Valhalla, 'with songs and flowing cups and everlasting mirth'. This became the first draft of a short story, 'The Soldier's Rest', which drew its inspiration from the Grail quest, one of Machen's literary obsessions. A British Tommy sacrifices himself to save his comrades from the Germans and suddenly finds himself in a strange hospice where he is ministered to by a monk in dark robes. He is offered wine from 'a great silver cup', which he is assured contains *vin nouveau du Royaume* as the clues that reveal his location fall into place for the reader. Finally, he experiences a vision of a figure in armour 'made of starlight, of the rose of dawn, and of sunset fires'. The identity of the figure is not given, but the context suggests he is Arthur, or St George, welcoming the gallant soldier to the next world. At this stage Machen found the idea unworkable, and put it to one side.[4]

A couple of weeks passed before Machen came up with the plot for 'The Bowmen' and sent it to Alfred Turner 'to take or leave'. The story filled 17 column inches on page three of the *Evening News* on Tuesday 29 September 1914, which fell upon the feast of St Michael and All Angels. This was one of a number of circumstances that led some readers to connect Machen's bowmen with angels, as St Michael was a patron saint of soldiers. No battle was specifically named, but the context of the story left no doubt that it referred to the stand made by the BEF at Mons one month earlier. In an article written for the *Daily Mail*, Machen summarized the story:

A British soldier finds himself one out of a thousand companions who are occupying a salient against a furious cannonade and the attack of ten thousand German infantry. The holding of this salient, for a time at least, is vital. Its capture means the turning of the Allied left flank, and that means ruin for France and England. The British see that the position is hopeless. Their guns are overwhelmed and shot to bits by the enemy's artillery; their numbers are reduced from a thousand to five hundred. They know that they are doomed to death beyond all hope or help; and they shoot on as calmly as if they were at Bisley.

Then the soldier – my soldier – remembers the motto that appears on all the plates in the vegetarian restaurant in St Martin's Lane: *Adsit Anglis Sanctus Georgius* – May St.

George be a present help to the English. He utters this prayer mechanically; and falls instantly into a waking vision. He hears a voice, mighty as a thunder-peal, crying, 'Array, array, array!' and the spirits of the old English bowmen obey the command of their patron and ours. The soldier hears their war-cries: 'Harrow, harrow! St George, be quick to help us.' 'Dear saint, succour us!' He sees the flight of their arrows darkening the air.

And the other men, to their amazement, see the Germans melting from before them. In a moment a whole regiment crashes to the ground. The men cannot make out what is happening; they suppose a reserve of machine guns may have been brought up. At all events, as one says to another, the Germans 'have got it in the neck.' And the soldier who is in the world of vision goes on shooting till the man next to him clouts him on the head and tells him not to waste the King's ammunition on dead Germans.[5]

The story ended with 10 000 German dead lying on the battlefield without any visible wounds on their bodies. The German General Staff, who are ruled by scientific principles, refuse to accept a supernatural explanation and instead decide the contemptible English must have used poison gas shells, 'but the man who knew what nuts tasted like when they called themselves steak, knew also that St George had brought his Agincourt bowmen to help the English.'[6]

Machen was not greatly impressed by his creation. At the newspaper, Machen's colleague Oswald Barron, who wrote 'The Londoner' column for the *Evening News*, read the draft, congratulated him, and asked why would English archers from the fifteenth century adopt French phrases for their battle cries. The only reply Machen could think of was that a *monseigneur* scattered here and there struck him as 'picturesque'. He pointed out that in fact many of the archers who fought at Crecy and Agincourt were mercenaries drawn from his homeland of Gwent who would have appealed to Celtic saints for protection. Their names would not have been recognized by readers of the *Evening News*.[7]

The story was not unique, as many readers believed, but was typical of Machen's literary style. Supernatural assistance to the war effort was a theme he would revisit again and again. In 'Drake's Drum' he wove existing folklore about the protective spirit of the Elizabethan hero into a story of a mysterious drumbeat heard when the German Navy surrendered at Scapa Flow in 1918. Another story from slightly earlier, 'Munitions of War', featured the ghosts of sailors from the Napoleonic wars helping sailors at Bristol docks in 1914.[8]

Machen's predilection for blurring the boundaries between fact and fiction is a familiar one today, but at the time it would have been clearly recognized only by those who knew his earlier work. Even by 1914, Machen's books were not widely read outside literary circles. This goes some way towards explaining what happened next. In writing 'The Bowmen', Machen said later that he was well aware of the traditions of supernatural intervention in battle that dated back to the time of the Crusades. He wrote that 'all ages and nations have cherished the thought that spiritual hosts may come to the help of earthly arms, that gods and heroes and saints have descended from their high immortal places to fight for their worshippers and clients.' He confessed that another direct influence was Rudyard Kipling's story 'The Lost Legion' (from *Many Inventions*, 1893) which told of a battalion of ghostly English soldiers who come to the assistance of a British force in Afghanistan. Kipling's tale went hand in hand with the medievalism of G.K. Chesterton that Machen said was never far from his mind. Medieval imagery influenced a number of writers and poets of the First World War. It even impressed itself upon the Prime Minister, Herbert Asquith, whose 1915 poem 'The Volunteers' spoke of London city clerks queuing to enlist 'to join the men of Agincourt'.

'The Dazzling Light' was another of Machen's 'legends of the war' published by the *Evening News* on 24 June 1915. At face value, it tells 'the story of a dream' experienced by a British soldier, Lieutenant Delamere Smith, before he goes to fight. Again Machen plays the role of journalist and narrator who describes how the soldier takes a holiday on the coast of South Wales days after the outbreak of war. One morning he scales the cliffs at Giltar Point, one of Machen's favourite places, and falls into a waking dream that is triggered by an odd sensation in the top of his head. This is followed by 'a sort of shock, something between a mild current of electricity and the sensation of putting one's hand into the ripple of a swift brook'. Simultaneously, the waves below him are transformed into an unfamiliar landscape where lines of soldiers in medieval armour are marching.

Readers of his earlier work would have immediately recognized the 'time-slip' depicted in 'The Dazzling Light' as typical of Machen's themes. Others may have been left feeling that perhaps Lieutenant Smith was a real soldier and not a product of the writer's imagination, especially as Machen wrote that his story could possibly be 'explained away ... it is merely one of the odd circumstances of these times'.

His fondness for adopting the persona of a journalist as a ploy in his fiction was inviting confusion and misinterpretation. Machen was now writing for a wider audience than his novels had ever reached during a period when the British people were experiencing a period of unprecedented anxiety. Indeed, Machen must have been aware of the danger, as he himself wrote in September 1914 of the 'remarkable delusion' that led thousands to believe in the Russian troop rumour. While he believed his short stories had very little literary merit compared to his earlier masterpieces, they undoubtedly caught the public mood at a critical time.

Fiction and fact

Much of the confusion that surrounded the ambiguous reality status of 'The Bowmen' can be explained not only by the content and construction of the story itself – but by the way it was published. 'The Bowmen' carried Arthur Machen's byline but many who read it could not decide if it was fact or fiction. This impression was the result of a series of accidents.

Although the paper regularly serialized works of fiction, readers had grown familiar with Machen as a news reporter, not a writer of fiction. Moreover, in the same edition that contained 'The Bowmen' there appeared 'A Scrap of Paper', by Alexander Cornford that was clearly marked 'Our Short Story'. This appeared to suggest that 'The Bowmen' was something different altogether. To make matters worse, the story itself was full of connotations that encouraged confusion. By opening with the phrase, 'If the authority of the censorship is sufficient excuse for not being more explicit', Machen referred to the draconian press censor with whom Fleet Street was engaged in a daily battle. His comment implied that it was only now, more than one month after the battle of Mons, that 'the truth' could finally be told.

At this stage in the war, the newspaper's readership had no access to factual description of what had really happened at Mons. In the middle of the controversy that followed, the *Evening News* summed up the state of mind that existed in England:

> People are still asking each other whether there were not some kind of miraculous intervention or strange event during the heroic retreat from Mons. 'After all,' they say 'it is admitted that the escape of our Expeditionary Force from destruction was a miracle. It seemed doomed. Something must have happened to save it.'[9]

Official censorship meant that newspapers were forced to rely upon the focused 'eyewitness' accounts of battle provided by the War Office and these were supplemented by the censored letters of soldiers at the front. Many of these had been 'tidied up' prior to publication by professional writers and Machen's story appeared to follow this tradition, employing an anonymous soldier as a focus of the action in a way that would be immediately familiar to his audience. These circumstances suggested to a proportion of the population that 'The Bowmen' was a story, if not wholly true, then at least partly true.

While Machen, and his newspaper, were ultimately responsible for muddying the waters, there is no evidence of any deliberate intention to deceive. Twelve days before publication he had already set out his patriotic intentions in the first fictional story he wrote for the *Evening News*. 'The Ceaseless Bugle Call' appeared on 17 September 1914, and Kevin McClure feels that it was 'virtually a trial run for "The Bowmen" '.[10] Like Machen's later fantasies it was intended as a piece of propaganda and it drew heavily upon Britain's martial and religious traditions. These were the very matter of Britain that appealed to Machen's imagination: the chivalry of King Arthur's knights, the quest for the Holy Grail, and the special favour of St George, which imparted divine favour upon the English at the battles of Crecy and Agincourt.

In 'The Ceaseless Bugle Call' Machen begins by waxing lyrical about the thousands of new recruits who were then swelling the British Army's training camps at Aldershot. Along the road by the camps stood the garrison church, dedicated to St George, and above the porch was a sculpture of the saint kneeling beside the body of the dragon. The dragon was equated with Germany, 'the Beast of our age', and soldiers with St George, its slayer. As Kitchener's growing army-in-waiting marches and turns a bugle call 'from some far off camp' rings a ceaseless call:

> It is as though it were the call of the trumpet that England has put to her lips, that summons shall soon sound and echo round all the regions of the world even till the final hour of victory. *Tuba mirum spargens sanum*: wondrous sound the trumpet flingeth. It shall resound till it call up the spirits of the heroes to fight in the vanguard of our battle, till it summon King Arthur and all his chivalry forth from their magic sleep in Avalon; that they may strike one final shattering blow for the Isle of Britain against the heathen horde.

Here Machen drew upon the Welsh tradition of how Arthur was not dead but lay sleeping inside a secret cavern, surrounded by his knights, waiting for the call that would wake them. In Britain, Arthur was a powerful symbol to invoke at a time of crisis but he was a peculiarly Celtic icon. For many soldiers, St George was a far more potent patron of the English military tradition, and he also had the blessing of the church, and this may explain why 'The Bowmen' had a greater impact than 'The Ceaseless Bugle Call'.

The chaos of war had momentarily lifted the veil that separated this world from that of myth and legend. Ancient forces were stirring and Machen was tapping into a national psyche that was ready to be exploited.

Dangerous rumours

Early in October 1914, within days of the publication of 'The Bowmen', Machen received a letter from an old acquaintance, Ralph Shirley, who edited the *Occult Review*. The *Review* was the leader in its field and its list of contributors reads like a roll-call of the leading spiritualists, occultists and theosophists in Edwardian London. Shirley enquired if his story had any foundation in fact and Machen replied that it was an invention entirely of his own making. Shortly afterwards David Gow, the editor of the weekly spiritualist magazine *Light*, wrote asking a similar question and again Machen assured him that he had 'made it up out of my own head'. It was not, as Gow suspected, based upon any rumour or hint or whisper of any kind the journalist had picked up from the Front. Writing in 1915, Machen was growing irritated by these stories:

> It has been murmured and hinted and suggested and whispered in all sorts of quarters that before I wrote the tale I had heard something. The most decorative of these

legends is also the most precise: 'I know for a fact that the whole thing was given him in typescript by a lady-in-waiting.' This was not the case; and all vaguer reports to the effect that I had heard some rumours or hints of rumours are equally void of any trace of truth.[11]

Two days before the German offensive at Ypres, on 10 October 1914, David Gow described Machen's story, in *Light*, as 'a little fantasy' and 'an imaginative piece of word-painting' but then compared it to stories of divine intervention from the Old Testament. He added:

> If in the present struggle any such interposition of the unseen world were to occur, we should doubtless regard it as a special intervention of Providence in our favour, but so far as we can see the unseen world does not work in that way. The spiritual hosts are probably better employed in ministering, as far as they can, to the wounded and dying, and receiving the great throng of spirits that are being ushered so violently into the spirit world.[12]

Shirley and Gow were not alone in their speculations. Machen was astonished when his oldest friend, A.E. Waite, said: 'I felt pretty sure you had some foundation for that story of yours.' Within days of publication, the *Evening News* learned the story was being discussed in military circles and 'one officer called and asked how much was true and how much fiction'.

Were the soldiers really talking of the vision in August and September 1914, as Brigadier-General Charteris claimed in his memoirs written at the time? Or did the first stories only begin to appear following publication of 'The Bowmen' on 29 September? If Machen's story was the only source, then how was the jump made from his bowmen and the appearance of St George to the more traditional arrival of angels? Some later accounts, such as the guide produced by the Belgian Tourist Office (see Chapter 2), have even combined the two strands and describe the angels as archers. These issues will be examined and explained in later chapters, with some interesting conclusions as to the veracity of supposed contemporary evidence from the highest sources.

As 1915 arrived, these rumours travelled rapidly along the trenches as soldiers settled down to endure the freezing cold that heralded the first winter of the war. It was during this fallow period that British troops began to adopt stories and rumours passed on by survivors from the original Expeditionary Force. This impression is supported by a testimony collected in the 1980s by historian Granville Oldroyd. His informant was a recruit who had joined Kitchener's army and arrived in France during October 1914.

> He heard nothing about angels either at home or on the Western Front but the story was going round before Christmas 1914. There were no actual eye-witnesses but a man from another regiment had seen something. He was adamant about this and since his recollections about other events of the war were accurate I had no reason to doubt him.[13]

For soldiers facing the grim reality of life in the trenches, the stories gave fresh impetus to the idea that they had supernatural protection, and encouraged faith in a divinely ordained British victory. These feelings were to live on in the hearts and minds of many thousands in England and France for the duration of the war. Military historian James Hayward recognized these were ideal conditions for the widespread acceptance of rumour. He wrote that:

> to the general public, in a less media-literate age than our own ... [the stories] may have tended to suggest that the bowmen described by Machen had actually appeared on the field, at a time when there was a pressing need in Britain to believe that the war had not been lost within the first eight weeks.[14]

Early in 1915, these ripples were spreading out rapidly like those from a stone that is dropped into a pool of water. Initially versions of Machen's story had been spread by rumour and gossip, and by discussions in the major esoteric newspapers. Soon these would be followed up by sermons and religious leaflets and a deluge of letters to newspapers and the religious press. Early in 1915, the orthodox clergy began to take an active interest in the rumours that had hitherto been the province of occultists. The editor of the *Evening News* received a number of requests from the editors of parish magazines who wished to reprint Machen's short story. He granted permission to all of them, without realizing what the consequences would be.

One of those making the request was a Roman Catholic priest, Father Edward Russell, who was deacon at the church of St Alban the Martyr in Holborn. Fr Russell was also chaplain to the nursing guild of St Barnabas and a 'conductor of parish magazines', one of which had reprinted the story in its February issue. Afterwards, Father Russell wrote to Machen to say the issue had sold out and, as demand was so high, could he reprint the story as a pamphlet along with a short foreword providing his sources for the tale. Machen readily gave permission for the reprint but said he could not provide any authorities as 'the story was pure invention'.[15]

Some time in April the priest wrote again – to Machen's amazement – saying he must be mistaken and 'that the main "facts" of "The Bowmen" must be true ... that my share in the matter must surely have been confined to the elaboration and decoration of veridical history.' Now he began to realize that the little fantasy he thought to be of no consequence

had been accepted by the congregation of this particular church as the solidest of facts: and it was then that it began to dawn on me that if I had failed in the art of letters, I had succeeded, unwittingly, in the art of deceit ... and the snowball of rumour that was then set rolling has been rolling ever since, growing bigger and bigger, till it is now swollen to a monstrous size.[16]

As a disciple of the Celtic church, Machen did not, unlike many in the Church of England establishment that he detested, dismiss the possibility that miracles could occur in modern times. As the *Times Literary Supplement* pointed out, anyone acquainted with the Welsh writer would know he was 'the last man to be sceptical about miracles', and his faith was such that the appearance of St George in Flanders would be to him 'no more surprising than the appearance of an omnibus in Regent Street'. His scepticism stemmed not from disbelief in miracles but because he appreciated the nature of the evidence required to establish that one had occurred. For him rumour and gossip were not sufficient substitutes for *real* evidence.

Machen maintained throughout the controversy that followed that he was author, not the historian, of the Angel of Mons. His friend and biographer John Gawsworth believed the stand he took against the wave of rumour that followed was brave and principled. At times Machen must have felt overwhelmed because even his editor, Alfred Turner, was unsure that his theory was entirely correct. As a writer, the moment of success brought him publicity but little money. It also generated jealousy and anger among rivals in the occult industry who were determined to undermine his version of events. Throughout the controversy, Machen saw himself as combating delusion and living up to the words he had written to a friend, the artist Paul England, at the outbreak of war:

> Depend upon it that he who loves making mysteries for the sake of mystery is ultimately and in big things a fool, and therefore dangerous.[17]

CHAPTER FIVE

The birth of a legend

It was all so entirely innocent, nay casual, on my part. A poor linnet of prose, I did but perform my indifferent piping in the *Evening News* because I wanted to do so, because I felt that the story of 'The Bowmen' ought to be told ... and then, somehow or other, it was as if I had touched the button and set in action a terrific, complicated mechanism of rumours that pretended to be sworn truth, of gossip that posed as evidence, of wild tarradiddles that good men most firmly believed.

Arthur Machen, 'Out of the Earth', *TP's Weekly*,
27 November 1915

The period when the rumours of supernatural intervention at Mons were slowly accepted as fact occurred between October 1914 and April 1915. In his study *Visions of Bowmen and Angels* (1993) writer Kevin McClure described these seven months as 'the missing link'. He asked why it was that:

the visions ceased to be reported in October 1914, having been given little or no credence, but then suddenly reappeared – in different forms, in different places – the following spring.[1]

It was the missing link that was 'the great mystery of the way the Mons stories unfolded'. This question still cannot be answered comprehensively. After five years of research I have found it impossible to reconstruct the precise chronology of this transformation, although many clues have come to light. The public had already been primed to accept the idea of angels protecting the Allies by a series of illustrations in the popular *King Albert's Book* published as a tribute to the Belgian king at Christmas 1914. The book contained drawings and pastels of angels and saints protecting Allied soldiers. One illustration served as the basis for a postcard published by the Church Army that showed:

> Christ on the Cross in the background; a sky full of angels and mailed, winged figure encouraging an infantryman and a sailor, both of them gripping rifles with fixed bayonets. The slogan on the card read: 'Enlisted under the Cross! Am I?'[2]

At the same time artist Arthur Forrestier adapted Arthur Machen's story of the bowmen of Mons as the theme of a dramatic pen and ink drawing published by the *Illustrated London News*. The idea of protective angels appearing on the battlefield had taken a firm root in the imagination, and new versions of Machen's story reappeared around St George's Day on 23 April 1915. The day before, the Germans had used poison gas to launch a surprise attack against Allied troops defending the front near Ypres – an action that broke all the accepted rules of traditional warfare. The perception of the enemy as a devilish foe was magnified by the publication, at the end of April, of rumours about a Canadian soldier allegedly crucified by the Germans during the battle for Ypres. The opening of unrestricted submarine warfare which culminated in the sinking of the *Lusitania* on 7 May added to the atrocities that were now laid at the door of the Germans.

For the Allies, 1915 was a year of failure and sacrifice for little gain. Frustrated by the deadlock in the West, in April the British War Cabinet decided to open up a second front against Germany's new ally, Turkey. The Gallipoli campaign ended in disaster and, ultimately, a humiliating withdrawal. The atmosphere of gloom was increased by a series of battles that cost the lives of hundreds of thousands of men and gained little ground from the Germans. From this background of gloom emerged the uplifting story of angels saving the day for the British Army. As a young girl in Yorkshire, Eva Lynch, recalled:

> Then the first German prisoners were captured and they had *Gott Mitt Uns* inscribed on their belt buckles. We were really indignant when we heard that. What cheek! God was on our side.[3]

Something was clearly needed to counter the bad news, and the story of divine intervention at Mons supplied the assurance that eventual victory was certain. Whether innocent or contrived, the part played by the church in nurturing the story helped to underline the idea of a 'moral truth' that lay behind the rumours. As the *Christian Commonwealth* observed at the time, such truth would:

> strengthen religious faith, which has been greatly weakened by the war, and ... reinforce belief in the justice of the cause for which so many men fell during that magnificent retreat and almost miraculous recovery on the banks of the Marne.[4]

What is missing from this equation are the contents of private letters that circulated between soldiers serving in France and the Home Front during Christmas and New Year. The postal service was one of the few things which the soldiers in Kitchener's army could rely upon. Letters contained not only vital supplies, but also kept the soldier in touch with news from home. Packages contained copies of newspapers and parish magazines that spread rumours to France which were then repeated in letters sent home. The role played by this ongoing but largely unseen mutual exchange is underlined by an entry that appears in the memoirs of Brigadier-General John Charteris. He was fascinated by the rumours he heard but, despite his seniority, he was unable to make much progress in tracing them to source. In a letter to his wife, dated 11 February 1915, published in his book

At GHQ, Charteris makes a second reference to the angel:

> I have been at some trouble to trace the rumour to its
> source. The best I can make of it is that some religiously
> minded man wrote home that the Germans halted at
> Mons, AS IF an Angel of the Lord had appeared in front
> of them. In due course the letter appeared in a Parish
> Magazine, which in time was sent out to some other men
> at the front. From them the story went back home with
> the 'as if' omitted, and at home it went the rounds in its
> expurgated form.[5]

Charteris was not the only British officer who had heard the
stories. He was followed by a number of other military officers
and prominent churchmen. One of the most impressive was the
son of the Bishop of Liverpool, who was a chaplain to the British
forces in France. The Reverend Christopher Chavasse was the
twin brother of Captain Noel Chavasse who was medical officer
with the Tenth (Liverpool Scottish) Battalion of the King's
(Liverpool) Regiment during the first three years of the war. Noel
became the only soldier to win the British military's highest
award for valour, the Victoria Cross, twice during the First
World War. He was killed in 1917 during the Third Battle of
Ypres (Passchendaele) while caring for wounded soldiers in a
first aid post.

Christopher reached France before Noel and, at the age of
30, served at the hospital in St Nazaire in the aftermath of the
retreat from Mons. While there he heard many rumours told
by the wounded soldiers from the BEF. In October 1915 the
Reverend Christopher Chavasse returned home to Liverpool
on leave and told a crowded congregation at Christ Church,
Claughton, that many trustworthy soldiers had sworn they had
seen 'visions' during the fighting. A newspaper account of the
sermon reported:

> They all knew the story of the angels of Mons, and on that
> subject he would like to ask them all to keep an unbiased

mind until they had direct evidence for or against to believe that it might be true.

Christopher Chavasse said he believed the war was the 'greatest event in history' next to the Incarnation, and therefore he would expect God to be present. As for the 'angels of Mons', he was reported to have said that:

> [he] never yet got first-hand evidence on the subject, but he had been told by a general, a brigadier, who was far from superstitious, that a captain and subaltern serving under him were certain they saw something at Mons. They were men who would never dream of seeing angels, but they said they saw something, some bright pulsating light, which came between the little company of Englishmen and a troop of charging Uhlans on their horses, which frightened the horses so that they scattered and bolted, while a little further along, where the British line was broken, the German troops refused to advance, saying that they saw so many English troops there, although there was not a man to oppose them. That story was spoken, too, by many that he had met, and he looked forward to the evidence being forthcoming to prove it was true.[6]

Who was the high-ranking informant, the 'general, a brigadier' referred to by the chaplain? Was it Brigadier-General Charteris? Christopher Chavasse never revealed the source of his information. He returned home after the war and rose through the ranks of the Church of England to become Bishop of Rochester in Kent. He died in 1962 without finding the elusive evidence for the 'angels of Mons' that he was confident would eventually come to light.

A letter published by *Light* in May 1915 illustrates how the rumour was reinforced on the Home Front by the stories told by soldiers and repeated by nurses and chaplains. An Irish woman described how a friend who was in London at the outbreak of war read Machen's story in the *Evening News*. Although she instinctively questioned the credibility of the story, her opinion changed when she met a wounded private who had returned from France.

> Directly she heard he had been at Mons, she asked, 'Oh, did you see the vision, and hear the shout?' He answered, 'I did not hear the shout, but I did see the vision, and' he added very emphatically, 'the Germans saw it too – they couldn't get their horses to come on!' He said that on comparing notes with his comrades afterwards they found that some had seen the vision, and some heard the shout, but very many had neither heard nor seen.[7]

Shining beings

Occultists, theosophists and clairvoyants played an important role in spreading stories of these rumours. For much of the summer, the pages of the pre-eminent esoteric journals – the *Two Worlds*, *Light* and the *Occult Review* – were filled with accounts of battlefield visions attributed to anonymous soldiers. In the May 1915 issue of the *Review* a founding member of the Theosophical Society, Alfred Sinnett, wrote of an intervention by 'spiritual beings' at Mons:

> During the retreat from Mons, on one occasion when a thin rearguard was awaiting attack, and an overwhelming host of the enemy was seen to be approaching, this host halted, was seen to be in some confusion and ultimately retired; why, no one on our side except the very few who had superphysical sight could comprehend. Those who could see said they saw 'a row of shining beings' between the two armies. On another occasion, much later on, when again a thin line of our troops seemed on the point of annihilation, an advancing body of German troops drew back for no obvious reason. Some of them a few days later were taken

prisoner, and asked why they fell back on the former occasion. They said, because they saw the enormous mass of reinforcements coming up behind our line! As a matter of fact no such reinforcements were really coming on.[8]

For Arthur Machen, it was Sinnett's reference to 'a row of shining beings' interposed between the two armies that marked the point of transition between 'The Bowmen' and the 'angels of Mons'. While angels are not referred to in the story, the fact that it was published on the feast of St Michael and All Angels suggested a connection existed. The ghostly bowmen appear in Sinnett's version as 'a long line of shapes with a shining about them'. To Machen the meaning was implicit:

> In the popular view shining and benevolent supernatural beings are angels and nothing else, and so, I believe, the Bowmen of my story have become 'the Angels of Mons'.[9]

On 18 April the *Weekly Dispatch* published further stories sourced from London occult and theosophical circles. Alice M. Callow, secretary of the Higher Thought Centre in South Kensington, told of 'strange stories of visions seen by British soldiers at the front'. She would not provide names but claimed an officer had sent members of the centre a detailed account of a vision that had appeared to himself and others when fighting against fearful odds at Mons.

> He plainly saw an apparition representing St George, the patron saint of England, the exact counterpart of a picture that hangs to-day in a London restaurant. So terrible was their plight at the time that the officer could not refrain from appealing to the vision to help them. Then, as if the enemy had also seen the apparition, the Germans abandoned their position in precipitate terror.[10]

The appearance of the 'London restaurant' in this version betrayed its origins in Machen's story, but in other instances mentioned by Callow, men had written about seeing 'clouds of celestial horsemen hovering over the British lines'. A nurse at the front, 'under the auspices of the theosophists', told how on one occasion she noticed that a number of wounded men were less forthcoming than usual. When asked why they were so strangely silent, they replied: 'We have had strange experiences which we do not care to talk about. We have seen many of our mates killed, but they are fighting for us still.' The soldiers believed the visions were hallucinations but the theosophists could not dismiss them so easily.

Then the stories suddenly became respectable in the most surprising places. One was published by the Roman Catholic newspaper, the *Universe*, on 30 April, with the headline: 'ON A WHITE HORSE, St George and Phantom Army'. The narrator was a Catholic officer at the front who had written to 'an accredited correspondent' of the paper who was 'precluded from imparting the names of those concerned'. He said:

A party of about thirty men and an officer was cut off in a trench, when the officer said to his men, 'Look here; we must either stay here and be caught like rats in a trap, or make a sortie against the enemy. We haven't much of a chance, but personally I don't want to be caught here.' The men all agreed with him, and with a yell of 'St George for England!' they dashed out into the open. The officer tells how, as they ran on, he became aware of a large company of men with bows and arrows going along with them, and even leading them on against the enemy's trenches, and afterwards when he was talking to a German prisoner, the man asked him who was the officer on a great white horse who led them? For although he was such a conspicuous figure, they had none of them been able to hit him. I must also add that the German dead appeared to have no wounds on them.

The correspondent said the officer involved was a friend of his. He did not see St George on the white horse, 'but he saw the archers with his own eyes'.

In April *Light* published a similar story, again drawing upon the St George motif, but this time told from a Protestant perspective. Its source was a sermon preached by a contributor to the *Occult Review*, the Reverend Fielding Ould, Vicar of St Stephen's, St Albans:

I heard a story last week from three sources, and which I think may be true. A sergeant in our army had frequented a house of the Young Men's Christian Association, and had seen there a picture of St George slaying the dragon. He had been deeply impressed by it, and when, at the front, he found himself in an advanced and rather isolated trench, he told the story of St George to his men – St George, the patron saint of England, whose name the warriors have shouted as their war-cry in the carnage of Crecy, Poitiers and on many another glorious field. When shortly afterwards a sudden charge of the grey-coated Germans in greatly superior numbers threatened the sergeant's trench, he cried, 'Remember St George for England!' to his men as they advanced to meet the foe. A few moments afterward the enemy hesitated, stopped and finally fled, leaving some prisoners in our hands. One of the latter, who seemed dazed and astonished, demanded to be told who were 'the horsemen in armour' who led the charge. Surely they could not have been Belgians dressed in such a way![11]

Drip, drip drip. All these versions contained elements that could be traced back to the contents of 'The Bowmen'. The Catholic version was one of the few that contained a specific reference to the bowmen from Agincourt. The Protestant version revives the theme of a soldier calling upon St George at a critical moment. The story circulated by the theosophists was even more derivative – the picture of St George was the one in a real vegetarian restaurant near Leicester Square, the very same location used in 'The Bowmen'. Those who spread these stories were aware of these facts, but they maintained they had suspended disbelief

because they had received the same information from several independent sources.

Mysterious clouds

One of the first articles to mark the divergence between the Bowmen/St George and what would become known as the 'Angels of Mons' appeared in the pages of *Light* on 24 April. In 'The Invisible Allies: Strange Story from the Front', editor David Gow referred to the growing body of rumour. A well-known publisher had been in contact asking if the magazine could tell him anything about the origin of the story 'as statements were being made that it was founded on fact'. Gow had satisfied himself that it was indeed a product of the writer's imagination, but:

> a few days ago, however, we received a visit from a military officer, who asked to see the issue of *Light* containing the article in question. He explained that, whether Mr Machen's story was pure invention or not, it was certainly stated in some quarters that a curious phenomenon had been witnessed by several officers and men in connection with the retreat from Mons. It took the form of a strange cloud interposed between the Germans and the British. Other wonders were heard or seen in connection with this cloud which, it seems, had the effect of protecting the British against the overwhelming hordes of the enemy.

The account of the mysterious military officer was confirmed by correspondents in Ireland. Mrs F.H. Fitzgerald-Beale, from Queen's County, wrote to say she was pleased to tell the editor it was true.

> We have among other wounded soldiers home from the war a soldier of the Dublin Fusiliers who was injured at Mons. I told him of the story and asked him if it was true. He said,

'Yes, I saw it myself – a thick black cloud; it quite hid us from the enemy.[12]

A second Irish correspondent told of a ladyfriend who met the family of an officer, 'General N', who had been present at Mons. His story resembles that overheard by the Reverend Christopher Chavasse, and may refer to the same incident, or rumoured incident. The officer told her that during the rearguard action there had been one especially critical moment when:

> the German cavalry was rapidly advancing, and very much outnumbered our forces. Suddenly, he saw a sort of luminous cloud, or fog, interpose itself between the Germans and our forces. In this cloud there seemed to be bright objects moving; he could not say if they were figures or not, but they were moving and bright. The moment this cloud appeared the German onslaught seemed to receive a check; the horses could be seen rearing and plunging, and they ceased to advance. He said it was his opinion that if that check, whatever its cause, had not come, our whole force would have been annihilated in twenty minutes.[13]

More confirmation came from another friend, who had a visit from a relative, a young officer, who was on leave from the front. He said the account of 'General N' was correct.

> He had seen the luminous cloud and the sudden check to the enemy's cavalry, exactly as General N. had described it, and he said, 'After what I saw that day, nothing will make me doubt for one moment but that we shall win in this war.'

In June 1915, variations of these stories were circulating among the families of soldiers who were hungry for news from the Front. The rumour spread among the upper classes of society, among officers and members of the aristocracy. A writer in the *Church Family Newspaper* said he knew for a fact that the British Commander-in-Chief, Sir John French, would soon reveal what he knew about them. A certain Mrs Crossley of West London informed the *Hereford Times* that the story she heard had been corroborated by five widely different sources. Unfortunately, these were third- and even fourth-hand. One came from a servant of hers who was married to a chauffeur who was the driver for a King's Messenger of Dispatches serving in France. He told of an officer whose men were outnumbered by the enemy. As he was debating whether he should surrender and save the lives of his men, 'he saw a white horse and a commander sitting upon it, also leading a small army which blended with his. When the Germans saw it they fled!' She continued:

> One of our clergy here copied for us a letter from an officer to his wife telling of his regiment being ordered to take up an isolated position for the English. On arrival he found it full of Germans in overwhelming numbers. His men were praying earnestly for help when a large white cloud came quickly down between the forces, and as it thinned they saw a multitude of Heavenly Hosts. The English knelt with faces covered in reverence, and when they looked up the enemy had disappeared and all was clear.[14]

She added that 'a vision of Christ' had also been seen 'as a knight in blue armour in the trenches'. The appearance of this vision was greeted by the French with exclamations of 'Le bon Dieu! Le bon Dieu!' while a figure in white was seen tending the English wounded who called him 'the White Comrade' (see Chapter 8).

A troop of angels

Two versions of the battlefield visions were now circulating. First there was the version where St George appeared on a white horse and was sometimes accompanied by phantom cavalry or bowmen. Second, there was the 'mysterious cloud' that hid the British from the Germans. While the two 'new' versions appeared to diverge from Machen's story their ultimate source

1 **St George at Mons**.
Illustration by Alfred
Pearse. A figure on a
white horse holding a
flaming sword halts the
German advance at Mons.
British soldiers believed
the figure was St George
whereas French troops
claimed they saw
St Michael and Joan of
Arc.

Reproduced by permission of
the Mary Evans Picture
Library.

2 **The Angels of Mons**. From an illustration by Alfred Pearse published in
   A Churchwoman's *The Chariots of God* (1915). Shining angels throw a
   protective curtain around men from the Lincolnshire Regiment at Mons.
   Reproduced by permission of the Mary Evans Picture Library.

3 **A Russian vision.** From an illustration by Alfred Pearse published in A Churchwoman's *The Chariots of God* (1915). Russian troops are comforted by a vision of the Blessed Virgin Mary on the eve of victory at Augustovo in September 1914.
Reproduced by permission of the Mary Evans Picture Library.

4 **'Angel of Mons Waltz'.** The cover of sheet music composed by Paul Paree and published by the Lawrence Wright Music Company of London during 1916. The legend was also adapted for piano solos, plays, films and in more recent times by the rock guitarist Steve Hackett (Clocks: The Angel of Mons, Spectral Mornings, 1979).
Reproduced by permission of the Mary Evans Picture Library.

5 *The Bowmen and Other Legends of the War* **by Arthur Machen**.
The book appeared at the height of the Angels of Mons controversy in August 1915. In the introduction Machen explained how his short story, 'The Bowmen', gave rise to the legend, but few believed him at the time.
Reproduced by permission of the Mary Evans Picture Library.

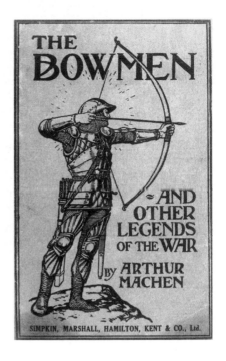

6 *Back of the Front*. The cover of a book published by Phyllis Campbell in September 1915. Campbell served as a Red Cross nurse in France during the Battle of the Frontiers in August 1914 and claimed to have cared for soldiers who saw angels and saints leading them against the Germans.
Reproduced by permission of the Mary Evans Picture Library.

7 **Arthur Machen**. Machen was a journalist working for the London *Evening News* in 1914 when he wrote 'The Bowmen' and a series of other short stories that mixed fact and fiction together.

8 **Brigadier-General John Charteris**. Charteris was Chief Intelligence Officer at GHQ France 1915–17. In his memoirs he recorded rumours about the Angel of Mons circulating among British soldiers in France during September 1914.
Reproduced from *At GHQ* by Brigadier General Charteris, 1931 Cassell & Co., London.

9 **'The Bowmen of Mons'**. Arthur Machen's story of ghostly bowmen from Agincourt helping British troops at Mons in 1914 was depicted by artist Arthur Forrestier in 1915 for the *Illustrated London News*.
Reproduced by permission of The Fortean Picture Library.

10 **Royal Fusiliers at Mons.** A company of the Fourth Battalion Royal Fusiliers resting in the Grand Place on 22 August 1914 before the Battle of Mons the following day.

Reproduced by permission of the Imperial War Museum (Negative No. Q70071).

11 **Angels of Mons leaflet, 1915**. An example of one of the many leaflets, religious pamphlets and sermons published during the First World War and circulated on the Western Front, in England and in the colonies.
Reproduced by permission of St Albans Church archives.

From the painting by W. H. Margetson
"THE ANGELS OF MONS."

THE REAL ANGEL OF MONS.

"An angel in all but power is she!"
"Un ange,—mais une force!"

12 **Postcards of the Angel of Mons**.
Reproduced by permission of Stan Suggitt, Bedale, North Yorks.

was indicated by the lack of names, locations or specific dates. They were not first-hand accounts but second- and even third-hand, the product of rumour and gossip. As Mark Valentine remarked, while at face value they differed from 'The Bowmen', they were 'suspiciously close to the pattern, if not the exact content of Machen's tale'.[15]

But there is one story that had a dramatic and enduring impact on public opinion and can truly be referred to as the 'Angel of Mons' in order to separate it from the earlier rumours concerning mysterious clouds and phantom horsemen. The first specific reference to angels occurred in a story published by a provincial newspaper a month before Sinnett wrote of 'shining beings' in the *Occult Review*. On 3 April 1915 the *Hereford Times* published what it called 'an extraordinary incident in the British retirement from Mons'. The source was third-hand even at this early stage. A Hereford clergyman, who was not identified, had received a letter 'from a relative in Cheltenham' who heard the story from a Miss M—, the 'daughter of Canon M—'.

> She told me she knew the officers, both of whom had themselves seen the angels who saved the left wing from the Germans when they came right upon them during our retreat from Mons. They expected annihilation, as they were almost helpless, when, to their amazement, the Germans stood like dazed men, never so much as touched their guns, nor stirred, till we had turned and escaped by some cross roads. One of Miss M—'s friends, who was not a religious man, told her he saw a troop of angels between us and the enemy, and has been a changed man ever since. The other man she met in London last week and she asked him if he had heard of the wonderful story of the angels. He said he had seen them himself, as while he and his company were retreating they heard the German cavalry tearing after them. They ran to a place where they thought a stand might be made with some hopes of safety, but before they

could reach it the German cavalry were upon them, so they turned round and faced the enemy, expecting instant death – when, to their wonder, they saw between them and the enemy a whole troop of angels, and the hordes of the Germans turned round terrified out of their senses, and regularly stampeded, the men tugging at their bridles, while the poor horses tore away in any direction from our men. He swore he saw the angels who the horses saw plainly enough, if not the German soldiers, and this gave our men time to reach the little fort or whatever the shelter was, and save themselves.

A copy of this account reached the Reverend M.P. Gillson who was Vicar of All Saints' Church at Clifton in Bristol. It was reprinted in the May 1915 issue of his parish magazine. The previous issue had been dedicated to the legend of St George and, along with many other parish magazines at the time, he republished 'The Bowmen' without introduction or comment.[16] Its readers – drawn from the hinterland of Bristol – were unlikely to have realized the story was fiction, and fewer still would have been familiar with the original story in the London *Evening News*. The publication of the 'troop of angels' led to what Gillson described as 'remarkable interest'. Writing in *Bladud*, 'the Bath Society paper', he revealed how:

> our modest little Parish Magazine has suddenly sprung into almost world-wide notoriety; every post for the last three weeks has brought letters from all over the country, not asking merely for single copies but for dozens of copies, enclosing a quite embarrassing number of stamps and postal orders, the more so since as there were no more magazines to be had.[17]

Gillson then criticized those who had expressed astonishment and disbelief at the stories of angels appearing on the battlefield. He believed such people were adopting 'the thoroughly materialistic and rationalistic outlook' of modern Christians who refused to accept that miracles still happened. Gillson compared this attitude of mind with the scientific theology popular in Germany that sought to explain away miracles 'to save us from any strain the Bible makes upon our faith'. Disbelief in the angels, therefore, was tantamount to adopting the mindset of the enemy. Gillson continued:

> Why should it seem more strange that a regiment of Prussian Cavalry should be held up by a company of Angels, and their horses stampeded, and our infantry delivered from a hopeless position, than that an Angel with flaming sword should have withstood Balaam, or that St Peter should have been delivered from the hand of Herod by the intervention of an Angel? Do they really relegate all such miracles to 'Bible Days' and believe that when the Church made up the Canon of Holy Scriptures she also brought to a close the age of miracles?[18]

Due to overwhelming demand, the story was reprinted again in the June issue and it then appeared in newspapers that had until this point ignored the rumours. The story was also taken up in church pulpits across England as proof of the rumours about a miracle at Mons. A letter telling of a sermon at St Martin's Church in Worcester added further grist to the mill. The preacher had many relations fighting in France, and:

> He told ... about this vision of Angels, which had been seen by so many of our soldiers, on that Saturday in August, when the situation looked so hopeless, that *The Times* correspondent wired that the British Army 'had been no annihilated,' and the Sunday papers all published it, and if it had not been for the angels there would have been no contradiction of it in Monday's papers! In particular he spoke of twelve men in a quarry, who *all* saw the angels, and among the mass of the army some saw and some did not. Two Colonels he spoke of, who said they had seen them, one of whom had until then been an unbeliever. But

all saw the unlooked for salvation of the remnant of the army. From another source I heard that many prisoners were taken that day who surrendered when there was no call for it. At home it was suggested that they were under-fed and did not want to fight. Some of the German prisoners were afterwards asked why they surrendered, 'for there were many more of you than of us; we were a mere handful,' they looked amazed and replied, 'but there were hosts and hosts of you.' It was thought that the angels appeared to them as reinforcements of our ranks.[19]

Several new themes emerged: the angels appeared spontaneously, without invocation, at the most critical point in the retreat; no violence is shown towards the German troops but a protective curtain is thrown around the British which frightens the enemy horses. The vision is curiously selective. It is seen by some and not by others and it strengthens the faith of those who see it. In some of the stories there is a suggestion that the Germans did not see the vision, but were discouraged from advancing by the sight of what appeared to be masses of British reinforcements where none existed. These 'phantom reinforcements' reappear in variations of the story circulated later in the war. For his part, the Reverend M.P. Gillson was happy to accept the Angel of Mons as fact and the earlier rumours concerning St George and the bowmen as fiction. He concluded:

> It has been enquired into, and apparently it is only based on a perversion of the story of the angels, and that I do believe. The only very astonishing part of it is that so many men were allowed to *see* them.

Rumour becomes legend

In London, the headquarters of the Society for Psychical Research (SPR) was inundated with inquiries that all appeared to have been sparked off by the story published in the All Saints' parish magazine. The society appealed to its members for first-hand information and decided to investigate the growing mystery. Its report revealed they had received a number of similar accounts that were attributed to different authors. Their wording was identical, or almost identical, to that attributed to 'Miss M—', whose real identity was revealed by the *Occult Review* in July. Sarah Marrable was the daughter of a leading member of the Roman Catholic Church and her story therefore appeared all the more credible. The SPR realized that Marrable was the key source, as the one thing all the narratives had in common was the claim that she personally knew the officers involved. They were surprised to find this was not in fact the case. In reply to a letter from the SPR Marrable responded on 28 May 1915: 'I cannot give you the names of the men referred to in your letter ... as the story I heard was quite anonymous, and I do not know who they were.'[20]

Miss Marrable was now being pursued relentlessly by journalists, and in desperation she sent a note to the *Evening News* which read: 'I will be much obliged if you will inform the Editor of *The Occult Review* that I know nothing whatever of officers or men who saw the angels.'[21] She explained the origins of the story further in a letter published in the *Church of Ireland Gazette*:

> Allow me to correct a mis-statement which has been published widely in England in several papers, without our permission, i.e. that we know, or have met, the officers who saw the angels at Mons. We do not know them, nor their names, but simply heard the story, and may have mentioned it in the hearing of the lady who wrote to a clergyman in Hereford, who sent her letter to a newspaper there.[22]

Marrable qualified her statement by noting that she 'did not wish to express doubt as to the truth of the original', which reminded her of the story of the siege of Dothan in the Old Testament. For someone as deeply religious as Marrable, the truth of the story was self-evident, even though the soldiers who saw the angels could not be identified. It was 'what we may expect in answer to our prayers for men constantly exposed to such danger'. The origins of the account published in the *Hereford Times*, reproduced in the All Saints' Parish Magazine, and then across the nation were then laid bare. Far from being first-hand, it was simply a rumour heard from 'a friend of a friend'. Few of those caught up in the expectant atmosphere of the times realized the significance of Marrable's statement. Again it fell upon Arthur Machen to spell it out to readers of the *Evening News*:

> So what it amounts to is this: Miss Marrable heard the story – as we have all heard it – and sees no reason to doubt it. And the fact of Miss Marrable's hearsay – common to us all – has been used as the sure foundation, the certain, convincing evidence on which the whole tower of rumour has been built! It is nothing less than amazing.[23]

As a result of its own inquiries, the SPR recognized the reports based on the authority of Marrable broke down at a crucial point and 'prove to be no more than rumours which it is impossible to trace to their original source'. Another correspondent reported on his attempt to track down yet another version of the rumour and, having failed to do so, concluded that 'somehow, first-hand knowledge seems to be purposely withheld'. Ralph Shirley took an entirely different standpoint. He believed all the accounts, including that attributed to 'General N' were 'variants of ... the same story'. Shirley said he found it difficult to accept that *all* the accounts could be traced to 'The Bowmen'. If that was indeed the case he expected elements from Machen's fantasy would be prominent within them. In fact, he argued, the bowmen appear in only one of the narratives. The others described troops of angels, figures on horseback and mysterious clouds that hid the British from the German onslaught. Shirley pointed to the 'mysterious cloud' mentioned in several of the new accounts:

> in one case the apparition appears merely as a strange cloud, in the second ... as a cloud with bright objects moving

within in it, and in the third, fourth and fifth it appears definitely as a company of angels.[24]

He believed all these accounts referred to a specific incident during the Battle of Mons, while others – such as the account of the Roman Catholic officer – related to other, separate incidents elsewhere on the battlefield.

Shirley also introduced a new story sourced to 'a letter from a soldier at the front', read out by the Reverend Lancaster of Weymouth, Dorset, in a sermon on 30 May. The soldier was in the retreat from Mons when:

> his regiment was pursued by a large number of German cavalry from which they took refuge in a large quarry, where the Germans found them and were on the point of shooting them. At that moment, stated the writer of the letter, the whole of the top edge of the quarry was lined by angels, who were seen by all the soldiers and the Germans as well. The Germans suddenly stopped, turned round, and galloped away at top speed. The narrator adds that this is vouched for not only by the Tommies, but by the officers of the regiment.[25]

Versions of the 'troop of angels' and the 'angels in the quarry' were widely republished and accepted as fact by thousands. In leaflets and pamphlets produced by the religious press, Miss Marrable's name was removed and her retraction ignored. Rumour had become legend, and a myth was in the making.

For more than six months during 1915, the Angel of Mons provided the British press with a sensation that filled thousands of column inches with articles, stories, letters and editorial comment. The British press censor did nothing to suppress coverage because the stories were undoubtedly seen as beneficial towards the war effort. In Germany the imperial authorities held almost total control over the output of the major weekly and evening newspapers. A survey I conducted of the three most influential Berlin newspapers published during the autumn of 1914 and summer of 1915 failed to locate a single reference to visions on the battlefield.[26]

A letter published by the *Daily Mail* at the time suggested rumours were circulating in Berlin at the time of the retreat from Mons that German cavalry were halted by some form of invisible barrier. The writer claimed that:

> a lady who was in Berlin up to the end of September [1914] said there was a great stir there because a regiment told off to do a certain duty at the battle of Mons failed to carry out its orders. When severely reprimanded the German soldiers gave this explanation: 'We did try to carry out our orders, but those devils of Englishmen were up to some of their devilry, and we could do nothing – we were powerless.' My friend asked a lieutenant of the regiment what really happened, and he said: 'I cannot tell you. I only know that we were charging full on the British, and we were suddenly stopped. It was most like going full speed and being pulled up sharp at a precipice, but there was no precipice there – nothing at all, only our horses swerved around and fled, and we could do nothing.'[27]

The informant claimed this story was heard in Berlin at the end of August 1914, 'and as my friend did not leave Germany till the end of September she had heard nothing of any English account until she arrived in England.' Unfortunately, her letter was not published until 1915 after the story had become well known, lessening its value as contemporaneous evidence. It was not the only story to claim that some of the German soldiers believed the British had employed a devilish spell that had created an 'invisible barrier' they were unable to cross. This is a common theme in supernatural folklore and it reappears in some of the stories that were circulated at a later stage of the war. We know from the accounts of German officers such as Captain Walter Bloem how General von Kluck's army were stunned by the rapid fire they faced from the Lee Enfield rifles of the British troops at Mons.

This gave them the *impression* they faced a much greater force than was in fact the case and because it caused the Germans to come to a halt, it may account for the stories about 'invisible barriers'.

Another account of rumours that circulated among the German troops resurfaced in a pamphlet written by John J. Pearson, *The Rationale of the Angel Warriors at Mons*, published in 1916. Pearson believed the war was a sign that the biblical apocalypse was near and claimed the visions at Mons were products of the struggle between the forces of good represented by the Allies and those of evil, represented by the Germans in their unholy alliance with the 'unspeakable Turk'. Pearson claimed that shortly after the commencement of the retreat from Mons he heard a 'fiercely fanatical' prisoner of war in London refer to visions seen by German troops during the advance in France. The POW:

> informed me that the day was approaching when we [the British] would be called to strict account for using some strange and horrible devices, previously unknown in warfare, and by means of which thousands of countrymen had been done to death, having been found dead without wound or scratch, or any other indication as to how they had come by their deaths. They had, the German Medical Staff decided, succumbed to some untraceable cause, and had not been killed in fair honest fight. He also averred that the British and French had, by means of some terrifying spectral illusions, stampeded the horses of the Prussian Cavalry Corps, just as they were on the point of pressing home a successful charge upon our retreating troops, and that, as Germans were known as the most advanced chemists in the world, they would soon 'give us a dose of our own physic' perhaps stronger and more effective than ours had been.[28]

At the time Pearson had regarded this outburst 'as being merely an explosion of German rancour' against his British captors, but in the light of the information that was circulating of the visions at Mons he had been led to reconsider. Although his was an intriguing story, it did not appear until two years after the events it claimed to describe. In addition, Pearson's reference to German troops 'having been found dead without wound or scratch' can be traced directly to 'The Bowmen' and betrays its origins in the rumours that followed its publication. One such rumour was traced to 'an eminent occultist' who claimed that dead Germans with arrow wounds had been found on the battlefield at Mons. For some people this appeared plausible because a number of German troops *had* been killed by deadly steel arrows used by British and French airmen operating over the Western Front as early as September 1914. Aerial bombardment of troops was a completely new concept at the outbreak of war and in the first month of hostilities steel darts or 'arrows' known as *flechettes* were dropped from aircraft as the Germans advanced on the River Marne. In one action, canisters containing around 250 *flechettes*, which were around five inches long and three-eighths of an inch in diameter, were fixed under the fuselage of aircraft as they flew above enemy lines.[29] The London *Daily News and Leader* of 21 September 1914 described how:

> Two airmen flew over a German regiment at the frontier, at a height of 500 feet and dropped a shower of arrows as the soldiers were in camp. It is estimated that the two airmen shot 50 arrows, killing and injuring 13 soldiers. The arrows were made of steel and were not poisoned.

The *flechettes* were released by the pilot pulling a wire attached to the bottom of the canister. In order to cause harm they had to score a direct hit and it was soon realized they were a far less formidable weapon than a bomb. Nevertheless, reports about the use of *flechettes* appeared immediately following the publication of 'The Bowmen' and led some to suspect that reports of Germans killed by arrows was another indication that the story was based on some elements of fact.

The church and the angels

By the late summer of 1915 these early versions of the rumour had begun to coalesce into a legend that was acceptable to all religious and spiritual denominations. The bowmen and St George were largely forgotten although they continued to circulate in some Roman Catholic publications. Other stories were never recorded in print. The SPR, for instance, referred to a rumour which told of 'the Black Prince and his bowmen marching to help their fellow countrymen' at Mons. As the year progressed, the phantom horseman and the 'mysterious clouds' that followed them were replaced by 'angels' as the medium of supernatural intervention. Angels were more acceptable to the various Christian denominations that were busily engaged in spreading the story via Sunday sermons and religious pamphlets.

By September, the *Evening News* was reporting that 'not a Sunday passes' without the angels being the subject of a sermon somewhere in London. Arthur Machen observed that the pulpits both of the established church and of nonconformity had been busy. Among those who included the angels in their sermons were the Chaplain-General Bishop Taylor Smith, Bishop Welldon and Dean Hensley Henson. Sir Joseph Compton Rickett, President of the National Federation of Free Church Councils stated that soldiers at the front 'had seen visions and dreamed dreams, and had given testimony of powers and principalities fighting for them and against them'. Most influential of all was a sermon delivered at Broughton Church in Manchester on 13 June by the Reverend Dr R.F. Horton, an eminent Congregational minister, whose views commanded wide respect. Horton's remarks were widely published, and added further momentum to the rumours. He agreed with the Reverend M.P. Gillson in rejecting the view that the miracles were confined to the days of the Bible, but he placed a subtle spin on what actually constituted a miracle.

Miracles do not happen; but the same things happen which once were called miracles, the same astonishing deliverances, the same unexpected and unexplained alteration in the accustomed order of things, the same appearances, visions, manifestations, the same sudden realisations of the forces behind Nature, of the personal agencies which are at work unseen, the same discovery that palpably across the scene of human life God passes ... these events, or phenomena, produce just the same effect as they always did.[30]

Dr Horton revealed the source of his faith in supernatural intervention as the same rumour that had been heard by everyone else, the story attributed to 'Miss Marrable'.

When, therefore, soldiers and officers, who were in the retreat from Mons, say that they saw a batch of angels between them and the enemy, and that the horses of the German cavalry stampeded, and that thus our troops were saved from destruction, no thoroughly modern man is foolish enough to disbelieve the statement, or to pooh-pooh the experience as hallucination.

He also had direct evidence of unseen forces at work during the Allied assault on the Turkish positions at the Dardanelles. A sailor aboard one of the troop transports told the minister in a letter about an occasion when a German airship appeared over the ships, dropping bombs. The captain asked all his men to pray and 'as they knelt on the deck the Lord delivered them'. All the 18 bombs delivered by the airmen fell harmlessly into the sea. The lesson was simple.

These stories from the front, therefore – I should not myself call them miracles – are the unveiling of the real Power on which we depend; their result is to lead an increasing number of us to turn to the true springs of strength and victory. If God is for us, who can be against us? If God is not for us, all our munitions, all the heroism of our men, will not avail to secure the victory.[31]

Arthur Machen was bemused to find a distinguished Non-conformist making a public declaration that spiritual intervention in the war was possible. So much so that he visited Dr Horton and published his interview in the *Evening News*. When Machen confronted the minister with the facts, Dr Horton conceded that there 'may be something in my theory of derivation'. He accepted that Miss Marrable's account was not first-hand and agreed to suspend judgement pending the appearance of more direct evidence. But he asked Machen to take the following into account:

> Such phenomena – and we may call them phenomena – are a constant fact in history; we have many instances of supernatural beings appearing and exerting an influence on human life ... I was more particularly disposed to believe in the story of the angelic apparition during the retreat from Mons, from what I heard myself from an Army reader. He told me that all the men who were in that retreat were changed men. They had all prayed, and they had all felt a sense as of spiritual uplifting; and so the tale seemed to me congruous with their experiences.[32]

The Reverend Alexander Boddy and the angels

Unlike Dr Horton, who relied upon the evidence of hearsay, the Reverend Alexander Boddy claimed he had collected evidence for the existence of 'real angels' directly from soldiers themselves. Boddy was an Anglican minister from Sunderland who became the leader of a religious revival that spread to Europe from America in the late nineteenth century. He was 61 years of age and nearing the end of his ministry when he spent two months as a chaplain to soldiers serving with the British Army in France. This gave him the opportunity to investigate the stories he had read about in the English newspapers. In Flanders he found evidence of angelic visions not only from the time of Mons but from the Second Battle of Ypres in April, 1915. The Reverend Alexander Boddy described these stories to a crowd at an open air service on his return to Sunderland and his claims were widely reported in the newspapers as further evidence for miracles in the trenches. Unfortunately they were, without exception, all second- and third-hand accounts that added little to the body of rumours already circulating.

In one case Boddy struck up a conversation with a group of soldiers in a trench as they were tidying the graves of comrades. A soldier with the Third Canadians, claimed that after the Second Battle of Ypres, when their battalion was retiring through communication trenches towards their rest camp, they had passed a group of men from a West Riding battalion. There they stood for some time and overheard one of the Yorkshire soldiers telling those near him that he had seen on some occasion 'a very wonderful sight in the air' that seemed at first to be like a ball of fire. Then it took the form of an angel with outstretched wings hovering between the British first line and that of the enemy.

> We were standing near the graves of some 1,700 to 1,800 of our departed heroes, and this Canadian soldier, who was recovering from wounds, said: 'Why shouldn't these things happen to-day? I believe we are better now than in Old Testament times, when they often saw the angels. There's more reason for them appearing now.'[33]

Alexander Boddy also had evidence from a soldier of the First Battalion West Riding Regiment who took part in the retreat from Mons and was recovering from wounds in a hospital in France. The vision he spoke of took place on the second day of the retreat from Mons.

> We were hard pressed and were making for a ruined barn or something of that kind when I heard a comrade in the ranks speaking excitedly. I didn't know him, and I didn't hear all

details, as we soon were separated. But this man couldn't get away from one thing – it was that he had seen in the sky something quite 'above nature', something 'supernatural'. His manner and tone and reiterance impressed my informant so much that he could never forget it.

Boddy believed such signs were to be expected if, as he believed, the End Times were approaching. He told the *Sunderland Echo*:

The evidence, though not always direct, was remarkably cumulative, and came along channels which bore a stamp of veracity. Supernatural angel forms had, he believed, been seen. He was reminded of one of the prophecies that pointed towards a great crisis which many believed to be impending 'great signs shall there be from Heaven.'

The idea of the world war as the prelude to the biblical apocalypse was a theme taken up by other religious and occult writers of the time. While official propaganda encouraged the idea of the German soldiers as baby-killers, others portrayed the Kaiser himself as the antichrist. Ralph Shirley in his *Prophecies and Omens of the Great War* traced the idea to prophecies made by an obscure seventeenth-century French monk, Brother John. Shirley said this identification was not entirely without justification 'in view of his [the Kaiser's] barbarous methods of warfare and the wholesale destruction of sacred buildings by the German troops'.[34]

During the course of 1915, the early rumours of supernatural intervention during the retreat had grown and gained credibility with the stories told by soldiers, officers and others whose word could be trusted. By the autumn of that year Boddy's stories and Shirley's speculations were added to a mass of sermons, tracts and booklets on the angel theme that were rushed into print by many different religious denominations. This was in addition to the writings of spiritualists, theosophists and other occultists. The end result was the appearance of a body of self-perpetuating literature. A cult of the Angel of Mons was now in the making, but even some of its adherents had become confused and over-whelmed by the mass of competing and contradictory stories. The movement lacked coherence and needed a charismatic and respectable figure around which all the believers could rally. In August this person was located. One of Alexander Boddy's informants was 'a lady nurse of undoubted integrity, a worker among our soldiers' who was of aristocratic birth and 'of very good position'. She had spoken to a wounded soldier from Mons who claimed that:

> he saw at a critical moment an angel with outstretched wings – like a luminous cloud between the advancing Germans and themselves. The Germans could not advance to destroy them. This lady was subsequently speaking of this incident in the presence of some officers, and was rather incredulous. A colonel looked up and said, 'Young lady, the thing happened. You need not be incredulous. I saw it myself.'[35]

The lady nurse was Phyllis Campbell. Encouraged to tell her story by the unlikely combination of an evangelical priest and an occultist, she stepped forward into the glare of the media spotlight with the most dramatic testimony of all.

CHAPTER SIX

Ministering angels

I saw several wounded soldiers who had been in the battle of Mons and I asked them if they had heard the story of the Angels of Mons. 'Tell us what you have heard,' and when I had finished they said, 'Yes, that's right. We did not see them, but we have met many who have, and not only then, but on other occasions.' Mrs Curex Wilson, speaking to some girls on their work in connection with the war, told the story as she had it, from an officer who saw the Angels. The story never varies in the telling and evidently impressed all who witnessed it as a proof of divine intervention.[1]

This letter, published by the *Sheffield Telegraph* in August 1915, is typical of the stories that circulated at that time among volunteer nurses working in England and France. At the outbreak of war, many women were caught up in the wave of patriotic nationalism that drove men to the recruitment stations, but the Government's war plan provided only for a small number of medical units and auxiliary hospitals. In August 1914 there were just 300 trained nurses among Queen Alexandra's Imperial Military Nursing Service and these were quickly overwhelmed by the numbers of casualties arriving from the Front. Thousands more were on reserve but most important of all were the volunteers. Many young, middle-class women left their jobs to enlist with the Voluntary Aid Detachment (VAD). It was originally assumed the VAD would be called into action only in the event of an invasion of Britain. However, heavy casualties and a shortage of trained nurses made it inevitable that the volunteers would be called up to serve in France.

The nurses and volunteers who worked in the military hospitals served with a level of courage and devotion that matched the bravery and sacrifices made by the soldiers. Nurses symbolized everything the Tommies believed they were fighting for: God, king and country embodied in one profession. More directly, the presence of women at the Front, even in their unflattering apparel, represented for the men a vital link with home. The design of the seven-piece Victorian-style uniforms worn by the women had not changed since the days of Florence Nightingale. The flowing white veil and cap, white cuffs and coveralls decorated with a red cross were designed to conceal feminine beauty and cultivate a religious image of the women as 'nuns' or 'ministering angels'. Some women found it difficult to live up to these lofty ideals and there were a series of love affairs between nurses and their patients.

The best-known volunteer nurse was Vera Brittain who, at the age of 21, gave up her place at Oxford University to join the war effort. In 1914 she met and fell in love with Roland Leighton who was a friend of her only brother, Edward. At the outbreak of war both joined the British Army. Vera and Roland were engaged but only four months later he was killed on the Western Front. Before the end of the war her brother and many of their friends joined the list of dead and missing. As she coped with her loss, Vera devoted herself to nursing the wounded both in England and France. Her autobiography *Testament of Youth* (1933) describes how as casualties mounted the VADs, who were supposed to be providing basic support, found themselves acting as untrained nurses in hospitals along the front line.

An English nurse who served with the French Red Cross is a key figure in this story. Phyllis Campbell was 19 years old at the outbreak of war. She was a young woman caught up in a world dominated by soldiers and journalists, but within a year she electrified the English press with her stories of intimate conversations with wounded soldiers during the retreat from Mons. These stories were all the more influential because she claimed the soldiers had been inspired by visions as they halted the German advance on Paris. At the time, few people were inclined to question the word of a woman who was widely regarded as a heroine.

Like Brittain, Campbell was no ordinary nurse. She was the daughter of a novelist, Francis Campbell, and came from an aristocratic Scottish family background. Her aunt, Lady Archibald Campbell, was a noted occultist and medium who wrote regularly for the *Occult Review*. Phyllis was born in Australia and, although her parents settled in England when she was seven, she and her older sister were sent to schools in France. After leaving school, Phyllis continued to live there, dividing her time between Paris and Brittany. In 1913 she wrote two articles on French ghost stories that were published in the *Occult Review*. In a field dominated by men, Phyllis chose to hide her age and gender under the byline 'Phil Campbell'. Her interest in the occult was encouraged by her aunt and in France she was influenced by the mystical philosophy of the theosophists. Furthermore, her talent for writing was fired by intense patriotism and a hatred for the Germans.

Phyllis Campbell's angel stories were radically different from the rumours that spread during the spring of 1915. At face value they appeared to be first-hand, verbatim statements from soldiers, all anonymous. Campbell's stories outshone all those that preceded her. Her knowledge came not only from British soldiers but also from French and Russian sources. Furthermore, she was well placed in society and had extensive contacts with the royal families of Europe via her aristocratic friends. She was educated, and highly literate and it was said she had been decorated by the French Government.

Her account first came to light in the July 1915 issue of the *Occult Review*. The editor, Ralph Shirley, said that 'a few days ago' he had spoken to two English ladies at a hospital in St Germain-en-Laye, near Paris, nine miles from the most westerly point reached by the German army. One of these was Phyllis Campbell:

> In the course of our conversation the story circulated with
> regard to the alleged phenomena at the Battle of Mons
> cropped up, and I mentioned the fact that they had been
> alluded to in *The Occult Review*, but that certain organs of
> the London Press had held the alleged incidents up to
> ridicule, as being merely founded upon a romance that had
> appeared in the English papers. It was pointed out to me in
> reply that in France they were not merely implicitly
> believed, but were absolutely known to be true, and that no
> French paper would have made itself ridiculous by disputing
> the authenticity of what was vouched for by so many
> thousands of independent eye-witnesses.[2]

The ladies assured Shirley that whole battalions of French soldiers
had seen apparitions which they identified as Joan of Arc, while
others claimed to have seen St Michael the archangel. He added:

> Many of the British soldiers declared they had seen St
> George, but whether St Michael and St George were
> different interpretations, according to nationality, of the
> same apparition, did not seem clear.

From this point Shirley began to rely upon Campbell as an
authority on the visions. He was clearly impressed by the
intelligent, beguiling young nurse. Machen's adversary Harold
Begbie also drew heavily upon her testimony in his book, *On the
Side of the Angels*, published in September 1915. He described
Phyllis as an 'extremely pretty, child-like and sensitive' woman
who, despite her youth, 'has been through scenes that would drive
many people mad and has helped in surgical operations which
would try the nerves of a trained nurse'. This determination and
strength of character was again on display in an interview she
gave to the *Evening News*. The newspaper described how the nurse:

> submitted cheerfully to a rigorous cross-examination, and
> made no attempt to bolster up possible weak points in her

narrative; while, on the contrary, she resisted the most subtle attempts, by leading questions and suggestions, to varnish or embroider her story in the slightest degree.[3]

When in August 1915 Campbell returned to England, Ralph Shirley persuaded her to describe her experiences in the *Occult Review*. Her article appeared in the August issue and proved so popular it was reprinted again in September. Its popularity can be judged by Shirley's comment that 'owing to the great demand for the last issue hundreds of readers were unable to obtain copies'. However, the article is short on specifics of any British Army units, battles or places, making the stories impossible to verify from independent sources. The accounts of visions she described relate not to the Battle of Mons, but to 'the terrible week that brought the Allies to Vitry-le-François'.

Vitry is a town on the River Marne that was chosen by the French Commander-in-Chief, General Joffre, as his campaign headquarters. It is the only place name identified in Campbell's account. Her emphasis on Vitry, 'where the Allies turned', dates her stories to the beginning of September. In addition, Ralph Shirley wrote that the men Campbell referred to were casualties of a battle fought on 8 September. This was within three days of the date on which Brigadier General John Charteris noted in his memoirs that rumours of the Angel of Mons were circulating among the men of the BEF.

The Place in the Forest

Shortly before the outbreak of war, Phyllis Campbell was studying music in Germany but with international tension increasing she left with her aunt for Paris on 4 July. There she took a fast-track surgical course and volunteered for work at the Front. Her duties began on 15 August as *ambulancier auxiliaire* at a railway dressing station along one of the railway halts in the Forest of Marley which she knew only as 'the Place in the Forest'. At 'the first stopping place' were six other volunteers, and their *president*. Here, Campbell claimed she first heard about the visions. The German advance was unrelenting and the commandant of the dressing station warned the nurses to prepare for evacuation at a moment's notice as train after train crept into the forest. The carriages were unlighted and the nurses were obliged to climb into cattle trucks and carry lanterns in order to reach the mass of wounded soldiers lying on straw inside. A key passage in Campbell's account describes a scene at four-thirty one morning as an ambulance train pulled onto a platform:

We forgot our weariness in a race against time, removing the dead and dying, and attending to those in need. I was bandaging a man's shattered arm with the *majeur* instructing me, while he stitched a horrible gap in his head, when Madame de A—, the heroic President of the post, came and replaced me. 'There is an English in the fifth wagon,' she said. 'He demands a something – I think a holy picture.' The idea of an English soldier demanding a holy picture struck me, even in that atmosphere of blood and misery, as something to smile at, but I hurried away. 'The English' was a Lancashire Fusilier. He was propped up in a corner, his left arm tied up in a peasant woman's head kerchief, and his head newly bandaged. He should have been in a state of collapse from loss of blood, for his tattered uniform was soaked and caked in blood, and his face paper-white under the dirt of conflict. He looked at me with bright courageous eyes and asked for a picture or a medal (he didn't care which) of St George. I asked if he was a Catholic. 'No,' he was a Wesleyan Methodist (I hope I have it right), and he wanted a picture, or a medal of St George, *because he had seen him on a white horse*, leading the British at Vitry-le-François, when the allies turned.

There was an R.F.A. [Royal Field Artillery] man, wounded in the leg, sitting beside him on the floor; he saw my look of amazement, and hastened in, 'It's true, Sister,' he said. 'We all saw it. First there was a sort of a yellow mist like, sort of risin' before the Germans as they came to the top the hill, came on like a solid wall they did – springing out of the earth just solid – no end to 'em. I just gave up. No use fighting the whole German race, thinks I; it's all up with us. The next minute comes this funny cloud of light, and when it clears off there's a tall man with yellow hair in golden armour, on a white horse, holding his sword up, and his mouth open as if he was saying, 'Come on, boys! I'll put the kybosh on the devils.' Sort of 'This is my picnic' expression. Then, before you could say knife, the Germans had turned, and we were after them, fighting like ninety. We had a few scores to settle, Sister, and we fair settled them.'

'Where was this?' I asked. But neither of them could tell. They had marched, fighting a rearguard action, from Mons, till St George had appeared through the haze of light, and turned the Germans. They both *knew* it was St George. Hadn't they seen him with his sword on every 'quid' they'd ever had?[4]

That night their stories were confirmed by three mortally wounded men of the Irish Guard, one of whom stood over 6 feet 5 inches tall. As one took the sacrament from a priest, he told of a vision of St George 'riding on a white horse between them and the Germans'. This vision happened at 'the most critical point of the retreat'. Among the eyewitnesses to this event were 'officers of high rank, a Roman Catholic priest, and English and French soldiers'. Afterwards she compared notes with the other nurses at the dressing station and found that just one of them had *not* heard of the 'Angelic Leaders' and she was guarding wounded German prisoners. Campbell continued:

On discussing the matter between the trains of wounded, we remarked: First, that the French soldiers of all ranks had seen two well-known saints – Joan of Arc – to whom many of those delirious with the torrid heat and loss of blood were praying – that she was in armour, bareheaded, riding a white horse, and called 'Advance,' while she brandished her sword high in air; and St Michael the Archangel, clad in golden armour, bare-headed, riding a white horse, and flourishing his sword, while he shouted 'Victory!' Second, the British had seen St George, in golden armour, bareheaded, riding a white horse and crying while he held up his sword, 'Come on!'

After the Battle of the Marne, Campbell was moved from the ambulance post to a hospital nearer Paris where she met Ralph Shirley and the Reverend Alexander Boddy. She assured them that 'everybody has seen them who has fought through from Mons to Ypres'. The stories were told in a quiet, secular and matter-of-fact fashion, 'as if it were usual and quite expected occurrence for the lords of heaven to lead the hosts of earth'.

Of the retreat from Mons, Campbell painted a vivid picture of men marching day and night, collapsing in exhaustion and being dragged along by officers. Hungry and thirsty, under a fierce heat, and pursued by the German cavalry, the men reached a point of collapse before the trumpet call that called them to stand and fight. One of them said:

> The Germans were coming on just the same as ever, when suddenly the 'Advance' sounded, and I saw the luminous mist and the great man on the white horse, and I knew the *Boches* would never get Paris, for God was fighting on our side.

These anecdotes were thrown into the heady mix along with gory accounts of atrocities committed by the German troops whom Campbell identified with the forces of darkness. A typical passage from her account illustrates her real agenda:

> Poor Dix, when he came into hospital with only a bleeding gap where his mouth had been, and splintered hand and arm, he ought to have been prostrate and unconscious, but he made no moan, his pain had vanished in contemplation

of the wonderful things he had seen – saints and angels fighting on this common earth, with common mortal men, against one devilish foe to all humanity. A strange and dreadful thing, that the veil which hangs between us and the world of Immortality should be so rent and shrivelled by suffering and agony that human eyes can look on the angels and not be blinded. The cries of mothers and little children, the suffering of crucified fathers and carbonized sons and brothers, the tortures of nuns and virgins, and violated wives and daughters, have all gone up in torment and dragged at the Ruler of the Universe for aid, and aid has come.[5]

The Maid of Orleans

Phyllis Campbell was living and working in France at a time of enormous suffering and bereavement. By the close of 1914, the French army had suffered almost one million casualties, and had lost 10 per cent of its officers. 1915 brought more slaughter, with a further 1 430 000 casualties. At one stage the French President was warned the army could not continue as 'the instrument of victory is being broken in our hands'.

These disasters were in stark contrast to the optimism that followed the 'Miracle of the Marne'. The Allied success in halting the German advance before Paris was achieved by soldiers fighting with a level of bravery and passion that was fuelled by a determination not only to stop the Germans but also to turn the retreat into an advance. The French armies fought ferociously to defend Paris. They were driven in part by an appeal to the mythic past symbolized by the example of Joan of Arc who fought the English invaders five centuries earlier. Phyllis Campbell was caught up in this feverish atmosphere and she incorporated much of the folklore that surrounded Joan's legend into her own stories. During the battles, Catholic soldiers from all sides carried medals and images of saints, and assistance from Joan was widely invoked by the French armies. Campbell claimed that the French wounded she tended during the retreat from Mons were 'dumb, stricken and paralysed' whereas the later arrivals, coinciding with the victory at the Marne, were in a 'curiously exalted condition', a 'self-contained rapture of happiness' as though uplifted by some spiritual experience. This she attributed to the direct intervention of Joan and the saints. One soldier told her:

> 'Yes,' it was quite true. The *Boches* were in full retreat, and the Allies were being led to victory by St Michael and Joan of Arc. 'As for petite Jeanne d'Arc,' said one soldier, 'I know her well, for I am of Domremy. I saw her brandishing her sword and crying "Turn! Turn! Advance!"' Yes, he knew others had seen the Archangel, but little Joan of Arc was good enough for him. He had fought with the English from Mons – and little Joan of Arc had defeated the English – *par example!* Now she was leading them. There was a combination for you. No wonder the *Boches* fled down the hill.[6]

Both Campbell and Ralph Shirley claimed these stories were common knowledge in France during August and September 1914. Five centuries after her death, Joan of Arc remained a living legend in France. The mysterious nature of her mission and her conversations with angels contributed to the mystique that surrounded her life. During the nineteenth century, Joan was slowly reinstated as a national heroine, a process that began with her formal exoneration from the medieval charges of witchcraft and heresy. She was finally canonized by the Vatican in 1920 at the end of a long process of rehabilitation that was accelerated during the Franco-Prussian War. By 1914 she had become a symbol of national self-sacrifice par excellence that appealed to both religious and nationalist instincts of the French. Joan's story symbolized to many soldiers the eternal battle between good and evil that was reflected in the earthly struggle between France and the German invaders.

Reports from war correspondents indicate that behind the lines French ministers were encouraging soldiers to invoke Joan in battle. One English reporter, Frank Adkins, described the scene at a great open-air commemoration of Joan at Harfleur in Normandy. Thousands of soldiers and local women attended the event in May 1915. Many of them wore Joan medallions or carried her colours of light blue and white. The crowd was addressed by a Belgian minister and then by Catholic chaplains from the BEF. Mass was followed by a rousing oration from a French curé. Adkins reported:

> He boldly claimed the turning of the Germans back from Paris as a miracle. He said that the password for the critical day was 'Joan of Arc' and that it was Joan herself who, unseen, rode at the head of their charging Frenchmen. Could they utter the password without feeling the tightening of their inspiration?[7]

Joan had become a rallying icon for the battered French armies, and images of her appeared throughout the war in art, literature and propaganda. The opening scenes of the earliest film of her life-story, Cecil B. de Mille's *Joan the Woman* (1916), depicts a battle in Flanders while Joan of Arc and angelic warriors hover protectively in the sky above the Allied trenches. Henry van Dyke's *The Broken Soldier and the Maid of France* (1919) has a vision of Joan appear before a deserter from the French army. He is returned to the faith and rejoins his companions who are defending Verdun against the Germans. Both artistes drew upon the legend of the Angel of Mons as the source for their inspiration. Many others would follow in their footsteps.

Campbell vs. Machen

Phyllis Campbell's claims were widely published in English newspapers during the summer of 1915. They also received favourable coverage in the occult and spiritual press, but they failed to impress Arthur Machen. In the chivalrous age in which he lived, it was not possible to question the motives of a heroine who had dedicated herself to the war effort. Campbell also escaped direct criticism from the *Evening News* and instead its editor allowed her and Machen equal space to put their case in a series of articles.

Arthur Machen continued to believe he was the creator of the legend, and began to grow weary of contradicting those who claimed otherwise. We have seen how in June 1915, in his interview with Dr Horton, he confronted the clergyman with the facts and in another issue of the *Evening News* refuted the angel story attributed to 'Miss Marrable' (see Chapter 5). In July his frustration was illustrated by the headline which accompanied another article: 'NO ESCAPE FROM "THE BOWMEN", My Sympathy with Frankenstein'.

In August he responded first to the claims made originally by Phyllis Campbell in the *Occult Review* and then to Harold Begbie. Ralph Shirley allowed Arthur Machen to see page proofs of Campbell's article shortly before the first edition of Machen's book, *The Bowmen and Other Legends of the War*, went to press. This allowed him to respond quickly, both in his book and in his newspaper. The problem with the stories collected by the nurse, Machen wrote, was that they were all second-hand:

If Miss Campbell had proffered herself as a witness at the Old Bailey and said, 'John Doe is undoubtedly guilty. A soldier I met told me that he had seen the prisoner put his hand into an old gentleman's pocket and take out the purse' – well, she would find that the stout spirit of Mr Justice Starleigh still survives in our judges. The soldier must be produced. Before that is done we are not technically aware that he exists at all.[8]

Machen highlighted what he believed were two glaring absurdities in Campbell's account. How was it, he asked, that two soldiers claimed to have seen St George leading the Allies at Vitry-le-

François and yet, one paragraph later in Campbell's account, when asked 'Where was this?' responded that 'neither of them could tell'. Equally puzzling was their claim that the figure on the horse was St George because of his likeness to the figure that appeared on the English sovereign. The vision seen by the soldiers was a bareheaded man in golden armour. Yet the St George depicted on English coinage wore a helmet and was naked, other than a short cape flying from the shoulders. Such a mistake, Machen implied, would not have been made by two streetwise Tommies, but might easily have been made by someone who visited England infrequently.

Campbell's claim that 'everybody' who fought from Mons to Ypres saw apparitions was to Machen the clincher. While he accepted that many soldiers who had fought at Mons had been killed or succumbed to their wounds, others *had* returned home. In fact, many letters from the front had been published in newspapers. Yet no one had spoken of angels. If such a great number existed, Machen noted,

> It is again odd that nobody has come forward to testify at first hand to the most amazing event of his life. Many men have been back on leave from the front, we have many wounded in hospital, many soldiers have written letters home. And they have all combined, this great host, to keep silence as to the most wonderful of occurrences, the most inspiring assurance, the surest omen of victory.[9]

Campbell's response to Machen's point-by-point demolition of her claims was feeble. She claimed the soldiers she interviewed came from 'widely-separated points of the field of battle' and neither she, nor they, could give the names of the places: 'They had been retreating and fighting for days and nights. None knew where they were.' The two Tommies who saw St George, recognized him from the figure's *tout ensemble*, 'which to their minds represented St George'. Most amazing of all was her explanation for the lack of named witnesses. This was the result, she claimed, of 'an embargo of silence' imposed on the British Army by the

War Office press censor:

> It is untrue to say 'nobody has come forward to testify at first
> hand.' Such evidence exists: it has been published in the
> daily papers, and when the war is over and the embargo
> of silence upon soldiers is removed Mr Machen will be
> overwhelmed with corroborative evidence.[10]

Campbell's claims were adopted by her champion, Harold Begbie
who, in his book *On the Side of the Angels*, claimed there was 'a
definite military order that soldiers are not to speak of their
experiences at the front ... until after the war'. Working from his
privileged position in Fleet Street, Machen had inside knowledge
of the many topics that were subject to censorship. The angels
were not among them. In any case, he asked, why should the
British Government suppress such wonderful news that was a
positive benefit to the war effort? 'I have heard of no such order,'
he concluded. 'I do not believe in the existence of any such order.'

Despite her protestations, Campbell was unable to provide
substance to the claim that her stories preceded what Machen
called 'the snowball of rumour' that followed the publication of
'The Bowmen'. In her *Occult Review* article, Campbell claimed:

> Much of what I have written here is not new to the
> Editor ... because when I had a moment to spare I wrote to
> him after August 4 last year [1914], and much also I wrote
> to friends whose names I enclose with this, mentioning these
> things as they came, with the time.[11]

She was unable to name these friends because they were shy of
publicity but Ralph Shirley was aware of their identity. Harold
Begbie believed that Machen's theory was 'very badly damaged'
by Campbell's claims and he wrote: 'There is either a conspiracy
between Miss Campbell and Mr Shirley to deceive the British
public (object not stated!) or Mr Machen's theory does not hold
water.'[12]

If it was indeed the case that Campbell had written of visions
seen by British soldiers in August 1914, the production of her

dated letter would have put an end to the controversy. Oddly, Begbie did not ask to see this letter. He was satisfied with Shirley's assurance that 'Miss Campbell is a credible witness, and he has assured me that he is entirely satisfied in this respect.' If Shirley possessed a letter from Phyllis Campbell, dated August 1914, that referred specifically to angels witnessed by British troops, it is curious that he should make no mention of such a vital piece of evidence in his writings on the subject. Nevertheless, despite this curious lack of direct evidence, claims that stories and rumours were circulating among the BEF *before* Machen's short story appeared continued to be widely accepted and believed. The actual evidence of this fact did not come out until the publication of the Charteris letters in 1931 – if those letters stand up to investigative scrutiny.

Campbell certainly had connections with the 'very best of sources'. One of her claims related to a letter 'received by her friends in France in September 1914, written by a Russian princess'. This claim at least did have some substance, as versions of this story were published shortly after the battle of Augustovo on the Eastern Front (see Chapter 2). Unfortunately, her own contribution to the debate in the *Evening News* failed to provide testimony that could be independently checked. Readers were instead asked to accept the stories on her word alone. In her response to Machen she made her own personal agenda explicit:

> I believe that these experiences of the Allied soldiers have been of great spiritual comfort in thousands of bereaved homes; and I want, if may be, to help to keep alive that divine spark of consolation. I think it wicked to write or say anything that may tend to stem the great wave of spirituality which these awful days have caused.[13]

How reliable was Campbell's evidence and was there any independent corroboration of the stories? There were claims of nurses who had independently collected stories from soldiers, but the majority of these were of the 'friend of a friend' type. Campbell's own stories are placed in context by the memoirs of

Vera Brittain, who nursed both in England and France from 1915 to the end of the war. In *Testament of Youth*, she writes of sisters who 'seemed to try and outdo one another in telling stories of war horrors' and adds:

> In those days I knew, of course, nothing of psychology ... I was still too young to realise how much vicarious excitement the War provided for frustrated women cut off from vision and opportunity in small provincial towns, or to understand that the deliberate contemplation of horror and agony might strangely compensate a thwarted nature for the very real grief of having no one at the front for whom to grieve.[14]

At the time of his very public clash with Campbell, Machen held back what he really believed. After the war, when he was asked to comment on the controversy by a US admirer, he was less reticent. Campbell, he said, had 'become a conscious liar in the matter'.[15]

Melvin Harris was the first modern writer to scrutinize Campbell's testimony with the hindsight provided by history. He was even less sympathetic towards her motivations. According to him, among the women volunteers held in high regard were a few sensation-seekers 'who forced such stories as that of the angels onto wounded soldiers', and in his opinion Phyllis Campbell fell into this category. Although he could not prove his theory, Harris pointed to a number of examples from the war where 'sweet young ladies' proved to be quite capable of inventing elaborate accounts of events that never took place.[16]

The most notorious example was the strange story of nurse Grace Hume. On 16 September 1914, newspapers in England and Scotland published an astonishing story that produced outrage against the Germans. The allegations were that Grace was working at a hospital in Vilvorde in Belgium when the Germans overran the town. The hospital was burnt to the ground, its patients were brutally murdered and Grace herself was mutilated. In her last moments she wrote a final note to her younger sister Kate in Scotland, and this was carried home by faithful friends including one 'nurse Mullard'.

The press and public were rightly enraged, but the story was not true. Within days Grace Hume was found alive and well in Huddersfield. She had indeed volunteered for nursing in France and Belgium but had never been called upon to leave the country. When police investigated the claims, it emerged that the source for the story was a letter forged by Kate Hume who had become mentally unbalanced by the loss of her brother on the *Titanic*. The 17-year-old was charged and stood trial at Dumfries. After three months in custody she was released when the jury heard evidence from a doctor who testified that Kate had heard so many lurid stories about German atrocities that she had come to believe her sister really had been killed.[17]

Of course it was not only a minority of the nurses who tried to outdo one another in the telling of stories. The soldiers themselves were capable of creating stories of their own that were often highly elaborate and personalized versions of rumours that circulated in the trenches. Melvin Harris believes that some Tommies were motivated to spread and embroider stories because they found that by telling them they could enjoy attention from 'posh' female nurses. Vera Brittain reproduces in almost verbatim detail a conversation she overheard while working in the hospital camp at Etaples during the German offensive of spring 1918.

"Ave yer come down from Albert way?' inquired a sergeant of a corporal in the next bed, who, like himself, wore a 1914 ribbon.

'Yus,' was the reply, 'I have. There's some mighty queer things happenin' on the Somme just now, ain't there, mate?'

'That there be,' said the sergeant. 'I can tell yer of one that 'appened to me, meself.'

In hushed silence, the soldier told how a much-loved sergeant killed in the first days of the Somme had become a guardian angel for his men. Before his death he had pledged to return whenever the lads in his platoon found themselves in peril. When they became trapped by a German advance in Albert, 'Suddenly I turns round, and there I sees 'im with 'is bright eyes and 'is old smile, bringin' up the rear.' As the enemy were beaten back, the phantom sergeant disappeared. After the story was told, a Lancashire boy from an opposite bed leaned forward. He said, 'I can tell yer summat that'll beat that.' Afterwards, Brittain said she began to recognize her world 'for a kingdom of death, in which the poor ghosts of the victims had no power to help their comrades by breaking nature's laws'.[18]

This elaborate rumour mill did not exist in August 1914 when those first desperate and fluid battles were fought on the Franco-Belgian border. One of the few first-hand accounts of this time is by a Church of England and Wesleyan chaplain, Owen Spencer Watkins. He served with the Fourteenth Field Ambulance attached to the Fifth Division of II Corps which crossed to Le Havre on 22 August and reached Valenciennes as the Battle of Mons began. Watkin's detailed account of the battle and the retreat, *With Field-Marshal French in France and Flanders*, was published early in 1915 before the Angel of Mons rumour began to spread. Watkins ministered to soldiers who had been mortally wounded at Le Cateau and wrote:

> I was received by our devout lads with enthusiasm, and all, even the most careless, after the experiences of the past days, were only too glad to talk with me on the deep and most sacred things of the Spirit.[19]

Despite being caught in the thick of the action described by Phyllis Campbell, Watkins fails to mention stories of angels or supernatural visions, even in the form of rumours. Even more telling is the diary of a French Army chaplain, Abbé Felix Klein, who was attached to the Ambulance Division of the American Hospital in Beuilly, northeast of Paris. During the fast-moving campaign from 3 August to 28 December 1914, the abbé maintained a detailed diary of his experiences and the 'lively impressions' he collected from the wounded troops on the battlefield. During his daily journeys to and from the Front ferrying the wounded to field hospitals, the priest heard many of the rumours that were circulating among the Allied troops, including that of the 'Russians with snow on their boots'. But again there is no mention in his diary of angels or any other supernatural visions mentioned by either French or British soldiers.[20]

Negative evidence is seldom conclusive, but the writings of Watkins and Abbé Klein do provide what Melvin Harris calls 'telling evidence' when set against Campbell's second- and third-hand stories. Abbé Klein's diary, *La guerre vue d'une ambulance*, was published in January 1915 and was a contemporaneous record of events as they happened. The most serious problem with Campbell's evidence is shared by all the other sources for the Angel of Mons. Her account was not published until a year after the events she described. When one looks more closely at the context in which the story was collected, here was a nurse who by her own admission had hardly slept in a week, or had a change of clothes. She was 'too weary to undress, or to eat' when casualties arrived at her ambulance station. Yet after a year had passed she was still able to repeat in verbatim fashion the stories told by soldiers in their last moments inside a dark hospital train.

Back of the Front

Nurse Campbell's stories were quoted extensively and uncritically by Begbie, Shirley and others who wished to keep alive the claims of 'divine intervention' in the war. They continued to be reproduced as 'fact' in many later accounts. In 1915 it was claimed that the 'overwhelming evidence' that Campbell had promised during her spat with Machen would be revealed in a book she was writing. This never materialized, but a pocket-sized book called *Back of the Front* was published in October 1915 by George Newnes & Son, of London. A picture of Campbell dressed in her Red Cross uniform appeared on the dust jacket, and Harold Begbie proclaimed in the blurb that 'I am on the side of the angels and on the side of Miss Campbell'. By this time the Angel of Mons had been sidelined by fresh stories of alleged German atrocities in France and Belgium. Nevertheless, various officials were quoted in prefaces and letters endorsing her stories including Gabrielle Larroque, the chief superintendent of a ward at the hospital at St Germain-en-Laye, Paris. She contributed a signed statement which read:

> The wounded have spoken of apparitions of Joan of Arc after the battle of the Marne. This would be in the same places where she showed herself again with St Michael. But I know that all these facts have been recorded, and that the matter will be explained, the dates, places and irrefutable evidence, after the war. That is all that one can say at the moment.

The introduction was supplied by one W.L. Courtney who shared Campbell's predilection to accept without question accounts of German atrocities. Referring to Campbell's obvious belief that the Germans represented the forces of darkness and that their brutal behaviour proved it:

> It is the more necessary for me to give this testimony, because I understand that some doubts have been expressed as to the credibility of a narrative which to my mind carried conviction from its first page to its last, and in reality requires no external proof ... [but] ... of course it may be difficult in some cases to distinguish between memoranda taken at the time and the results of mere memory.[21]

As for the 'visions' that wounded soldiers described to Miss Campbell, Courtney's comments were hardly a ringing endorsement. He wrote: 'Frankly I do not know what to say about [them] ... it is a beautiful legend ... let us leave it at that.'

A reviewer in the *Times Literary Supplement* agreed, noting:

> She [Campbell] has perhaps erred from a desire for an excessive realism, and not seen the difference in carrying conviction between an exact record and the writing up into a story of a host of memories.[22]

There is no better summary of the contents of Campbell's book than that provided by Melvin Harris, who wrote that it gave a dramatic insight into a mind 'driven by a fanatical patriotism, which led her to accept and repeat every atrocity story that came her way'. As a result, she did not think it was necessary to check the truth of stories she overheard. Although she did not claim direct experience of the angels in *Back of the Front*, her earlier claims were now upstaged by her imaginative and gory descriptions of hospital trains containing mutilated Belgian civilians.

> In one wagon, sitting on the floor, was a naked girl of about 23. One of her suffering sisters, more fortunate than the rest in possessing an undergarment, had torn it in half and covered up the front of her poor body; it was saturated with blood from her cut-off breasts. On her knees, under her blistered hands, lay a little baby – dead.[23]

Throughout the book Campbell catalogues the horrors she claimed to have personally witnessed in France. These included priests burned alive, women violated and little children torn from their mothers' arms and bayoneted. The claims she made are severely tainted when set in the context of her undisguised hatred of the Germans that led her to repeat and, it appears, create stories of atrocities against civilians. While appalling massacres of civilians did occur during the German army's brutal march through Belgium, no real evidence has emerged to support the exaggerated claims of mutilation, rape and bestiality that were circulated by the Allied propaganda machine during the war.

Stories of German atrocities had the tacit support of the British press censor and they played upon the sense of moral outrage and sympathy for the plight of the Belgian civilians. Vera Brittain wrote of how her first experience of nursing German soldiers was coloured by the stories she had heard of baby-killing, rape and crucifixion in Belgium. Eventually, after months caring for the endless procession of dead and wounded, it dawned on Brittain and her fellow nurses that 'the Germans looked – how strange! – like other men'.

Phyllis Campbell's prejudice towards the enemy is starkly highlighted by a paragraph in her book that describes how she went about holding her nose when German prisoners were nearby. The German army were to her 'millions of men in grey with the faces of the devil'. She added:

> I thought they were distinctly a race that is something apart from Humanity, as we understand the word. When they stood blinking in the sun with their square heads and putty-coloured faces, colourless eyes and lashes – furtive yet unspeakably sinister in their grey uniforms – they suggested to me a creation of some monstrous spirit of evil. Is it strange that saints and angels should fight against this dreadful foe?[24]

Towards the end of her book the list of atrocities laid at the door of the German army reaches a crescendo with her claim that 'all the wickedness, the lust, the hate and cruelty and greed – the filthiness unimaginable that exists can be summed up in one word: *German*!' To Melvin Harris, this gave more than just a glimpse of Nurse Campbell's secret. To her, the Germans were so evil that anything could be used as a weapon against them. That included half-truths, rumours and even lies.

CHAPTER SEVEN

Angels that refuse to die

You saw, O friend, the forms, the light, the sheen?
   Our foes, their horses, saw; they turned and fled,
As troops of silent angels filed between
   Our broken ranks and theirs, and stilled our dread.

They did not come to spare your life, nor mine,
   To save man's pride, to write a nation's name;
But for some secret victory divine.
   Of universal love the spirits came.

'After Mons', *Light*, 15 May 1915

During 1915 the Angel of Mons grew from rumour and gossip into a summer sensation. The controversy provided a momentary distraction from the casualty lists and the growing feeling in Britain that the war was not going as well as had been predicted. The newspaper stories that had initially fuelled the tale were followed by a whole series of new articles, books and pamphlets that were rushed into print to satisfy the demand. First off the press was a 15-page penny pamphlet published by the Newspaper Publicity Company, London, with the elaborate title:

The Angel Warriors at Mons:
Including Numerous Confirmatory Testimonies,
Evidence of the Wounded and Certain Curious Historical Parallels,
An Authentic Record.

Compiled by Ralph Shirley, this was the first attempt to collect stories of angels and bowmen together alongside the historical precedents for supernatural intervention in war. Prominent above all other evidence for the Mons visions were the stories told by Phyllis Campbell who, as we have seen in Chapter 6, both Shirley and Alexander Boddy had met in France. At the same time, the flow of 'angels' correspondence addressed to the *Evening News* had become an overwhelming flood. When a London publisher offered to re-publish 'The Bowmen' in book form along with a selection of Machen's other war stories, the newspaper saw it as an opportunity too good to resist. Both Machen and his editor were hopeful that publication of the book would draw the debate to a close. In the event, it simply added more fuel to the fire.

The Bowmen and Other Legends of the War was published by Simpkin, Marshall, Hamilton, Kent & Company of London as a card-covered pocket book on 10 August 1915. At the price of one shilling it became an immediate best-seller. Within days it was difficult to obtain a copy from the first print run of 50 000. By the end of the year its success was followed up by an expanded second edition and worldwide sales topped 100 000. Unfortunately for Machen, the deal struck between his newspaper and the publishers brought him little personal financial benefit. When he left the *Evening News* he wrote somewhat sarcastically that 'It is always a satisfaction to feel that one has put a little money into the pockets of good men'.[1]

Machen's original contribution to the book took the form of a lengthy introduction where he carefully and patiently explained that the story from which the legend had grown was the product of his own imagination. His argument was lost on many of his readers who were equally determined to believe; and ironically the decision of the publishers to subtitle the book 'The Angels of Mons' tended to suggest there was some substance in the stories outside of fiction. Machen came to appreciate that many people were happy to accept what they read because it was published in a newspaper, and he became fascinated by the influence which a fictional story could exert upon the collective imagination. The power of the written word and its potential to spark off mass hysteria was a theme he returned to often in later writings. In 1917 the *Evening News* serialized Machen's 'shilling shocker', *The Terror*. This told of a series of mysterious attacks on humans by wild animals driven to a frenzy by the horror of the world war. In *The Terror* the British Government is fully aware of the outbreak but fears the disastrous effects the news would have on morale if the truth was allowed to leak out. A cover-up is the result, with all reports of the mysterious events suppressed by rigid censorship.[2]

Once again, Machen demonstrated an uncanny gift to predict future events. Some of those promoting the idea of divine intervention claimed that soldiers were forbidden to talk about what they had seen by an official order until the conflict was over. The notion of a Government cover-up of 'secret knowledge' of angels and later flying saucers and UFOs would eventually become one of the most enduring conspiracy legends of the late twentieth century. Another comparison which can be made with the 'flying saucer' belief was recognized by Machen's publishers in 1915. On the day of publication of his book, the *Evening News* carried an advertising feature which demonstrated how many people wanted to believe in and see angels. It read:

> Letters have come in from the most widely divergent classes of readers. Two Duchesses and several Countesses have sent direct the necessary stamps for copies. Letters have come in from hospital nurses, marked 'urgent,' requesting copies by return because wounded soldiers in their wards are asking eagerly for the book. Soldiers' wives and Tommies themselves are amongst today's applicants for copies direct ... One remarkable point about a large number of these letters is that the writers state they firmly believe in the 'Angels of Mons' ... 'I know the Angels saved our men at Mons,' writes a hospital nurse ... A soldier's wife writes for 'The Bowmen' to send to her husband 'somewhere in France' because she 'knows he saw the Angels'.[3]

For much of the summer, Machen's protests against this groundswell of belief fell on deaf ears. He was widely disbelieved and publicly rebuked for displaying 'impudence and arrogance' in claiming credit for the creation of the legend. One 'lady of substance' wrote to his editor asking if Machen was also claiming authorship of the Second Book of Kings. But the most ferocious attack of them all came from the patriot Harold Begbie, who accused Machen of 'amazing effrontery'. Begbie was a popular writer who produced both science fiction novels and works of non-fiction on social and political matters, such as his biography of the Secretary of State for War, *Kitchener: Organizer of Victory*, published in 1916. Begbie was, like Machen, fascinated by the supernatural and became a prominent member of the Psychic Society. His interest in telepathy and 'second sight' became apparent in 1904 when he produced a series of short stories for the *London Magazine*. In 'The Amazing Dreams of Andrew Latter', Begbie's hero is able to visit an alternative reality or 'dreamland'. In one of the stories Latter is able, by entering this alternative state, to witness the chain of events leading up to a series of vicious murders in London and his powers attract interest from Scotland Yard. Psychic detective work is now an established genre in TV and film, but in 1904 this idea was entirely an original concept.[4]

Begbie's interests coincided with Machen up to a point, but his use of evidence fell well below that of his rival. This difference in approach became apparent when in 1915 Begbie became champion of the pro-angels lobby. He felt the Angel of Mons was an inspiration to the war effort and a comfort for the bereaved, and was determined to defend it by challenging Machen's version of events. His book, *On the Side of the Angels – the Story of the Angels at Mons – an Answer to 'The Bowmen'*, commissioned by Hodder & Stoughton of London, appeared in September 1915. The popularity of the book can be judged by the fact that it was reprinted in five editions, the last of which appeared in 1917.

The book opened with an attack on Arthur Machen, Begbie's 'sinister genius'. He then appealed to the emotions of his readers, chiding Machen for what he felt was 'a most lamentable failure upon his part to realise the acuteness of human suffering and the intense eagerness for consolation which are now lying at the heart of English existence'.[5] Begbie's mission was to undo what he saw as the mischief wrought by Machen's 'grinning and inaccurate introduction'. He did not set out to prove 'that Angels appeared at Mons, but that before Mr Machen had written his fiction British soldiers in France believed that Angels had appeared to them'. To explain how Machen had spontaneously produced a piece of fiction that had accurately reflected 'real' events, Begbie proposed an ingenious theory:

> Mr Machen, on that Sunday morning, when he read with supreme sympathy that 'awful account' in [a] newspaper ... [he] may have received from the brain of a wounded or a dying British soldier in France some powerful impression of the battlefield at Mons.[6]

Here Begbie displayed not only a lack of critical faculties but also a lack of familiarity with Machen's careful account of the circumstances by which 'The Bowmen' came to be written. Machen had been powerfully affected by the accounts of the retreat published on 30 August, a week after the battle, but had waited a month to put pen to paper. If 'a powerful impression' from the brain of a wounded or dying soldier had indeed exerted an unconscious influence upon his writing, as Begbie opined, it was odd that such a dramatic message had been delayed in its transmission across the English Channel by almost a month.

The public debate between Machen and Begbie appeared acrimonious, but the two men had a grudging respect for one another. The world of journalism has always been an intimate one and in wartime London, with many young reporters leaving to join the army, it became even smaller. The older news hounds all knew each other, and gossip travelled fast on the grapevine. Machen and Begbie may have been poles apart in their values and beliefs, but their public clash obscured the fact they were both part of a very tight-knit social network based loosely around Fleet Street. This was highlighted in 1918 when a US admirer asked Machen for his views on Begbie's book. In reply he wrote:

> I don't think anything about Harold Begbie or his books. *On the Side of the Angels* was a publisher's commission; I don't think that Harold believes in a word of it. I don't think he's fool enough to do so.[7]

In response to a similar question, in 1930, Machen revealed that both he and the *Evening News* enjoyed the publicity 'and the more parodies and protests there were – the better the ad'. Throughout the controversy, he said, 'I told the truth as I knew it; but I was not a bit cast down if people chose to take fancy for fact.'[8]

Harold Begbie, on the other hand, relied heavily upon a mass of hearsay evidence and specifically the dubious testimony of Phyllis Campbell, so the argument with Machen quickly became a circular one. His stories were independently scrutinized by the Society for Psychical Research (SPR), whose own rigorous investigation of the story was then underway. Mrs Salter, the SPR investigator, found that some were second-hand:

> ... and in others have been described by the percipients only after an interval many months since the date of the experience, so that due allowance must be made for inaccuracy of memory, the force of suggestion, and other common sources of error.[9]

Attempts were made to obtain further information from the more promising of Begbie's informants, but the results were small as 'in one way or another many possible witnesses have passed out of reach, and other witnesses do not feel themselves able to assist us'. The only direct evidence was that of the wounded Lance Corporal whom Begbie interviewed in the Netley Hospital. The remaining testimony was all third-, fourth- and even sixth-hand statements attributed to 'a soldier', 'an officer' or 'a nurse', all of whom were untraceable. In *The Bowmen and Other Legends of the War* Machen summarized their value succinctly:

> Someone (unknown) has met a nurse (unnamed) who has talked to a soldier (anonymous) who has seen angels. But

THAT is not evidence; and not even Sam Weller at his gayest would have dared to offer it as such in the Court of Common Pleas.[10]

While Begbie deplored what he called 'police-court methods', Machen countered that the object of such methods is to ascertain the truth 'and this object seems to me a harmless one'. Harold Begbie's attempts to prove his case by relying upon accumulated testimony and by the reputation of 'credible witnesses' is a familiar one. A similar argument is used by UFO believers in the present day who claim that so many reliable people have reported seeing flying saucers that they must exist. But as science writer Isaac Asimov observed, maybe they do: 'It's not what you see that is suspect, but how you interpret what you see.'

Private Cleaver and the angels

The threadbare nature of the testimony presented in *On the Side of the Angels* was demonstrated when revelations about a new piece of allegedly first-hand evidence cast doubt upon the authenticity of the other stories. This came in the form of an affidavit sworn and signed by Private Robert Cleaver, of the First Cheshire Regiment. The stand made by the Cheshires against the advancing Germans during the rearguard action at Elouges on 24 August 1914 was one of the heroic moments during the retreat from Mons. In the following year George Hazlehurst, a Justice of the Peace in Flint, North Wales, heard rumours that Cleaver 'frequently spoke to his friends in the canteen of what he had seen at Mons' and decided to track him down. The JP travelled 40 miles to find him and Cleaver duly signed an affidavit which read:

> I, Robert Cleaver (No. 10515), a private in the 1st Cheshire Regiment of His Majesty's Army, make oath and say as follows:- That I personally was at Mons and saw the Vision of Angels with my own eyes.

Sworn at Kinmel Park, in the County of Flint, this 20th day of August, 1915. Before me, Geo. S. Hazlehurst, one of his Majesty's Justices of the Peace acting for the County of Flint.

Hazlehurst, quoted in the *Daily Mail*, said Private Cleaver struck him as 'being a very sound, intelligent man' who volunteered his statement and had no hesitation in signing a legal document.

He said that things were at the blackest with our troops, and if it had not been for this supernatural intervention they would have been annihilated. The men were in retreat and lying down behind small tufts of grass for cover. Suddenly the vision came between them and the German cavalry. He described it as 'a flash.' I asked him if the Angels were mounted or winged. He could say no more than that it appeared as 'a flash.' The cavalry horses rushed in all directions and were disorganized; the charge frittered away.[11]

Cleaver's evidence was quickly endorsed by the pro-angels lobby. David Gow in *Light* described it as 'striking confirmation'. The story appeared in time for Harold Begbie to include it in the first edition of *On the Side of the Angels*. Both men would quickly regret their endorsements. The few senior officers who knew the facts would have recognized two errors of fact in Cleaver's story. The Cheshires' stand at Elouges was part of a rearguard defence sent forward to halt the German advance and at no time during the battle were the men in retreat. They were not attacked by cavalry but were overwhelmed by an artillery barrage and waves of advancing infantry. The truth emerged in a letter published by the *Daily Mail* on 2 September. In it, Hazlehurst said he became suspicious after hearing rumours that Private Cleaver was not at the Battle of Mons. He contacted the regimental headquarters at Shrewsbury for confirmation of the soldier's movements. In reply, Major Hicks said Cleaver was mobilized at Chester on 22 August 1914 and posted out to the First Battalion, Expeditionary Force, France, with a draft on 6 September. He returned to England on

8 December, sick. A disappointed Hazlehurst added:

> The battle of Mons was in August 1914, and readers will draw their own conclusions. Information sworn on oath is usually regarded as sufficiently trustworthy for publication, but apparently not in this case. Will none of the officers who were at Mons and saw the angels, of whom Miss Marrable speaks, come forward and confess it?

The exposure of Cleaver's story as a hoax did nothing to dampen down the controversy, but his sworn testimony was removed from the second edition of *On the Side of the Angels*. During the autumn of 1915 *The Bowmen and other Legends of the War* became a worldwide best-seller. Copies of the second edition quickly sold out in London and orders poured in from the overseas dominions. Readers in Australia, New Zealand, Canada and South Africa received shipments and the story was translated into Hindustani for the Indian subcontinent. Copies made their way to Japan, Hong Kong, Chile and Petrograd, and G.P. Putnam & Sons of New York announced plans for a US edition.

In the updated introduction to the second edition of his book, Machen wrote that until the day of publication he had not seen 'a single morsel of evidence' to show anything of supernatural nature had occurred during the retreat from Mons. However, the very next day a journalist from the *Daily Mail* interviewed the wounded British Lance Corporal who claimed he saw a vision of three figures in the sky following the battle of Le Cateau. Of this testimony Machen conceded that:

> The story told by the lance-corporal constitutes the first piece of evidence – as distinguished from gossip, hearsay, tittle-tattle, and tarradiddle – that was advanced to show that there had been supernatural manifestations during the retreat from Mons.[12]

Soon after this he received a second piece of evidence, in the form of a letter from a 'distinguished officer', a Lieutenant-Colonel, who saw squadrons of phantom cavalry following the Battle of

Le Cateau in August 1914 (see Chapter 2). Machen's honest answer to those who asked what he made of this new evidence was simple, but unsatisfactory. He simply did not know what to make of them, but he had a theory: 'that the visions, both of the corporal and the colonel, were the hallucinations of men utterly worn out and exhausted, in both body and mind'.

These hallucinations may have combined in the two narratives that impressed him, 'with a mistaken judgement as to the actual forms of mists, trees, clouds and light'. In these instances the actual experience took place long after the moment of danger had passed and in the case of the Lance Corporal the 'apparition' remained visible for 35 minutes. Both involved soldiers who were physically and psychologically worn down by the stress of combat, a recurring theme in much of the first-hand testimony gathered during the war.

The showmen meet the angels

Later in the war Arthur Machen and Harold Begbie became the subject of a sarcastic parody by the satirist T.W.H. Crosland, whose previous contributions to literature were titled *Lovely Women* and *The Unspeakable Scot*. His *Find the Angels: The Showmen, A Legend of the War* was skilfully constructed in imitation of Machen's book and added a touch of humour to the clash of swords between the author and his detractors. *The Showmen* told the story of two British Army privates, Sweets and Cheese, who are 'ministered to by a female angel' but it is of lesser interest than the contents of the introduction and appendices. These parodied Machen, his tormentors and even Kipling, whose 'White Feather Legion' became the subject of a supplementary sketch. In his introduction, Crosland asks:

How did I come to write *The Showmen*? What moved me to put down on paper a fiction which turns out would be so true that people go about asserting that it was intended by Heaven for a war correspondent rather than a writer of poignant short stories? From first to last it has been the oddest of odd affairs. As you will see for yourselves, the story itself is nothing; yet the hubbub and bother it has raised impinge on the phenomenal. Everybody is talking about it: everybody swears that Pte Sweets and Pte Cheese are real persons; that they were really visited and succoured in their extremity by a real angel; that the angel has been seen by all manner of sober folk in all manner of places ... and that when I say, as I do say, that to the best of my knowledge and belief there is no angel (save and except a certain charming young lady to whom I send violets fresh from Piccadilly Circus every morning) I am an unmitigated promulgator of falsehood, or in plain terms, a liar. What is one to do?

On Machen's predicament, Crosland was equally scathing:

Good people, do you know, that this excellent man, who sat down to write a story out of his own head and for the perfectly legitimate purpose of earning an honest shilling (an exceedingly rare thing among journalists, by the way) ... do you know that this good, great and innocent man has been so pestered and harassed by the persistent attacks of people who know of their knowledge that the story is true, that he is actually beginning to believe they may be right when they call him a liar? Isn't it terrible that this sensitive person of genius ... now goes about under a sinister cloud, suffering from the benumbing consciousness that while he knows and I know that he wrote it clean slap bang out of his head and nothing else, there are hundreds, nay thousands who think they know better than both of us, and don't scruple to tell us so.[13]

Crosland was the first of a series of writers and artists to adapt the Angel of Mons into fiction, music and film. Artists and propagandists were also quick to set their imagination to work upon the vivid descriptions of angels and phantom armies described in the writings of Machen, Begbie and Campbell. The most popular illustrations using the angel theme were by artist Alfred Pearse, who produced a series of colour plates that were used to illustrate a book by a Christian writer who called herself 'A Churchwoman'. *The Chariots of God* (1915) mixed biblical stories with accounts of angels protecting British troops at Mons, Ypres and other battles of the war. These were interspersed with Pearse's dramatic artistic impressions. Prints and postcards depicting the Angel of Mons and the 'Comrade in White' were equally popular with soldiers and civilians (see Chapter 8). In October 1915, a firm of London publishers brought out a series of six coloured prints depicting elements of the legends, which were sold in a specially designed envelope. An advertisement published in the *Evening News* read:

> The pictures are of incidents in Mr Machen's book, *The Bowmen*, and in the testimony of Miss Phyllis Campbell, as published in *The Occult Review*. One, 'Heaven's Knight Aid Us!' shows the shining apparition of St George and the Bowmen of Agincourt during the retreat from Mons ... other illustrations are of St George leading the British, St Michael and the Blessed Joan of Arc.[14]

Angels on film

Public entertainment during the war was centred around the theatre, the music hall and, increasingly, the cinema. Musicians were some of the first entertainers to set the stories from Mons to verse. One of the first to appear was a piano solo called 'Angels of Mons (*Rêve Mystique*)' by Sydney C. Baldock (Gould & Bottler, Oxford Street, 1915). The sheet music cover featured a robed and winged angel, with sword and shield, hovering above a British soldier. It quickly became a 'hit' and as late as 1982 a reader of *This England* recalled spending Sunday evenings in the First World War gathered with his family around the piano as his sister and cousin played 'a beautiful piece of music called The Angels of Mons'. Baldock's composition was quickly followed by the 'Angel of Mons Waltz' by Paul Paree published by the Lawrence Wright Music Company, Charing Cross Road in 1916.[15] The splendid colour cover was inspired by the stories collected by Phyllis Campbell. It featured a winged angel-knight, mounted upon a white charger emerging from a white cloud above the trenches. Beneath the warrior angel was a panorama of shell-bursts above a landscape of trenches and advancing soldiers.

Moving pictures made their first appearance on the travelling fairgrounds of late Victorian England, and by the First World War cinemas were showing silent films on a variety of topical themes in many towns and cities. It was here that the legend made the leap from the literary imagination onto celluloid. In September 1915 the director Fred Paul released a film, *The Angels of Mons*, that was one of a large number of productions featuring his comedy character, Pimple. The film is described in the *British Film Catalogue* as 'A War Drama based on popular topical myth' but unfortunately, all surviving copies have been lost.[16] However, the symbolic link between angels and the First World War has been made continually by film makers in the present day.

In 1994, director Bill Bryden incorporated the legend into his epic production *The Big Picnic* that was staged at the Harland and Wolff sheds in Glasgow and later broadcast on BBC TV. The drama told the story of a Scottish regiment's experience of trench warfare and focused upon the symbolism of No Man's Land and the destruction of soldiers at the hands of the impersonal machinery of war. For the production Bryden employed a theatrical device known as the 'deus ex machina', which was used in medieval theatre to lower actors playing gods and goddesses onto the stage. In *The Big Picnic* the 'God from the

Machine' is a mobile crane which represented:

> the remorseless, inhuman tide of destruction as it cruises back and forth, like a giant bird scavenging over the battlefield. Its central icon is the Angel of Death, here called the Angel of Mons. She is a distillation of the many (over 10 000) sightings and mass hallucinations reported by allied soldiers, who saw visions of angels and folk heroes, saints and lost relatives in the sky over the Western Front. For us, she is the arbitrary hand of fate and the bringer of release from this hell.[17]

Bryden's play helped to give new life to the legend while at the same time perpetuating inaccuracies, such as the claim of 'many (over 10 000) sightings' of the angel. The BBC production of *The Big Picnic* was followed in 1997 by a big-screen adaptation of another famous supernatural mystery from the First World War, the Cottingley fairy photographs. *Fairytale: A True Story* was set in Yorkshire in 1917 and is based upon the true story of how 12-year-old Elsie Wright and her cousin, eight-year-old Frances Griffiths return from the bottom of their garden with photos of fairies taken on Elsie's father's camera. In the film, the pictures come to light at a lecture organized by the Theosophical Society in Bradford to discuss the Angel of Mons. They are examined by photographic experts who dismiss the possibility of hoax. Although the public lecture depicted was entirely fictional, it was based upon descriptions of soldiers' meetings described in Harold Begbie's book. In one scene a soldier describes his own sighting of the angels in a form of words which is based directly upon the report of the wounded Lance Corporal published in the *Daily Mail* (see Chapter 2). In this subtle fashion, stories from the First World War are recycled for a new generation to interpret in their own way.

Both these films were made during the 'angel revival' of the mid-1990s that began in the United States and spread to the British Isles, bringing with it a new wave of books, articles and films. Many writers of New Age angel literature copied their accounts of the Angel of Mons from earlier books, including those by Begbie and Campbell, compounding errors and perpetuating the myths in the process. Few of these accounts chose to describe Arthur Machen's seminal role in creating what became a living legend. This mass of popular literature has helped to perpetuate a number of myths and falsehoods, such as Private Cleaver's angel experience.[18] As a result, the Angel of Mons has found new life presented as 'fact' for a new audience of believers almost a century after the end of the First World War.

It was inevitable, given the revival of interest in the First World War, that the Angel of Mons would eventually become the subject of a Hollywood feature film. In 2001 rumours of such a film appeared to be substantiated by a story published in the *Sunday Times* under the headline: 'Brando inspired by vision of Mons angel'.[19]

The article claimed that director Tony Kaye, working in partnership with Hollywood megastar Marlon Brando, had paid £350 000 for some original black-and-white film footage that appeared to contain an image of 'an angel'. The film, it was claimed, had been discovered by accident two years earlier in an antique shop in Monmouth, South Wales by Danny Sullivan, an author of books on ley lines and ancient mysteries. Danny said he found the old canisters while browsing in the shop in Agincourt Square and acquired the collection for a mere £15. He also bought a mass of military memorabilia along with letters documenting the former owner's extensive correspondence with various mystical societies during the interwar period. Danny claimed he put the material aside for a year and it was not until the autumn of 2000, when he began to read the letters, that he suddenly realized he had stumbled upon a gold mine.

The papers appeared to describe the quest undertaken by a West Country soldier, William Doidge, who was born in Monmouth in 1896 and joined the Scots Guard at the outbreak of the First World War. Danny claimed that Doidge had fought at the Battle of Mons and fell in love with a local woman while serving in Belgium. The letters told how he lost contact with her during the campaign and after the war he devoted his life to finding the 'Angel of Mons', which he believed could reunite him with his lost sweetheart.

If this romance wasn't sufficient to attract the interest of a Hollywood director, there was more. As he pieced together the fragments of papers, Danny discovered that Doidge's quest to find the angel finally ended in 1952 when he received a letter from a US army veteran. This man, identified in the letters only as Doug, described an angel experience from the time of the D-Day landings, when US and Canadian soldiers were training in the grounds of Woodchester Park in the English Cotswolds. In his letters to Doidge, Doug described his sighting of a 'spook' in the grounds of the Gothic mansion the night before a pontoon bridge on a lake collapsed, which dragged 20 US soldiers to their deaths.

On receiving Doug's letter, William Doidge began a nightly vigil in the grounds of Woodchester, hoping this angel of death would return. Among the collection, in addition to the film footage, Danny found a black-and-white photograph, 'which clearly incorporates the image of an angel' floating in front of a background of gravestones and tombs. The photo, marked '1950 E. Bennett', was examined by professional photographers who – in a clear reference to the Cottingley fairy photograph controversy – found 'no hint of forgery about it'.[20] The question was: Did the photograph show the angel of Woodchester and did William Doidge take it?

These finds inspired Danny to create an Internet website dedicated to spreading the story of the mysterious Doidge, a man who he said 'has a strong claim to the title of the UK's very own Indiana Jones'. *The Angel Homepage* made a direct link between the Woodchester phenomena of 1952 and the Angel of Mons. In addition it implied that Doidge was one of the anonymous soldiers quoted in 1915 by Harold Begbie in *On the Side of the Angels*.[21] When the website appeared, Danny was inundated with emails from people who believed they were relatives of Doidge and others who wanted to describe their own experiences with angels. It was *apparently* as a direct result of the appearance of the website that Danny was introduced to Tony Kaye, a British film producer who was based in Los Angeles. On seeing the footage, Kaye was so enthusiastic that he offered Danny 'half a million dollars for both film and papers saying the angel film would form the centrepiece of a major Hollywood movie starring Marlon Brando'. It was this endorsement by a big name in the movie industry that gave the story a touch of credibility. At least it was sufficient for the *Sunday Times* to take the bait.

Their article was followed up by the tabloid, the *Sun*, who, in a double-page spread, published what it called 'the ghostly "angel" photograph, which has now been sent off to Hollywood to be checked out by experts'. Tony Kaye was quoted as saying:

> I want to include Doidge's footage of the apparition at the heart of the movie ... it will be a spine-tingling moment. This is the nearest we have on film to proof of an angel.[22]

Events took an even stranger turn when Danny returned to Bonita's junk shop in search of additional clues. He was disappointed to discover that any additional material had long disappeared. But four days after the *Sun* published the angel photo, musician John Reynolds of the pop group Ghostland posted a message on Danny's Internet site. It read:

> You may be interested to know that some time ago, on a trip to Monmouth, I was wandering around an antique shop and bought an old trunk which contained a whole load of weird stuff – wax cylinders, film canisters, papers & diaries. Could this be the same shop ... maybe even the trunk you have been looking for? Your angel photograph is very similar to the most amazing images I found on the film, which I have since painstakingly restored.[23]

Reynolds claimed the images he found on the film had 'a profound influence' on his musical compositions. Strangely enough, the picture that subsequently appeared on the cover of Ghostland's album *Interview with the Angel* was similar to the 'still photo' Danny Sullivan claimed to have found among Doidge's papers.

This final 'coincidence' had all the hallmarks of a carefully timed publicity stunt. But what of William Doidge and 'Doug', the mysterious character which the *Sun* assured its readers Marlon Brando was keen to play in the forthcoming film?

As is the case in other successful hoaxes, the clues that should have exposed the facts were always out there waiting for someone to piece them together. The discovery of the angel film in Agincourt Square was a coincidence that would have been significant to anyone familiar with Arthur Machen and 'The Bowmen'. The story itself was riddled with numerous other absurdities. As one commentator pointed out, if Doidge had joined the British Army in August 1914 as Danny had claimed, he could not have fought at Mons as he would have been undergoing basic training in England when the battle was fought. These inconsistencies were overlooked at the time the story was published. According to Danny:

> At no time did any one seriously question the credibility of the story. It was simply accepted ... as far as the press were concerned I doubt whether the truth of the matter was ever an issue.

The truth was exposed in 2002 during a BBC Wales production for Radio 4, *The Making of an Urban Myth*. Originally the programme planned to discuss Arthur Machen's role in the original legend. But when reporter Chris Morris followed up the *Sunday Times* article he was intrigued to find Danny Sullivan's story apparently confirmed by both the owner of the antique shop and a public relations agency linked to Brando. But when Morris challenged Danny about the whereabouts of the film he admitted the whole story was a publicity stunt concocted to promote a book he had written on the occult history of Woodchester Mansion. By a stroke of genius, the story was given historical credibility by the link with the Angel of Mons. Danny told Radio 4 he suspected the journalists involved never believed the film actually showed an angel:

> ... but I think what swayed it was the fact that the story was made to stand up by a third party coming in and saying that

they had paid me a lot of money for this film, and that was Tony Kaye. And that meant the Marlon Brando connection, the Hollywood connection, big money connection and rags-to-riches, good luck story, you know ... ordinary bloke finds half a million pound film in junk shop for fifteen quid.[24]

Given this confession it is unsurprising that attempts by others to trace 'the real William Doidge' failed. According to Danny, his website helped to demonstrate what he calls 'the strength of public belief or wanna-belief in the angel myth':

Many people offered suggestions as to the identity of William Doidge and I came very close to finding a man who never existed outside the imagination. I had to abandon the inquiry to avoid upsetting some genuine people.[25]

The Doidge saga is an example of a piece of fiction that created a reality of its own in a fashion similar to the rumours that were widely believed and acted upon during the First World War. Interviewed by Radio 4, junkshop owner John Read Smith said he remembered an occasion when Danny visited his shop and purchased several reels of film. 'Among the films was a canister with a number of letters securely attached to it, and written on them was the word angel,' he said. But when quizzed about this claim, Danny replied: 'No. I have never bought anything from Bonita's at all. I mean I have been in there several times but I have never actually bought anything.'

Arthur Machen faced a similar problem in that the more he protested that the story was untrue, the more people were determined to believe it. Like Machen's bowmen, Doidge's angel refuses to die. Despite the very public exposure some continue to believe the story contains a kernel of truth. While rumours about a big-budget movie continue to circulate, Danny is philosophical about where the story will go next. Shortly before his death, Arthur Machen came to accept that it was impossible to distance himself from the legend he had created. Like Frankenstein's monster, the Angel of Mons had outlived its creator.

CHAPTER EIGHT

Phantoms of No Man's Land

It seemed that out of battle I escaped
Down some profound dull tunnel, long since scooped
Through granites which titanic wars had groined.

Yet also there encumbered sleepers groaned,
Too fast in thought or death to be bestirred.

Wilfred Owen, 'Strange Meeting' (1918)

At the opening of the First World War, stories of visions tended to be on a large scale. Dramatic and inspiring stories were told of bowmen, cavalry, St George and angel hosts, which helped to save the day and proved both to soldiers and those at home that they were fighting on the side of light and goodness. But as the war entered its dark stalemate phase and the casualties mounted, the stories changed and became more personal. At home, bereaved families turned to spiritualism to make connections with the dead in order to grieve and make sense of the slaughter. Meanwhile, in the trenches and on the Front, weariness and fear led many soldiers to find comfort in stories of ghosts and mystical guardian spirits.

Although the Angel of Mons was the best-known supernatural story to emerge from the battlefields of Europe during the First World War, it was not unique. Another equally widespread story concerned a mysterious individual who roamed the Western

Front comforting soldiers who lay wounded and dying. This supernatural being was immune to the effects of shells and bullets alike and became known as 'the Comrade in White', or 'White Helper'.

The rumours surrounding the Comrade in White can all be traced back to a short story, 'In the Trenches', written in March 1915 by the Reverend W.H. Leathem of Aberdeen. It was published in *Life and Work* magazine in June and widely reprinted in newspapers and the occult press. In the re-published versions it was portrayed as a true story told by a soldier who had been rescued by the Comrade in White. It read:

Strange tales reached us in the trenches. Rumours raced up and down that three-hundred mile line from Switzerland to the sea. We knew neither the source of them nor the truth of them. They came quickly, and they went quickly. Yet somehow I remember the very hour when George Casey turned to me with a queer look in his blue eyes and asked if I had seen the Friend of the Wounded. And then he told me all he knew. After many a hot engagement a man in white had been seen bending over the wounded. Snipers sniped at him. Shells fell all around. Nothing had power to touch him. He was either heroic beyond all heroes, or he was something greater still. This mysterious one, whom the French called the Comrade in White, seemed to be everywhere at once. At Nancy, in the Argonne, at Soissons and Ypres, everywhere men were talking of him in hushed tones. But some laughed and said the trenches were telling on men's nerves. I, who was often reckless enough in my talk, exclaimed that for me seeing was believing, and that I didn't expect any help but a German knife if I was found lying out there wounded.

It was the next day that things got lively on this bit of the front. Our big guns roared from sunrise to sunset, and began again in the morning. At noon we got word to take the trenches in front of us. They were two hundred yards away, and we weren't well started till we knew that the big guns had failed in their work of preparation. It needed a stout heart to go on, but not a man wavered. We had advanced one hundred and fifty yards when we found it was no good. Our captain called to us to take cover, and just then I was shot through both legs. By God's mercy I fell into a hole of some sort. I suppose I fainted, for when I opened my eyes I was all alone. The pain was horrible, but I didn't dare to move lest the Germans should see me, for they were only fifty yards away, and I did not expect mercy. I was glad when the twilight came ...

The night fell, and soon I heard a step, not stealthy, as I expected, but quiet and firm, as if neither darkness nor death could check those untroubled feet. So little did I guess what was coming that, even when I saw the gleam of white in the darkness, I thought it was a peasant in a white smock, or perhaps a woman deranged. Suddenly, with a little shiver of joy or fear, I don't know which, I guessed that it was the Comrade in White. And at that very moment the German rifles began to shoot. The bullets could scarcely miss such a target, for he flung out his arms as though in entreaty, and then drew them back till he stood like one of those wayside crosses that we saw so often as we marched through France. And he spoke. The words sounded familiar, but all I remember was the beginning, 'If thou hadst known,' and the ending, 'but now they are hid from thine eyes.' And then he stooped and gathered me into his arms – me, the biggest man in the regiment – and carried me as if I had been a child.

I must have fainted again, for I woke to consciousness in a little cave by a stream, and the Comrade in White was washing my wounds and binding them up. It seems foolish to say it, for I was in terrible pain, but I was happier at that moment than ever I remember to have been in all my life before. I can't explain it, but it seemed as if all my days I had been waiting for this without knowing it. As long as that hand touched me and those eyes pitied me, I did not seem to care anymore about sickness or health, about life or death. And while he swiftly removed every trace of blood and mire, I felt as if my whole nature were being washed, as if all the grime and soil of sin were going, and as if I were once more a little child.

I suppose I slept, for when I awoke this feeling was gone. I was a man, and I wanted to know what I could do for my friend to help him or serve him. He was looking towards the stream, and his hands were clasped in prayer; and then I saw that he, too, had been wounded. I could see, as it were, a shot-wound in his hand, and as he prayed a drop of blood gathered and fell to the ground. I cried out. I could not help it, for that wound of his seemed to be a more awful thing than any bitter war had shown me. 'You are wounded, too,' I said faintly. Perhaps he heard me, perhaps it was the look on my face, but he answered gently: 'This is an old wound, but it has troubled me of late.' And then I noticed sorrowfully that the same cruel mark was on his feet. You will wonder that I did not know sooner. I wonder myself. But it was only when I saw his feet that I knew him.[1]

In writing his story, Leathem's aim was to bring comfort to the families of soldiers who were praying for the safe deliverance of loved ones from the battlefield. In a preface to a collection published in 1916 he wrote that he knew nothing about the alleged supernatural happenings at Mons when he wrote the story 'and the opening words were, like the rest, entirely imaginative'. In what would become an uncanny echo of Arthur Machen's words, he added:

It did not occur to me that anyone would take my story to be other than an interpretation of spiritual truth; though I firmly believe that such supernatural interventions have happened in the past, and may happen again.[2]

Almost immediately, readers accepted 'In the Trenches' not as the 'spiritual truth' Leathem intended, but as literal fact and many clearly *wanted* to believe the story was real. David Gow, the editor of *Light*, told spiritualists that 'we are not told whether it is a piece of imaginative writing or is intended to convey statements of fact'. Quite innocently, Leathem had adopted a similar narrative device to that used by Arthur Machen in 'The Bowmen' and laid the foundation for another wartime legend. As the story spread, the narrator was identified as a real person. Ralph Shirley was aware of the story's true origins when he published a poem, 'The White Comrade', in the *Occult Review*, but in a preface he wrote:

> Whatever view we may take with regard to it ... I have the statement of my contributor that [the poem] was inspired by an account taken down by an officer from the lips of one to whom the vision was manifested.[3]

Harold Begbie also believed that George Casey was a real person. In *On the Side of the Angels* he claimed the story had been 'sent home by a British officer, who took it down from the soldier's own lips, a man named Casey'. To establish the credibility of the officer, Begbie noted that he held 'a Court appointment' at the outbreak of the war.[4]

In June 1915 the factual basis of Leathem's fiction was given a further lease of life in the widely republished sermon by Dr Horton in Manchester (see Chapter 5). Horton, whose statements on the Angel of Mons did much to establish the story as 'fact', referred in the same sermon to testimony from the Front that suggested 'miracles' were constantly happening. He had received several letters from soldiers which described how:

> occasionally a wounded man on the field is conscious of a comrade in white coming with help. One of our men was sceptical, but when he himself lay wounded he, too, saw 'the White Comrade.' At first he thought this might be a stretcher bearer or hospital attendant, but soon realised his mistake, because the bullets were flying thick around the comrade, who was untouched. The man lost consciousness for a moment and on recovering seemed to be out of danger.

The comrade in white stood by him and he saw that there was a wound in his hand, and he said: 'You are wounded in your hand.' 'Yes,' was the reply, 'that is an old wound that has opened again lately.' The soldier says that, in spite of the peril, he felt a joy he had never experienced before.[5]

This 'factual' version, endorsed by a senior clergyman, circulated rapidly in correspondence between the battlefields and Home Front. As it was repeated, new versions appeared and accounts of those who had met the Comrade in White were published. A Church of England priest, the Reverend Ernest Fitzroy, read out to his congregation a letter received from a nurse at a military hospital in Saffron Walden. It said:

There is a wonderful story of a man called by the soldiers 'A Comrade in White,' who is going about at the front helping the wounded. A man told my sister that, though he had not seen Him himself, he knew many soldiers who had. He was supposed to be 'The Angel of the Covenant,' our Lord Himself. He has been seen at different places.[6]

The message for Christians was that Jesus Christ had visited the Western Front and the appearance of God's son, supplemented by the vision of angels at Mons, was a reassuring sign from heaven. This evidence could not be ignored, and it further encouraged the feeling that the Allies would eventually be victorious, but only if commitment to the faith remained true. Belief in the Comrade in White spread from the British to the French armies, who produced new versions more suitable to a Gallic audience. Harold Begbie quoted a British Army chaplain who heard French soldiers speaking of a mysterious nurse who appeared to them as the Virgin Mary. She was seen during the First Battle of Ypres, tending the wounded and comforting the dying.

In October 1915, 'In the Trenches' had become so popular that it was reprinted by the British publishers H.R. Allenson Ltd as part of a collection by W.H. Leathem under the title *The Comrade in White*. Leathem wrote in his foreword that he felt it was his duty to make it clear that all his stories 'are of no evidential value whatever' but his retraction came too late. When a US edition was published in 1916 the disclaimer was removed from the book. Publication in the USA had an equally dramatic effect upon a new audience as the country prepared to enter the war on the side of the Allies. Among those who drew spiritual strength from it was the musician and poet Robert Haven Schauffler (1879–1964) who had been commissioned as a Second Lieutenant in the US Expeditionary Army. He participated in the Allied offensive in France and was decorated with the Purple Heart on return home.

Schauffler's poem 'The White Comrade' was published in 1917 and helped to ensure the survival of belief in miracles among US troops long after the end of the First World War. Variations on the 'divine intervention' theme circulated in the folklore of US veterans between the wars. Another widely believed story attributed the survival of the Ninety-first Infantry Brigade to a daily recitation of Psalm 91, which their commander, a devout Christian, had printed on a card distributed to every soldier. The 'Psalm of Protection' was carried by many soldiers, both religious and agnostic, as a protective charm that was sometimes pinned over the heart. Legend has it that while other US units suffered up to 90 per cent casualties during the bloodiest battles of 1918, the Ninety-first Brigade escaped without a single loss. More recently, research by Michael E. Hanlon of the Great War Society revealed there never was a Ninety-first Infantry Brigade, as the army's highest brigade number was 88. There was, however, a Ninety-first Division that took part in the Meuse-Argonne offensive of 1918, but they suffered heavy casualties. Curiously, there are identical stories from other sources which also attribute the survival of various Canadian and British infantry units to the recitation of Psalm 91. This suggests the stories began, like the Angel of Mons, as gossip or rumour and eventually became a piece of military folklore. Hanlon comments on the US legend:

> In one variation, the source of the story is the father of the late actor James Stewart, who served in the non-existent

91st Brigade. The story continues to suggest that father passed it on to son when James Stewart departed for World War Two. I have never been able to verify the truth of any of this. However, it is quite credible that the 91st Psalm was distributed to some soldiers by their commanders before battle. It has many comforting thoughts for those in jeopardy.[7]

The remarkable longevity of the Comrade in White in its various incarnations is demonstrated by its reappearance in more recent collections of stories concerning the Angel of Mons. When in the 1980s Hilary Evans and Kevin McClure collected and published accounts of battlefield visions that circulated during the First World War, they were unaware their ultimate source of stories surrounding the Comrade in White was the short story produced by Leathem. They did recognize, however, that although they might not be factually true, they were similar to more traditional accounts of religious visions such as those of the Blessed Virgin Mary. In his *Visions of Bowmen and Angels* (1993), McClure compared the Comrade in White with more recent stories of angel guardians where mysterious figures have appeared from nowhere to guide or rescue people at times of danger or at the moment of death. He recognized that:

> whatever we call these accounts – wishful thinking, imagination, hallucination, spirit or divine intervention, or whatever – they are perhaps closer to traditional forms of religious experience than the visions involving interventions by non-human figures in military battles. They made popular reading, and no doubt brought hope and some comfort to those at the front in France, and to those at home.[8]

The spiritual revival

The Angel of Mons and the Comrade in White were two legends enthusiastically accepted by all denominations of religious belief and helped to maintain faith in a time of great doubt and despair. Equally, occultists and spiritualists adopted them as further evidence for the presence of the supernatural on the battlefield. In March 1915, the *Weekly Dispatch* reported on a lecture given by Robert King, a theosophist and 'well-known authority on occultism' to the International Club for Psychical Research in London. His presentation, *Occult Aspects of the Battlefield*, described the experiences of clairvoyants who claimed to have visited the scene of the fighting in their astral bodies. Here they had encountered, in the lower levels of the astral world, 'swirling groups of combatants who had left the body, locked together in an intense emotional stress, fancying they were still engaged in slaughter'. Those with psychic power could see 'masses of astral matter of intense colourings, rotating at rapid rates and moving about in all directions' above the battlefield.[9]

Clairvoyants also spoke of two opposing spiritual forces, representing good and evil, who were locked in battle. The latter were referred to as 'the Brethren of the Shadow' or the 'Black Host' which penetrated the battlefield like a fine mist and intensified the horrors already present. The forces of good were represented by what the clairvoyants called the 'Great White Spiritual Order' who worked to liberate human souls after death. These appeared as 'masses of opalescent silvery light, oval in shape'. King reported that many occultists and clairvoyants were actively using their powers to assist soldiers at the front. He knew of one case where 'a highly accomplished occultist' in England had used his powers to travel to the battlefield, where he was able to materialize in bodily form and bring water to the wounded. Was it merely a coincidence that King's claims were published in the same month that the Reverend W.H. Leathem wrote his fantasy about the Comrade in White, or were both men tapping into a similar shared idea?

The Theosophical Society, to which Robert King belonged, was founded by the Russian mystic Madame Blavatsky in the 1870s and, as we have seen, played a prominent role in spreading these beliefs via lectures and pamphlets. Theosophists drew heavily on Eastern traditions and believed the universe was permeated by a 'psychic ether' that stored information from the past and present. This ether could be accessed by mediums and explained a range of phenomena including clairvoyance and telepathy. One of the founders of the society, Alfred Sinnett, regarded the First World War as a reflection of a far greater struggle that was taking place on a higher plane between the forces of light and darkness. Arthur Machen believed the article Sinnett wrote in the May 1915 issue of the *Occult Review* was instrumental in the transformation of his bowmen into the Angel of Mons because it referred to the appearance of a 'row of shining beings' during the battle (see Chapter 5). Elsewhere in the article Sinnett wrote:

> Though much of the work that has to be done will be done for us on higher planes, on the physical plane the task to be accomplished is ours, and the duration of the war may be thought of as dependent on our own exertions. These are sometimes supplemented in emergencies in a way clairvoyant combatants have wonderingly perceived.[10]

Sinnett claimed that in all theatres of the war 'invisible supporters' had granted protection to the Allied armies in subtle ways that would not be obvious to those who 'can only think of the war in terms of millions spent and lives lost'. The unseen host did not make itself known 'in the sense of actually destroying hostile life with unseen weapons'. Instead, it acted in a more subtle way, appearing on the battlefield as mysterious clouds, 'unseen storms' and angelic forms that intervened at critical moments in the conflict.

In their writings and lectures, the theosophists and other occult groups were reinventing older beliefs and traditions for the benefit of a modern audience. At the same time they were subtly reinterpreting the visions and stories that members of the established church, such as Dr Horton, were endorsing. As the meaning and significance of the visions changed, the reports and stories could be used for a variety of other purposes.

The war saw a great revival in the burgeoning industry of spiritualism and the popularity of the séance room. In all countries where armies were locked in conflict the dead were contacted in order to provide comfort to the living. Although some mediums were frauds, many honestly believed in their power to contact the dead and, by passing on their messages, brought comfort to those who were bereaved.

The craze for visiting mediums and communicating with the spirits of dead people originated in the USA during the early nineteenth century. The new religion quickly spread to England and Europe during the Victorian period when a number of eminent scientists became fascinated by the claims of mediums. Unlike orthodox Christianity, spiritualism did not just preach about life after death but allegedly produced proof that could be verified in the form of messages from the spirit world. The Society for Psychical Research (SPR) was founded in 1882 by a group of Cambridge scientists and spiritualists who wished to apply scientific methods to the investigation of these claims.

The list of SPR members reads like a roll-call of the great and good in Victorian England, from Sir Arthur Conan Doyle to Charles Dodgson (Lewis Carroll) and William Gladstone. Its methodical approach to the investigation of psychic phenomena attracted interest from psychologists such as Freud and Jung as well as physicists such as Sir William Crookes and Sir Oliver Lodge. The growing interest of scientists and widespread popular belief in the possibility of communication with the dead reflected and seemingly endorsed the increasing fascination that people from all classes of society had for the supernatural. This was demonstrated by the crowds who gathered outside haunted houses, or queued to attend demonstrations by mediums. Popular interest was not, however, shared or approved of by the scientific and religious establishment. In the face of great disapproval from their peers, the SPR's founders did their best to apply scientific methodology to the claims of mediums and to the investigation of clairvoyance, telepathy, ghosts and hauntings. Their reports form some of the best examples of the common-sense approach to the investigation of the unexplained and were undertaken with a truly open mind.[11]

One of the most prominent public figures who sought comfort in spiritualism was Sir Arthur Conan Doyle. On the surface, as the creator of the detective Sherlock Holmes, he was the ultimate rationalist but in reality he was a believer in both spiritualism and fairies. In fact, as G.K. Chesterton pointed out, he was so gullible that 'it has long seemed to me that Sir Arthur's mentality is much more that of Watson than it is of Holmes'. Doyle's fascination with the supernatural increased with the loss he felt as a direct result of the war. His son Kingsley along with his brother and his brother-in-law were all killed in action, the latter being one of the first to fall in 1914 at the Battle of Mons. Ironically, Doyle was one of the first to chronicle the events of that battle in print and yet failed to report any angelic interventions.[12] Later in the war a female relative who lost three brothers told Doyle she received messages from them and his interest grew. She then began to play a key role in introducing the whole family to mediums and it was through them that Doyle claimed to have made contact both with Kingsley and his brother. The latter said his only regret was dying before seeing the Allied victory.

After the war, Doyle's quest for proof to validate his beliefs led him to endorse the 'fairy photographs' taken by Elsie Wright and Frances Griffiths in 1917. These were sent to Geoffrey Hodson, a prominent member of the Theosophical Society, who showed them to Doyle. When he saw them his initial scepticism was overcome by his growing will to believe and he was led to endorse them as genuine in his book, *The Coming of the Fairies*, published in 1922. Although many suspected trickery, the girls refused to reveal how they had produced the images. The photographs were not exposed as hoaxes until 1983 when Elsie, by then an octogenarian, confessed the fairies were in fact drawings based upon images in a children's book that they had mounted on cardboard and held up by hat-pins. The two women had kept their secret while Doyle remained alive as they feared his reputation would be destroyed by the revelation of fakery. But for Doyle, the messages received from mediums and the fairy photographs were ultimate proof of the way the world of the spirit mingled with the material world during the war, to produce what he believed to be a 'turning point in spiritual history'.[13]

Apart from Doyle's writings, the most important contribution to spiritualist literature during the war came not from an occultist, but from one of the greatest living scientists of the time. Sir Oliver Lodge was an eminent physicist and a pioneer in the development of wireless telegraphy. He also dabbled in spiritualism and became an important and respected member of the SPR. In the summer of 1915, Lodge received a message from a US medium who was known for her ability to produce automatic writing while in a trance state. The spirit message apparently came from a former colleague and SPR member, Frederick Myers, who had died in 1902. It warned of great sacrifices before the end of the war and of an unspecified calamity. This ominous warning had a dramatic effect on Lodge and his wife for soon afterwards they learned of the death of their son Raymond, aged 26, while serving with the South Lancashire Regiment on the Western Front.

Within days of receiving the shattering news, channelled messages claiming to be from Raymond began to arrive at the Lodge household from a number of different mediums. Grief-stricken, the family turned to spiritualism for comfort and attended regular séances with one of the best-known mediums of the day, Gladys Osborne Leonard. From Leonard they received a great deal of circumstantial personal and family detail that satisfied them that life after death was fact. Lodge put aside his scientific scepticism and compiled all the messages they received into a book, simply called *Raymond*, that appeared in 1916 following the Battle of the Somme. Its message of hope struck a chord with all classes of society and it became an instant best-seller. At the end of the war the book was in its twelfth printing, and continued to sell steadily for many years. The author's credentials tended to overshadow the criticisms that were made of the book, in particular the lack of evidence that could be independently validated and the absurd details contained in the messages. These included Raymond's description of officers asking for a whisky and soda on their arrival in the next world. In the preface to his book, Lodge wrote that his primary object was not to provide conclusive evidence for the existence of life after death but to bring comfort to other families who had been bereaved by the war. Although he did not recommend 'all sorts of people to visit mediums or try to investigate the subject themselves', he believed 'a considerable number of bereaved people have been helped' by resorting to their services.[14]

Raymond is the best-known example of a wide outpouring of spiritualist literature that appealed to the hopes and fears of a nation struggling to cope with bereavement and despair on a scale hitherto unknown. The theosophists, who promoted an early form of 'New Age' belief, also enjoyed a revival in popularity as a result, and the social and intellectual prominence of many of the movement's leaders makes it impossible to ignore the social and religious influence they exerted upon British society both during and after the First World War.

Ghostly soldiers

The supernatural was the subject of fascination not only to believers in spiritualism, but also to the soldiers themselves. Among those serving on all sectors of the front line there was a widespread belief in protective charms, ghosts and guardian angels. With the popularity of books like *Raymond*, many soldiers and senior officers carried their spiritual beliefs to the Front. The most prominent believer was Sir John French, Commander-in-Chief of the BEF in France during the Battle of Mons. French believed in the immortality of the soul and in March 1915 he told Lord Esher, who was visiting his HQ in St Omer, that he thought the room was 'thick with the spirits of dead friends' killed in battle and added, 'It was a solemn thought that at my signal all these fine young fellows go to their death.'[15]

A number of French's officers, NCOs and privates were spiritualists or members of mystical groups such as the theosophists who believed in an afterlife and the possibility of reincarnation. One officer, who held 'an important position in the army', wrote regularly for the weekly spiritualist magazine *Light* while serving in the trenches of France. Under the pen name 'Neagh', he described a number of curious psychic experiences. The following is typical:

> The evidence of my own senses many times repeated, and also that of several others, indicates that at a point along the roads approaching the fighting zone the atmosphere appears suddenly to get heavy – one, as it were, runs into it, and as the vicinity of the trenches is approached, it grows denser. This dense, murky atmosphere gives a sense of heaviness and depression difficult to describe ... when approaching the vicinity of the areas where the fighting troops are billeted, but still out of range of the usual shell fire, some describe a vague intangible feeling of fear.[16]

These beliefs supplemented orthodox religion and helped soldiers cope with the privations of life in the trenches. Officially, the Church of England refused to acknowledge what they regarded as popish superstitions, while atheists and agnostics improvised their own idiosyncratic methods of coping with the close proximity of the dead. There are many accounts of soldiers killed in battle returning to visit close friends at the moment of death, or merely appearing briefly and without warning. In supernatural folklore, this type of ghost is known as a 'wraith' or 'fetch'. To see one's own wraith was a sign of imminent death. Wraiths of dead friends or relatives appeared to soldiers imparting messages or giving warning at times of great peril. Neagh describes one which was so vivid that the Tommy who saw the apparition of a friend exclaimed, 'Hullo, I thought you were in another part of the line!' A day or two later, he heard that his pal had been killed.

Another man heard the words 'Don't, don't!' uttered in his ear, a warning that could not have come from another living soul, as he was alone in a trench at the time. According to Neagh, others 'get strong impressions to do or not to do certain thing, to go or not to go'.

These stories were circulated back to the Home Front in the steady flow of correspondence and via reports in newspapers and the occult press. What Paul Fussell described as the reinvigoration of ancient myths during the First World War is also apparent in the writings of wartime poets and authors such as Wilfred Owen and Rudyard Kipling. The short stories of the latter provided the inspiration for much of the military fiction of the war and he in turn was heavily influenced by a spiritualist agenda. Kipling's only son John, a lieutenant in the Irish Guards, was one of thousands of British troops killed at the Battle of Loos in September 1915. Kipling was a rationalist, but the death of John left him so overcome with feelings of guilt that he began to suspend judgement on the question of life after death. This is reflected in 'A Madonna of the Trenches' (1918), his first story to accurately portray the reality of life and death on the front. A platoon-runner called Strangwick is driven to the edge of insanity by an apparition he encounters in a trench called Butcher's Row that is filled with the corpses of French soldiers. He is convinced the ghost is real and not a hallucination, and tells his half-brother, a doctor:

> You see ... there wasn't a single god-damn thing left abidin' for me to take hold of, here or hereafter. If the dead *do* rise – and I saw 'em – why – why *anything* can 'appen. Don't you understand?[17]

Kipling was not the only popular author to incorporate supernatural themes into his wartime writing. Charles L. Warr, who later became a dean in Edinburgh, was inspired to produce a series of stories describing mystical visions he claimed were experienced by soldiers at the front. These were published in 1916 by Robert Grant & Sons of Edinburgh in a volume entitled

The Unseen Host. The story from which the book took its name followed the tradition established by Arthur Machen in 'The Bowmen' in attributing the German failure to break the Allied line during the First Battle of Ypres to divine intervention. The anonymous soldier who narrates the story hears 'a great host advancing' in the rear of the trenches as waves of Germans approach the thin line of British soldiers defending the trenches. As they reach the parapet the grey-coated enemy soldiers turn and flee, leaving the hero convinced that his life has been saved by angels and that:

> on his side that day fought Gabriel, the Captain of the hosts of Heaven, Michael, the Archangel, and all angels, with the powers and principalities of light – had fought for him, and did smite and win the victory.

In his preface Warr said he could not explain the stories but 'merely assert that to the best of my knowledge they are all true, and are in no case the figments of my own imagination'. Nevertheless he later wrote a collection of supernatural tales in a similar style which he admitted were indeed fiction.[18] The great popularity and spiritual influence of these stories can be judged from the fact that *The Unseen Host* was reprinted ten times, the last impression appearing in 1928, long after the war was over.

Other wartime ghost stories were set in No Man's Land, that eerie wasteland of craters, barbed wire and tree stumps that divided the Allied and German trenches. While normally the two front lines were separated by distances of between 500 and 250 yards, in some areas such as Zonnebeke it could be as little as seven yards. Tolstoy described No Man's Land in *War and Peace* as a 'terrible line of uncertainty and fear, like a line dividing the living from the dead'.[19] Symbolically as well as physically, No Man's Land marked the boundary between life and death for many soldiers. It was here that one was most likely to meet former comrades who had become phantoms. Some soldiers came to believe that the spirits of the dead continued to fight alongside them as 'angel helpers' at times of great peril. This appears to have been a psychological by-product of living in trenches so close to the dead, many of whom were buried in shallow graves or remained visible in the walls of trenches or in No Man's Land. Vera Brittain heard a number of stories of this kind while nursing wounded troops at the field hospital in Etaples. A British Corporal told her about a company of stretcher-bearers who had been blown to pieces by a huge German shell at the Somme, but:

> Last week some of our chaps sees 'em again, carrying the wounded down the communication trench. And I met a chum in the train who swears he was carried out by two of 'em.

After collecting several similar accounts she asked a group of wounded soldiers if they really believed they had met men that were dead. The reply left her stunned: 'Aye, Sister, they're dead right enough. They're our mates as was knocked out on the Somme in '16. And it's our belief they're fightin' with us still.'[20]

Signs in heaven

As the New Year of 1916 arrived, tens of thousands of new recruits poured into France along with millions of tons of munitions and big guns. Preparations were under way for the 'big push' by Britain's New Army that aimed to relieve pressure on the French who were defending the fortress at Verdun. The German plan was to 'bleed France to death' in a war of attrition. More than a million French soldiers had been killed or wounded and morale was dangerously low. In December 1915 Douglas Haig, now promoted to General and soon Field Marshal, replaced John French as Commander-in-Chief of the British forces in Flanders. His orders were to work closely with his French Allies to co-ordinate a new offensive that would break the stalemate on the Western Front. In February he met the French to finalize the date of a combined attack on German lines at the Somme, planned for 1 July 1916. Haig saw the Somme offensive as more than just another campaign of attrition. He hoped for a real breakthrough.

The new British Army that was assembled at the Somme included many of the famous Pals Battalions that were recruited by mayors and town corporations across Britain. The new recruits came from a variety of professions: stockbrokers, tradesmen, engineers and gamekeepers. They were motivated by a mixture of duty, patriotism and a desire to join their friends in a decisive battle they believed would bring an end to the war. Helping to train the fresh soldiers were survivors from the 'Old Contemptibles' who had fought at Mons, Le Cateau and Ypres, and the stories they told were passed on to the new armies awaiting action on the Western Front. In the lore of the battlefield the Angel of Mons was slowly transformed from a vision that rescued the BEF in the first weeks of the war to a divine force that protected both groups of soldiers and individuals in times of peril. The miracle at Mons was by now widely accepted and believed by men who joined the Pals Battalions in 1915 and 1916. As military historians Coulson and Hanlon found, the myth was 'not tested scientifically, it was not analysed: it was just accepted'. Furthermore, it was promoted by many supporters of the war because it was useful for 'maintaining the physic stability of Britain's soldiers, citizens and leadership'.[21]

As the Somme offensive bogged down in the trenches and victory seemed ever more remote, occult writers such as Ralph Shirley kept the story alive by claiming that divine forces had assisted British soldiers in the midst of other battles. A stream of new booklets and pamphlets devoted to the supernatural and the war were published that drew their material from stories circulating in the trenches and on the Home Front. A rich source for these was Rosa Stuart's *Dreams and Visions of the War*. In the book she claimed that, in addition to the Angel of Mons:

our men claim to have derived inspiration from apparitions and visions ... similar stories centre round the engagements at Nueve-Chappelle, Loos and other places the names of which will be handed down to history.[22]

By 1916 the Angel of Mons had become a catch-all phrase for a range of miraculous escapes from danger that were attributed to supernatural or divine forces. When a private serving with a Pals regiment from the West Riding of Yorkshire was saved from a sniper's bullet by a spoon in his tunic pocket, he said afterwards that his escape from death was because 'the Angel of Mons was looking over him'. There were many similar stories and anecdotes preserved in the oral traditions and in the various published memoirs of soldiers who joined the new armies. Several emerged even before the Somme campaign, such as from the time of the battle at Neuve-Chappelle in March 1915. The British plan had been to surprise the enemy with a sudden and intense bombardment of their trenches, followed up by an infantry push towards Aubers Ridge. Although the advance was initially successful, the British were halted by machine-gun fire and the offensive ended in another costly stalemate. Nevertheless Harold Begbie heard a reassuring story from a woman whose husband saw 'the angels all around us' as the men left their trenches. Another said his escape from an ambush was 'nothing short of a miracle'. Begbie explained:

> He was told to take a certain wood [but] on reaching a road at right angles to the one which he was to follow, to his surprise his horse stopped dead, and nothing would induce the animal to move. Turning to his A.D.C. he found the same thing had happened, and not only so, but to the whole troop – the horses refused to move; finding it useless to waste time, he followed a parallel road further on. Afterwards they found that a strong German ambush awaited them along the road from which they had been so strangely turned by the conduct of their horses.[23]

An even stranger story came from an anonymous officer who fought in the battle. He claimed that a phantom company intervened to rescue his men during a German counter-attack on the British lines. During the fighting he received an order to retire from a captured trench, but at that very moment he heard a voice behind him saying, 'Don't retire!' He turned round in amazement to see 'the figure of an officer in khaki with a large company of men behind him'. At that moment the Germans who were attacking the trench suddenly pulled back with a look of terror etched upon their faces. Afterwards, one of the prisoners who had been captured said they had been taken by surprise by a host of men who appeared from nowhere:

> The officer maintains that the apparition who addressed him and who was at the head of the ghostly warriors was that of a Boer General whom he knew in the Boer War, and what impressed him most was the wonder of the fact that a former foe should reappear from the dead to fight on our side.[24]

These inspiring tales led a researcher for the Imperial War Museum to comment, half a century later, that 'it may have seemed strange to some that, with all this angelic aid, our General Staff did not make a better go of things'. At the time scepticism was, in public at least, frowned upon, and the reassurance provided by these stories was equally as welcome in France as it was on the Home Front. Just days before the battle of the Somme, a London literary magazine, the *Fortnightly Review* published a stirring poem, 'The First Battle of Ypres' by Margaret Woods. It told how in October 1914 the thin line of Allied troops had been assisted by supernatural forces as they held back the Prussian Guard from overrunning Ypres and the Channel ports. At one point in the battle the British line was so weak that cooks and service men were hurried up to hold it against the advancing Germans. How were they held back? Like Charles Warr, Woods had no doubt:

> Marlborough's men and Wellington's, the burghers of
>   Courtrai,
> The warriors of Plantagenet, King Louis' Gants glaces
> And the young, young dead from Mons and the Marne river.

Old heroic fighting men, who fought for chivalry,
Men who died for England, Mother of Liberty.

In the world's dim heart, where the waiting spirits slumber,
Sounded a roar when the walls were rent asunder
That parted Earth from Hell, and, summoning them away,
Tremendous trumpets blew, as at the Judgement Day—
And the dead came forth, each to his former banner.

In her foreword, Woods disclaimed any connection between her poem and 'The Bowmen'. She claimed it was inspired by the testimony of 'a very competent witness' who said the Germans had broken through the Allied line on three occasions and then retired for no apparent reason.

On each of these occasions prisoners, when asked the cause of their retirement, replied: 'We saw your enormous Reserves.' We had no reserves. The story was incidentally confirmed by the remark of another officer on the curious conduct of the Germans in violently shelling empty fields behind our lines.

The publication of the poem led Arthur Machen to break his silence in an article for the *Evening News* that was, he forlornly hoped, 'absolutely my last word on the subject' (it wasn't). He pointed out that stories of 'enormous reserves' were nothing new and the witnesses to the Ypres miracle were all anonymous:

Pending the production of real testimony, I am strongly inclined to think that this brave poem of dead warriors rising in dreadful array and gathering again to their ancient banners is the most worthy and valiant offspring of an unworthy father: *The Bowmen*.[25]

Few people listened to Arthur Machen's protests. Reassurance was needed that higher forces were watching over the thousands who were preparing to go 'over the top' along a 14-mile front in France. On 1 July 1916 at the Somme, the British Army suffered the bloodiest day in its entire history, losing 57 470 officers and men. Of these, more than 19 000 soldiers were killed and a further 2,152 were missing.[26] These sacrifices were made without any significant breakthrough against the German lines, whose heavily fortified trenches had survived the ferocious artillery barrage. Many tens of thousands more would die on both sides as the two armies slogged on for another five hellish and rain-sodden months. The outcome was again stalemate and both armies were left depleted of men and worn down by the slaughter.

In the meantime, the signs and prodigies that appeared in the sky of the ancient world made a comeback. Three weeks after the Somme the *Illustrated London News* published a painting by A.C. Michael titled 'The Cross in the Heavens above the Trenches.' It was inspired by a story from the British lines prior to the battle that sparked comparisons with the Angel of Mons. A letter written by a sergeant to his mother in England read:

> This morning about 12.30 or one o'clock, we saw a most beautiful white cross in the sky. It sailed along until it reached the moon. I think everybody about here saw it, and for about 10 or 15 minutes there was not a shot fired. There was absolute silence on both sides. We are wondering what the vision means.[27]

The newspaper pondered whether the appearance of the cross was merely a natural phenomenon, a chance effect of moonlight among the clouds, or a miraculous sign set in the heavens by a divine power. More signs in the heavens were to follow as the Third Battle of Ypres, or Passchendaele, approached. In England, the bleak mood that followed the Somme was lifted temporarily by a series of wonderful sunsets that heralded the return of the Angel of Mons. Late in August 1917, strange tales began to reach London newspapers of 'Peace Angels' seen by the inhabitants of Grays in Essex. According to the *Grays and Tilbury Gazette* of 18 August, crowds of children gathered on the beach overlooking the Thames Estuary to gaze at the heavens. The newspaper said:

> 'Have you seen the angels?' is the latest topic which is arousing interest in Grays. Although stories are varied, and,

as usual, conflicting, most circumstantial tales are going
the round regarding alleged angelic visitations seen from
the beach on the evenings of Tuesday and Wednesday this
week. It is not a case of the 'Angels of Mons' this time, for all
the stories agree that those now seen are harbingers of peace.

Inquiries by the paper failed to find anyone who claimed to have
seen a vision. Some stories came from mothers who heard tales of
'angels' from their children. They believed the youngsters were
'getting a bit nervy in the present times of stress'. Nevertheless:

'All Ardent Street was out after them,' said one speaker.
'They appeared over the Exmouth, two of them sitting
on two rainbows with "Peace" in between. Then they
faded away, leaving only the rainbow.' This was on
Tuesday, when a rainbow did actually appear. 'I saw the
rainbow,' said a listener, 'but I didn't see the angels!' ... 'It
was three angels, I was told,' said one speaker ... 'They had
roses wreathed in their hair,' added another story-teller,
who had evidently heard a more detailed version. Everyone
agreed that they were 'Peace Angels' and one prophesied
that the 'Angels of Mons' were due to arrive next week.
On Thursday evening some hundreds of people, many of
them juveniles, thronged the beach to see the sight, and
even in the higher part of the town strollers appeared
on the look-out for some great spectacle. Needless to say,
so far as ordinary mortals were concerned, there was no
manifestation of the heavenly vision. Another version,
coming from a relative of one said to have witnessed the
apparition, states that the angels are generally seen about
9.30. According to her they are the 'Angels of Mons,' but
the description given is rather different from that of those
legendary beings. These visitants are three angels seated
and chained together, a long chain linking them up.[28]

A week later the newspaper managed to find a first-hand account
from a woman resident of Globe Terrace. She explained what she

saw on the Tuesday evening:

> I don't know about any angels, but I saw a wonderful cloud.
> We were out with my landlady and the children, and we
> were looking at the rainbow. Then I saw a cloud a little
> distance away. It was shaped just like a woman ... It quite
> unnerved me. My husband is away in the Army, and I
> thought it meant something 'over the water.' I couldn't
> sleep for thinking of it. It was a wonderful thing. I've never
> seen a cloud like it before and don't want to again. Then
> when we got home there was a crowd out and they asked
> me if we had seen the angels.[29]

A spectacular rainbow and peculiar clouds associated with it were
seen by many thousands along the Thames Estuary and East
Anglia but it was only in Grays that they were transformed into
a vision of 'angels'. The London *Daily Mail* consulted a scientist
who attributed the sky spectacular either to the Northern Lights
or a phenomenon known as the *rayons de crepuscule* or 'the rays
of twilight' that are created by sunlight striking clouds at an
unusual angle.[30] Whatever role the stress and anxiety of war
had played in the transformation of aerial phenomenon into
heavenly visions, the message delivered by the angels was one
of peace, and this seemed to transform hopes and prayers of
thousands into a visible symbol literally written in the clouds.

The White Cavalry

The war would soon be over, although senior figures on both
sides could not have anticipated how unpredictable the final
outcome would be. For the Allies, the one piece of good news was
the US declaration of war against Germany on 6 April 1917. At
this stage the military situation remained finely balanced and the
German High Command realized they must take this opportunity
to launch a major assault before US troops arrived in France in

great numbers. In December there were 175 000 US troops in France but they were yet to join the fighting. On 11 November 1917 the German leaders had met at Mons to formulate a new strategy. Chiefs of the General Staff Hindenburg and Ludendorff pressed for the launch of one or more major attacks against the British and French forces, who were now outnumbered by the German armies in the West. Ludendorff's code-name for 'spring offensive' – Michael – was significant. In German folklore St Michael had replaced the war god Wotan to become the patron saint and protector of Christian soldiers. In placing his offensive under the symbolic protection of the archangel warrior, Ludendorff may have been attempting to turn the tables on the Allies who had found comfort in their belief that God was fighting on their side.

The forces of the British Empire were now stretched almost to breaking point, with troops fighting on many fronts in different parts of the world. The desperation of the British Generals can be seen in the wording of a special order distributed to British troops on 11 April 1918. In the message Douglas Haig told them:

> There is no course open to us but to fight it out. Every position must be held to the last man: there must be no retirement. With our backs to the wall and believing in the justice of our cause, each one of us must fight to the end.

It was during this perilous period for the British Army, with its striking similarities to the events of August 1914, that a new legend of divine intervention was born. The German offensive began in the early hours of 21 March 1918. Along a line stretched for 43 miles, 6,500 guns and 3,000 mortars opened up against the British trenches. Waiting in the German trenches were thousands of storm-troopers armed with light machine guns and grenades, waiting to emerge and move quickly across No Man's Land to punch holes in weak points along the Allied defences. The advance took them many miles behind Allied lines and the Germans recaptured acres of territory that had been so painfully gained by the Allies during 1917. According to a British officer, Captain Cecil Wightwick Haywood, at the very moment when all seemed lost, help arrived from heaven. It was then that:

> We remembered the 'Angels of Mons' and once again the whole British Nation was called to prayer. The President of the United States summoned the American people to do likewise; and united prayer went up from all the English-speaking peoples.[31]

Captain Haywood claimed the events he witnessed during the German offensive in April 1918 were 'absolutely first-hand from personal experience'. At the time he was an intelligence officer with British I Corps, who were responsible for a section of the front line near the town of Bailleul, some 15 miles south of Ypres. His headquarters were situated in the French town of Bethune, which until that point had remained untouched by shellfire despite lying only three miles from the German lines.

During the offensive, shellfire shattered the little town, forcing the civilian population to evacuate. At a point in the assault, the deafening German gunfire lifted and shells began to burst above a slight rise on the outskirts of the town. This was followed by massed machine-gun fire that raked a deserted area with a hail of bullets. Captain Haywood and his men watched the scene with growing astonishment.

> 'Fritz has gone balmy, Sir,' said the Sergeant; 'what in the world is he peppering that naked ground for?' 'I can't think,' I replied. 'Get along down to the canal and see what is happening there.' I followed him shortly afterwards, being eager to see for myself, as there were obviously no troops within sight against whom the Germans could be directing their fire. As I made my way over the scattered debris of ruined houses, the enemy's fire suddenly ceased, and a curious calm fell on everything. I went on, wonderingly, and got outside the town ... [there] I saw my Sergeant and men standing on the edge of a shell hole waving their tin hats. They shouted out: 'Fritz is retiring!' Indeed he was.

Outlined on the slight rise by the La Bassee village, and as far as we could see, was a dense line of German troops, who a short time before had commenced a forward movement to victory, in mass formation. This line suddenly halted, and, as we watched, we saw it break! Before our astonished eyes, that well-drilled and seemingly victorious army broke up into groups of frightened men who were fleeing from us, throwing down their arms, haversacks, rifles, coats and anything which might impede their flight.

Haywood ordered his men to follow and bring back prisoners who might explain the meaning of this retreat. With a cheer his men crossed the pontoons still spanning the canal and pursued the fleeing Germans. When they returned, each Tommy had between two and four prisoners. Their faces 'had a curious strained look, as if they had seen something which had been terrifying and unusual'. Two German officers were brought in and Haywood set about interrogating them. He said their accounts could be summarized in the words of a Prussian officer, whose alleged statement Haywood quoted in his account of the incident:

The order had been given to advance in mass formation, and our troops were marching behind us singing their way to victory when Fritz, my lieutenant here, said: 'Herr Kapitan, just look at that open ground behind Bethune, there is a Brigade of Cavalry coming up through the smoke drifting across it. They must be mad, these English, to advance against such a force as ours in the open. I suppose they must be cavalry or one of their Colonial Forces, for, see, they are all in white uniform and are mounted on white horses.' 'Strange,' I said, 'I never heard of the English having any white-uniformed cavalry, whether Colonial or not. They have been fighting on foot for several years past, and anyway they are in khaki, not white.' 'Well they are plain enough,' he replied. 'See, our guns have got their range now; they will be blown to pieces in no time ... We saw the shells bursting among the horses and their riders, all of whom came forward at a quiet walk-trot, in parade-ground formation, each man and horse in his exact place. Shortly afterwards our machine guns opened a heavy fire, raking the advancing cavalry with a hail of lead; but on they came and not a single man or horse fell. Steadily they advanced, clear in the shining sunlight; and a few paces in front of them rode their leader – a fine figure of a man, whose hair, like spun gold, shone in an aura around his bare head. By his side was a great sword, but his hands lay quietly holding the reins, as his huge white charger bore him proudly forward. In spite of heavy shell and concentrated machine-gun fire the White Cavalry advanced, remorseless as fate, like the incoming tide surging over a sandy beach ... Then a great fear fell on me and I turned to flee; yes, I, an officer of the Prussian Guard, fled, panic stricken, and around me were hundreds of terrified men, whimpering like children, throwing away their arms and accoutrements in order not to have their movements impeded ... all running. Their one desire was to get away from that advancing White Cavalry; above all from their awe-inspiring leader whose hair shone like a golden aureole. That is all I have to tell you. We are beaten. The German Army is broken. There may be fighting, but we have lost the war; we are beaten – by the White Cavalry.'[32]

Captain Haywood claimed that between 1928 and 1939 he collected more testimony from independent sources but he was unable to name any others who were present. At face value his account has the appearance of being a rare first-hand account from a named soldier, in this case a senior intelligence officer with the British Army. However, there are big problems with its authenticity, the most important of which is the lack of any independent corroboration. The second is that Haywood's story did not appear in 1918 but at the height of another national crisis, in 1940 when Britain was again faced with defeat and invasion. It was published as a piece of propaganda to help strengthen British resolve against Nazi Germany. I suspect that, much like 'The Bowmen' and *The Comrade in White* which preceded it, the 'White Cavalry' was fiction, or a piece of officially inspired propaganda. The earliest version I have traced was an article titled 'God's Angelic Armies', which appeared in the *National Message* on 24 April 1940. This was reprinted in a number of pamphlets distributed by Christian groups such as the Seventh Day Adventists. In 1942 the story had become so well known that it was published in a British Army publication, the *Household Brigade Magazine*. By this time its reality status was less important than the timeless message it sent to British troops:

> Our own troops must always remember that even if their numbers and material resources appear insignificant and the situation hopeless, it is not hopeless on those occasions where they have done their utmost and their unflinching conduct has merited victory on one side or other of the grave. Where such conditions obtain, and where the issue is crucial to the cause of the forces of Light, it is not a hope but a certainty that invincible reinforcements will be allowed to intervene ... In spite of the great latitude allowed us for self-destruction, God Omnipotent does divert the course of history when it would destroy his designs or submerge his material strongholds of Light.[33]

In April 1918, German resolve wavered and the Michael offensive ground to a halt. History tells us this was not because of the appearance of supernatural cavalry but because of a carefully planned counter-attack by the Allies. From this point onwards the combined Allied armies, reinforced by thousands of fresh US soldiers, pressed forward in a well-planned offensive. This integrated tanks with infantry and a rolling artillery barrage, and steadily pushed the Germans back towards the Hindenburg Line. Fighting continued until November but the German resistance had been broken. Between April and November more than 300 000 prisoners and 6,000 guns were captured. The guns finally fell silent on 11 November 1918.

CHAPTER NINE

The hidden hand

After the First World War, scepticism of wartime propaganda grew, as did the impression that *all* wartime rumours and legends were equally false. Scepticism was increased with the publication in 1928 of MP Arthur Ponsonby's book *Falsehood in Wartime*.[1] This revealed, for the first time, the facts surrounding some of the best-known rumours and atrocity stories that were widely told as true during the war.

The most intriguing explanation for the Angel of Mons to emerge during this period attributed 'visions' seen by soldiers during the war to motion pictures created by German scientists. This claim emerged in 1930 when a New York newspaper published an interview with a man it claimed was a member of the Imperial German Intelligence Service. Colonel Friedrich Herzenwirth claimed the 'Angels of Mons' were in fact motion picture images thrown upon screens of foggy white clouds over Flanders by cinema projectors mounted on German aeroplanes hovering above the British lines. Colonel Herzenwirth claimed the German plan was to create 'superstitious terror' among the Allied ranks, which would lead British troops to panic and refuse to fight an enemy that appeared to have supernatural protection. But the plan misfired.

> What we had not figured on was that the English should turn the vision to their own benefit. This was a magnificent bit of counter-propaganda, for some of the English must have been fully aware of the mechanism of our trick. Their

method of interpreting our angels as protectors of their own troops turned the scales completely upon us. Had the British command contented itself with simply issuing an Army order unmasking our trickery it would not have been half as effective.

The officer said the deception was more successful when it was used on the Eastern Front in 1915. Pictures of the Virgin Mary with an uplifted hand were projected onto clouds, as if motioning to stop a murderous Russian night attack. Colonel Herzenwirth continued:

> As had been the case in Flanders, the German planes carrying the magic lanterns with enormously powerful Zeiss lenses flew above the enemy lines. A dense snowbank in the sky above the German Army was used as a screen. Entire regiments who had beheld the vision fell upon their knees and flung away their rifles ... The trick was repeated several times on the Russian front and was invariably successful. We knew from prisoners we took that in some cases companies actually killed their officers and flung their rifles away, shouting that they would not be guilty of firing upon an army over which the Mother of God hovered in protection.[2]

When the Germans attempted to use the same tactics against the French Army in Picardy, they miscalculated again:

> Instead of taking the figure of a woman that we threw upon the clouds one night as that of the Virgin or a saint protecting our army, the French promptly recognised Joan of Arc. The tables were turned upon us once more when we changed from a woman to a man in Flanders. The British said it was St George.

The Colonel's story appeared superficially plausible because similar illusions had been created on a far smaller scale by magic lanterns and in the first moving picture shows. In Paris during the

1790s, crowds were amazed by the Phantasmagoria, which used light and shadows projected onto smoke to produce images of ghosts and skeletons. With the invention of photography and then moving pictures, by the First World War cinemas were being built all over Europe and films were soon a familiar sight. New and ever more ingenious inventions were appearing on a daily basis and the use of clouds as a giant backdrop for moving images did not seem impossible. The question was whether the technology and motivation for such a scheme existed in 1914. This was where Colonel Herzenwirth's claims unravelled.

Doubt was immediately cast on his story by soldiers who fought at Mons and by technical experts who were aware of the limitations of projection technology that existed at the time. A major problem was the fact that the Battle of Mons took place not at night but in broad daylight on a bright August afternoon. Furthermore, the early reconnaissance aircraft used by the Germans during the war were incapable of lifting the heavy projectors and generators that would have been necessary to project pictures onto clouds. Even if it had been possible, such a plan would have required advance planning and a very detailed knowledge of the position of the British forces at the time of the battle. In hindsight we know that was not what happened. There was something not quite right about German officer's sensational claims. The day after they were published in the London *Daily News*, a message arrived from the paper's Berlin correspondent:

> A prominent member of the War Intelligence Department in the present German Ministry declares that the story is a hoax: Herzenwirth himself is a myth, or, if existing, a liar. It is officially stated that there is no such person.[3]

Furthermore, the *News* was assured by the British War Office that their wartime files 'contained no record to support any statement that an apparition was seen at Mons'. Colonel Herzenwirth's story was just another hoax that kept the angels alive in the popular consciousness and ensured they continued to live on after the war. The claims resurfaced again in 1997 when the *Sunday Times* claimed that on one occasion during the war the Germans had dissuaded French troops from firing upon them by projecting a picture of the Virgin Mary onto a farmhouse wall.[4]

Devilish new devices invented by scientists were a common theme of rumour and gossip during the Victorian era, and the theme became popular again during the interwar period. During the 1920s, a number of amateur scientists, magicians and inventors claimed they were busily working to develop a 'death ray' that was capable of destroying aircraft before they could bomb a city. The most famous of all was the Welsh-born Harry Grindell-Matthews, whose nickname was 'Death Ray Matthews' after his most famous invention. His 'death ray' was offered to the Air Ministry in 1923 but, despite massive publicity at the time, it was never demonstrated at work. Among Matthews' more successful inventions were one of the first processes for talking films, a submarine detector and a device that was capable of projecting still images onto clouds. On one occasion he used his 'Sky Projector' to shine his name and the Stars and Stripes 10 000 feet (3,000 metres) above New York City. On Christmas Eve 1930, he stunned shoppers in London by projecting the ghostly image of an angel onto clouds above Hampstead Heath. The scene was described in his biography, *The Death Ray Man*, by E.H.G. Barwell (1943):

> The busy shoppers, hurrying home with festive fare, forgot everything as they watched, more and more fascinated, a mysterious steely beam of light shooting through one cloud into another. At first it looked to be part of the mythical underside of dark patches of storm cloud, but the radiance intensified, and focussed, taking shape all at once in the form of a beautiful mystic figure with hair flowing out into the wind ... The apparition appeared to glide across the sky at terrific speed, with wings outstretched, lost at one moment in a cloud, only to reappear again from another one a moment later. She was formed out of mist, became

real, and then vanished into the mist again … as people watched with amazement, wondering where she came from, and the reason for this visitation.[5]

Barwell adds that during the performance every car that arrived on the scene stopped and within a short time there was chaos, with crowds spilling onto the streets to gaze into the sky. A number of people fell to their knees in prayer, believing they were seeing a real angel, but they were soon disillusioned when the image vanished and was replaced by a message which read 'Happy Christmas'. Grindell-Matthews' Sky Projector consisted of a large searchlight mounted on a motor chassis, with a truck carrying the power linked to the electricity supply at a nearby cinema. The choice of an angel for the Christmas Eve spectacular is intriguing as just six weeks later Colonel Herzenwirth's claims were published. Either the mysterious colonel was inspired by Death Ray Matthews' stunt or both events were part of a clever publicity drive to promote the Sky Projector.

While Matthew's invention could never compete with cinema, the concept captured the imagination of the military, who were interested in developing the idea for the purposes of propaganda and deception. As the Second World War approached, the British War Office was searching for a machine that could produce panic or fear among enemy soldiers. During the 'Phoney War' of 1940 the British secret services seriously considered a proposal to use a version of the sky projector against the advancing German armies in Europe. In February of that year a propaganda committee set up by the Foreign Office and MI6 discussed a War Office suggestion to deploy a projector that would 'throw messages or images on to clouds, though the messages must be short and the images simple'. A Brigadier Penney told the committee:

> The cloud conditions required are cumulous at 2,000 to 3,000 feet and the visibility from one to four miles according to weather conditions. With these conditions operations can start half-an-hour after sunset at a distance of half-a-mile from the front line, when the letters or images would be

projected onto the clouds over the enemy lines the right way up for the enemy troops to read and see.[6]

Sceptics on the committee pointed out that the beams would immediately reveal the position of the projector to enemy aircraft and gunners, making it a prime target. In the event the German blitzkrieg of May and June 1940 meant the opportunity to use the new apparatus never presented itself.

This false start did not mark an end to military intelligence interest in the use of magic and illusion in war. During the North African campaign of 1941–42, General Wavell, the Commander of British Forces, created a unit called the A-Force that was dedicated to counter-intelligence and deception. One of the men attached to the unit was a stage magician, Jasper Maskelyne, who was keen to put his sleight-of-hand techniques to use on the battlefield. In 1941 he took part in an elaborate operation to create a fake harbour that would divert German bombers targeting the British-held port of Alexandria. He also constructed a revolving cone of mirrors to produce a dazzling wheel of spinning light beams nine miles across to confuse enemy aircraft approaching the Suez Canal. Maskelyne's crowning achievement came during Operation Bertram, which aimed to mislead General Erwin Rommel before the Battle of El Alamein. During the preparations, Maskelyne's 'Magic Gang' was dedicated to what he called 'the mass production of tricks, swindles and devices'. This included producing elaborate camouflage for British forces and a range of special effects to confuse German airmen, such as dummy tanks and water pipes constructed in the desert.[7]

Military deceptions, like black propaganda, could never be officially admitted if they were to be fully successful. Maskelyne revealed the story of his desert deceptions in a colourful 1949 memoir, *Magic: Top Secret*, but his role in procuring the Allied victory in North Africa was never officially acknowledged. More recently it has emerged, through research by the military historian James Hayward, that during the Second World War British Intelligence was busy spreading black propaganda in several covert operations. The most effective of all was the rumour that an attempt by a German raiding force to land on the south coast of England in August 1940 had been halted by a mysterious wall of flame. This story was given added credence by the discovery in September of the bodies of several Germans in the sea between Hythe and St Mary's Bay and a claim that three destroyers had been lost in the North Sea.

As in the First World War, foreign newspapers were used to spread the rumour. The *New York Times* claimed that 80 000 German troops had burned to death in three failed landings. Others claimed the British possessed a secret weapon that was capable of setting the channel on fire and this idea appears to have been deliberately planted by British Intelligence both in Germany itself and in neutral newspapers. These false stories became so widely believed in occupied Europe that they became a contributing factor to the German High Command's decision to postpone the *real* invasion of Britain, Operation Sealion. James Hayward believes the rumour of the invasion that never was originated as 'unavowable black propaganda' created by MI6 working with the Special Operations Executive and the Directorate of Military Intelligence. Like other wartime rumours, the 'burning sea' displayed remarkable longevity as stories about it continued to circulate as late as 1992. According to Hayward, it was 'the first substantial deception and propaganda victory of the Second World War'.[8]

British Intelligence and the 'Angels'

In *The Great War of Words: Literature as Propaganda* (1989) Peter Buitenhuis notes that the most successful propaganda myths of the First World War were those created inadvertently and unofficially. During that war the British Propaganda Bureau was based at Wellington House in London and at its head was the writer Charles Masterman. Its duties remained highly secret but the majority of its work was aimed at the United States, where a skilful campaign was waged to persuade the Americans to join the war on the side of the Allies. It was between 1914 and 1917, when Masterman was replaced by the novelist John Buchan in the newly formed Ministry of Information, that the operational ground rules for propaganda were first established. According to Philip Taylor, successful propagandists soon came to appreciate the connection between positive (propaganda) and negative (persuasion) and that success relied upon controlling the flow of raw information.

> First and perhaps foremost is the relationship between propaganda and censorship. It is not just a question of what, how, why and when you say something but also of what you decide to leave out.[9]

These skills were honed from the first weeks of the First World War. In September 1914, the War Office allowed rumours about Russian troops reinforcing the BEF in France to be widely published. When, after the Battle of the Marne, the story outlived its usefulness, it was denied. Even before a shot had been fired, the British moved to sever the direct transatlantic cables linking Germany to the United States. After that all messages to the USA had to travel by indirect routes or via morse code that could be intercepted.

While there is no evidence that the nascent Propaganda Bureau were directly involved in the creation of the Angel of Mons, military intelligence may have played a role in keeping the story alive. The clues lie in the source of the information and the timing of its release. One of the earliest of the versions to emerge six months after publication of 'The Bowmen' was the story of the 'strange cloud' described by a mysterious 'military officer' who happened to call at the offices of the spiritualist magazine *Light* in April 1915. The timing was significant in that it coincided with bad news from the front and the acceptance that the war against Germany and her allies could not be won as easily as had been predicted. The Angel of Mons was revived at the same time as the publication of the Bryce Report on alleged German atrocities in Belgium. It also coincided with the stories of the crucified Canadian at Ypres (see Chapter 5) and the appearance of the Comrade in White on the battlefield (Chapter 8). Some of these stories were created inadvertently, others were officially inspired.[10]

Most intriguing of all is the role played by Brigadier-General John Charteris, the most senior British officer to mention the angels in his war memoirs. These were not published until after Colonel Herzenwirth's story appeared in the London press. In his memoir *At GHQ*, published in 1931, Charteris refers to rumours about the Angel of Mons among the BEF in a letter home apparently dated 5 September 1914. He mentions the rumour again in another letter dated 11 February 1915. The view of recent commentators such as Kevin McClure is that Arthur Machen may have believed his story was the source of the angel rumours, but the Charteris letters prove the rumours actually pre-dated the publication of his story. This stance is similar to the claims made by the pro-angels lobby, who maintained that soldiers were talking about visions in August and September 1914, weeks before Machen's story was published. At the time they were unable to produce a single piece of documentary evidence to prove their case. In hindsight, Charteris appeared to provide the elusive evidence that was missing in 1915. If his first letter was genuinely contemporaneous it would indeed pre-date 'The Bowmen' by 14 days. However, before we can accept this conclusion we have to question how much reliance can be placed upon his dating. Were the letters really written when they appear to have been and can it be merely a coincidence that a military intelligence officer who played a role in the spread of what became known as 'black propaganda' also played a role in keeping the Angel of Mons alive after the war?

I set out to answer these vital questions by examining the most important evidence, the original letters themselves. On doing so it quickly became apparent that the originals bore little resemblance to the polished versions published in *At GHQ*.

Historians such as McClure have accepted the dates provided by Charteris as apparently authentic and showing no sign of addition or revision.[11] However, in the introduction to his own memoirs, Charteris confessed they had indeed been revised:

> I had not kept a formal diary; but very early in my days at GHQ I found it necessary to keep notes of my views from day to day ... from these records I have compiled this volume ... *where records were incomplete, I have amplified them by my recollections.*[12] [my emphasis]

The impression given is that Charteris did not have a precise date for *what became known as* the Angel of Mons when, years afterwards, he began to compile a chronology of events during the campaign. The 'Angel of Mons' emerged around April 1915 from a collection of rumours concerned with supernatural intervention on the battlefield which had ancient precedents. These did not initially refer to angels, but to mysterious clouds and visions of bowmen, horsemen and saints. How then was it possible for an officer to refer explicitly to the Angel of Mons in September 1914 when this description was not used until the spring of the following year?

In his book, Charteris refers to a number of rumours and legends of the war, and military historian James Hayward regards all his comments and explanations as 'unreliable'. His suspicions are borne out by a careful reading of *At GHQ* and, more conclusively, by an examination of the primary source material that was used in the preparation of the book. Microfilm copies of Charteris' papers, comprising letters, telegrams and postcards to his wife Noel, dated 1914–18, are preserved in the Liddell Hart Centre for Military Archives at King's College, University of London.[13] When I examined the letters I failed to identify any dated 5 September 1914 and 11 February 1915. The collection for September 1914 is sparse, which is understandable given the circumstances of the retreat from Mons and the Battle of the Marne. Charteris' first letter home is dated 2 September. A postcard followed on 5 September, but this is brief and bears no comparison to the lengthy letter published in *At GHQ*. It does not refer to angels. Neither does a subsequent letter dated 7 September. Negative evidence can never be entirely conclusive, but the fact that the crucial letters do not appear in the collection of originals undermines the authenticity of the dated entries in *At GHQ*.

It is also important to take into account the nature of the responsibilities Charteris assumed during his service with the British Army. From 1915 to 1917 he was Chief Intelligence Officer at GHQ France and as such part of his activities lay in the embryonic field of black propaganda. This included the running of spies and double agents and the seeding of false information with the intention of misleading and demoralizing the enemy. It is within this context that we cannot overlook Charteris' murky involvement in a story that has been described as 'the master hoax' of the war, the Corpse Factory. This story alleged that the Germans were recycling the bodies of their own dead for use in shells and animal feed in a secret factory hidden behind the front line. It was an allegation that built upon the Allied propaganda which accused the German army of brutality and atrocities against civilians. Hayward traces the origin of the rumour to 1915 as part of the same group that originated in England at the time of British military reverses on the Western Front. It reappeared in 1917, when accounts from witnesses who had allegedly visited the horrible 'tallow works' were published in newspapers around the world. The story would not go away and was still in circulation during the Second World War when a labourer in Somerset insisted that he had been forced to work in the Corpse Factory, 'and gave graphic details of the British and German corpses he had to dismember'.[14]

When challenged in 1917 in the Commons, the British Government refused to credit the story, but Lord Robert Cecil, Under Secretary of Foreign Affairs, said he found 'nothing incredible' in the charges 'in view of other actions by the German military authorities'. Foreign Office papers lend further credence to the suspicion that the Corpse Factory was created by a branch of military intelligence for use against the Germans.[15] The connection with Charteris relates to a visit he made to the United States in 1925, by which time he had retired from the army and become an MP. During a lecture tour he entertained his audience with stories of spies and wartime intelligence. It was during one speech to the National Arts Club that he reportedly admitted the Corpse Factory, until then widely believed in neutral countries, was invented by British intelligence. In a report of an after-dinner speech given by Charteris, the *New York Times* alleged that he had personally claimed credit for its invention. Their report also alleged that he admitted that a member of his staff forged a diary of a German soldier who had been transferred from the front to work in the factory with the intention that it should be planted on a dead body, where it would be discovered by a friendly war correspondent. It was at this stage that Charteris stepped in and decided the deception had gone far enough. He was concerned that any error discovered in the diary could expose the story and 'Such a result would have imperiled all the British propaganda.'

These allegations were widely republished and, on his return to England, Charteris was summoned to the War Office to explain his remarks. He subsequently issued a statement denying the *New York Times'* report and claimed he was misquoted. In the London *Times* he described the claims as 'incorrect and absurd ... as propaganda was in no way under GHQ France'. His only connection with the story came 'when a fictitious diary supporting the Kadaver story was submitted, but when this was discovered to be fictitious, it was at once rejected'. Despite his reassurances the disclaimer was widely disbelieved and indeed, prior to his return from the States, Charteris told a US newsman he had no intention of challenging the report in the *New York Times*, 'Since any errors it might contain were only of minor importance.'[16]

I emphasize the importance of the Corpse Factory controversy as it *must* reflect upon the reliability of all the other evidence offered up by Brigadier-General Charteris on the origin of wartime rumours. Successful propagandists, as Taylor noted, were those who were skilful in using both negative (Corpse Factory) and positive (Angel of Mons) to best effect. Even if the origin of the Angel of Mons can be ultimately traced to Machen's story rather than a British Intelligence source, the trigger for its reappearance in 1915 and the mechanism by which it was then spread from Home Front to Western Front remains suspicious. To the Propaganda Bureau and the press censor alike, the angel stories would have been seen as having a positive effect in terms of establishing the rightness of the British cause, and no action would be taken to suppress them.

The absence of an original letter referring to the Angel of Mons among the Charteris collection leads me to conclude that the testimony provided by him dates not from 1914, but from 1931. Arthur Machen was indeed correct when he claimed there was not a single piece of contemporary evidence for the 'Angel of Mons' that could be dated before the publication of 'The Bowmen'.

The Battle of Britain

At the opening of the Second World War, the Angel of Mons was widely regarded as a harmless story that had helped to raise the spirits of soldiers in the last war when the odds appeared stacked against the Allies. On 30 November 1939 Russia, at that time allied to the Germans in a non-aggression pact, invaded its neighbour Finland. The Finns, like the British at Mons, were heavily outnumbered but their forces fought a heroic defence. The Red Army columns were halted by combining skilful tactics with the natural barrier provided by the lakes and peninsulas that separated the two countries. The survival of Finland against the Soviet offensive was portrayed in Free Europe as a miracle. As the hard-pressed Finnish troops defended the Mannerheim Line, they looked towards the heavens for a sign. According to the London *Daily Mail*:

> The most fantastic of all wars – the war where the
> weak defeat the strong, where the battlefield looks like a

Christmas card – grows even more strange. Instead of guns and bombs and tanks, the principle news to-day is of 'angels.' Battle-weary Finnish troops say they have seen them north of Lake Ladoga. They speak of gigantic white figures with arms stretched out in the sky as if to protect them from the repeated attacks launched from the Russian lines. Perhaps three days of fighting with no sleep or rest is having its effect. Perhaps weeks and months of patrol work in the silent forests has sharpened their imaginations. Whatever the explanation, they are as convinced as the thousands of British and French troops who 'saw' and believed in the 'Angels of Mons' during the last war.[17]

At the same time spiritualists were circulating stories of angels seen during the Japanese invasion of China that demonstrated how 'the powers of good' were widely at work in the world of war. A Christian missionary in China, Dr Charles Kimber, told the *United Church Record* that he had received two independent accounts of angels intervening to stop Japanese bombers from attacking a defenceless city. The first was a letter that told of a young airman who was ordered to lead ten bombers against the city. As he approached the target he saw in the sky before him 'a multitude of angels with drawn swords, blocking the way'. Believing these were merely cloud formations he flew on but found himself facing an 'invisible barrier' that proved so strong that he turned around and his squadron followed him. The airman was later executed for not carrying out his orders. The second letter contained a Chinese account of the fright experienced by the residents of the city on hearing the approach of the bombers. At that moment a Chinese pastor fell on his knees to pray to God to stop the planes.

For several hours he struggled in prayer, until he saw the squadron approach. Then suddenly he saw the leader irresolutely swerve from his course, as if beaten back, and turning round, he flew away, followed by the other nine airmen.[18]

These stories found a resonance in Britain in the spring of 1940 when prayers were being said for the deliverance of the British Expeditionary Force trapped by the German advance into France and the Low Countries. The time was ripe for a revival in the idea that Britain, and its army, had divine protection.

Following the fall of France in 1940, Britain again stood alone against the *Werhmacht* and it seemed only a matter of time before the Germans would launch an invasion of the British Isles. Although the escape of the BEF from the beaches at Dunkirk in June was proclaimed by Winston Churchill as a 'miracle of deliverance', the crisis was far from over. Throughout the summer the *Luftwaffe* was massing along the French coast in preparation for the planned invasion of Britain, Operation Sealion.

The Battle of Britain began in July 1940 and continued through the summer and autumn as the *Luftwaffe* targeted fighter airfields in southern England. The air defence of Britain rested in the capable hands of Air Chief Marshal Sir Hugh Dowding who was the Commander-in-Chief of RAF Fighter Command. Dowding was seen as a lonely and aloof character but privately he was a dedicated spiritualist who, in later years, expressed his belief that his men had been protected by higher powers throughout the air battle. Dowding's faith in the existence of protective spirits and, post-war, flying saucers, is often sidelined by history but his beliefs were certainly shared at the time by some RAF and US aircrew.

At the height of the battle on 7 September 1940 or 'Black Saturday' as it became known, hundreds of German bombers crossed the English coast and 300 tons of high explosive were dropped on the city of London. The bombers and their fighter escorts were met by squadrons of Hurricanes and Spitfires piloted by the famous few who fought on bravely despite the odds stacked against them. The RAF fighters were guided towards the bombers by Britain's 'secret weapon,' the radar early warning chain, that could detect enemy aircraft before they reached the English coast. Radar gave the RAF a tactical advantage in the battle of attrition that reached its climax during the mass daylight raid against

London on 15 September. On that day the *Luftwaffe* lost a total of 60 aircraft against 21 lost by Fighter Command. As a result, Hitler was forced to accept that air superiority over England could not be achieved. Operation Sealion was postponed but the blitz by German bombers against English cities continued.

Early on the morning of Sunday 27 October 1940, a formation of German aircraft crossed the English coast and was met by RAF fighters. As the action petered out, the white vapour trails left in the wake of the dogfight continued to hang in the clear blue autumn sky above the Sussex Downs. A shepherd tending his flock miles below on Firle Beacon happened to glance up to the sky. On 8 November the London *Daily Mirror* published his story under the headline: 'The Vision in the Sky':

> Old Fred Fowler, sixty-six, lifted his weather-beaten face skywards and pointed west way above the highest peak of the Sussex Downs. 'It be there when I see,' he said. 'There in the clear blue sky. A vision they calls it – it was the like of something which I never see before.' Then he said reverently: 'It be Christ I see.'

A journalist dispatched to the scene reported how the shepherd and several others in the village had, apparently quite independently, seen a vision of Christ and six angels they believed was a sign from heaven. The *Mirror* found Fowler with his two trusty sheepdogs sheltering from the October wind in a bracken shelter high on the beacon. He explained that he attended church every Sunday and was 'not one to see things'. He said:

> I'd just rounded up the flock that morning – it be about eleven. I says to meself it's a nice clear day and I looks up west at the sky. Then I sees it. There in the clear blue sky. A vision they calls it – it was the like of something which I never see before ... It be like what they tells me the cinema is like, but I thinks it be more real. There came a kind of panel across the sky. Inside the panel of white there was a cross, with Christ, his head to one side nailed on to it.

Round him were six angels. I counted 'em, and they wore white cloudy robes to the feet. I know it was to the feet because I even saw their feet. I even saw their toes.[19]

As the vision faded Fred ran down the hillside to his home in Firle, near Lewes, and told his story. There he found that a number of others had seen a 'peculiar cloud' above the Downs. Two sisters, Grace Evans and E.M. Steer, who had been evacuated to Sussex from London, confirmed the story as did a neighbour, Mrs Stevens. Mrs Evans told the paper they must have seen the vision 'a second or two before the shepherd did', because when she first looked at the sky it was clear blue.

Gradually I saw a panel of kind of white cloud appear. I called my sister because it looked so pretty, then all at once we saw the crucifix and Christ. I saw every detail, to the nails in his crossed feet and the angels rose around him. One held a harp, another an old fashioned pitcher with two handles. It was as clear as a picture and then, when I had got over my surprise, I called my neighbour to see the wonderful sight.

Her sister, Mrs Steer, later told the *Daily Mail*:

I was in the house when my sister called to me from the garden and there she was pointing to something in the sky. I looked up, and first of all there was a white line like a road in a cloudless blue sky. It was very bright, brighter than any cloud I have ever seen. Then before my eyes I saw figures beginning to take shape above the line. It did give me a turn. Well, I watched and then I could make out the figures. I saw the shape of the Cross, and on the Cross clearly I saw our Lord, and on either side of Him I made out the figures of six angels ... It was so real it almost frightened me. I am not one to imagine things, and I used to smile at the story about the Angels of Mons – I always thought the soldiers who saw them imagined things, but now I can believe it.[20]

But what appeared at face value to be independent testimony broke down when the *Daily Mail* reporter tried to check the shepherd's story. When Fowler was approached he said: 'No, I can't say I saw the cross and the figures they say they saw in the village, but also I have never seen a cloud anythin' like that over the Sussex Downs.' The Vicar of Firle, the Rev A.G. Gregor, smelled a rat. He said: 'I saw nothing and think the whole thing is nonsense.' In the villages, there was no doubt what ordinary people believed. Despite its doubts, the sceptical *Daily Mail* said there was no doubt the vision was 'the symbol of victory' the country had been waiting for after months of bombing.

For a week at the height of the blitz, the vision at Firle was the talk of London, and letters poured into newspapers from others who had seen apparitions in the sky. On the day the *Mirror* published its story an air-raid warden claimed she saw 'a vision of Christ with a crown of thorns on his head, dressed in flowing robes and with an angel on either side of him' rising above burning houses in Middlesex. She called a telephone engineer working nearby and both watched the vision for about five minutes. A man from Croydon said he had seen the figures of Christ and the six angels from a great distance on the same day as the people in Sussex. Although the vision was partly obscured by clouds, 'I did very clearly observe the harp in perfect detail for several minutes.' Meanwhile, Mrs H. Penton claimed she saw angels 'in beautiful flowing robes, with arms outstretched, pointing to the sky' high above the cliffs overlooking the sea at Boscombe Harbour. 'The vision appeared when the sun was setting in a lovely sky,' she wrote. 'They seemed to be appealing to those on earth.'[21]

The Angels of Mons had returned for one final display to mark the victory of the RAF against the German invasion of England. Or had they?

Rationalists had a better explanation. An RAF Flight Lieutenant wrote to say the 'sign' was merely an optical illusion produced by exhaust vapour trailing from aircraft at 30 000 feet. A dogfight had taken place early that morning and the white trails left behind remained for more than one hour. A man in Addlestone who watched the action added:

> During that time they turned, twisted, and tied themselves in such knots that before they finally cleared over the Sussex Downs there was such a fantastical design that you could see not only angels but any subject that was dear to your heart. I saw the whole phenomenon from its start to its closing stages.

Angels and clouds

The visions at Firle in 1940 can be compared with those seen in Essex during 1917 (Chapter 8). They are examples of people trapped in the midst of a desperate war spontaneously 'seeing' images of Christ and other divine beings in clouds or photographs of cloud formations. Many accounts of religious visions begin or end with the appearance of curious clouds, and in folklore mist and vapour is often associated with the materialization of fairies and other supernatural beings. The drive to find spiritual significance in celestial phenomena is widespread and received a boost with the invention of photography. In the twentieth century, mysterious images have appeared on pictures that thousands have come to believe show gods, angels and latterly aliens.

The First World War led to a growth in the industry of 'psychic photography' that produced the Cottingley fairy photos and images of dead soldiers conjured up in the séance rooms. The circumstances in which these and other photographs were taken are often mysterious or ambiguous. One famous example dates from the Korean War and features an image of Christ dominating the sky below an image said to depict US and Communist planes locked in combat. The photograph was widely circulated during the 1960s but all the stories that seek to explain its origins contradict each other and the photographer could never be traced.[22]

Another miraculous photograph, known as 'Christ in the Snow', has been widely copied and circulated since 1926, when a print was sent to Sir Arthur Conan Doyle by a woman who claimed she obtained it in Canada. When *Fortean Times* researcher Bob Rickard tried to identify the original source, he found dozens of prints in existence whose owners all believed it had been taken by a close relative under extraordinary circumstances. One version claimed it was taken by a housewife in Seattle in 1920 as she tried to photograph her daughter against a bank of flowers.[23] The shutter clicked of its own accord and when the roll was developed the image of Christ was present in one frame. Other versions claim the photo was of a snow scene in the Alps, taken from an aircraft. Inevitably, some have linked the picture with the visions reported during the First World War and the Angel of Mons. According to an account published by *Psychic News*, the miraculous photo was 'unexpectedly secured in the trenches in France' during 1917 by a priest.[24]

Supernatural clouds that hide soldiers from the enemy were a central feature of the stories from Mons and other battles during the First World War. One of the most famous mysteries of the war linked a sighting of mysterious clouds with the disappearance of an entire battalion of British soldiers, numbering some 260 men, during the disastrous Gallipoli campaign of 1915. Fifty years later, in 1965, two New Zealand veterans gave statements to a UFO magazine to the effect that they had seen a regiment of British soldiers marching into a solid-looking cloud that straddled a sunken road. The cloud then lifted off and the 'regiment' were never seen again. It later emerged that the soldiers, from a battalion of the Norfolk Regiment, had been massacred during a bungled attack on Turkish positions. The bodies of many of the men were discovered by a War Graves investigation in 1919 but the full circumstances of their deaths remained ambiguous. The 'disappearance' of the Norfolks is still attributed by some to extraterrestrial kidnappers, but the facts were revealed by

Nigel McCrery in his 1991 book *The Vanished Battalion*, to which readers are referred.[25]

Long before the mystery of the Vanished Battalion was solved, stories about clouds that appear suddenly, apparently in answer to unspoken need, became the central theme of wartime miracles. Following the evacuation from Dunkirk in May–June 1940, the London *Sunday Dispatch* claimed the English Channel had become: 'as calm and as smooth as a pond ... and while the smooth sea was aiding our ships, a fog was shielding our troops from devastating attack by the enemy's air strength'.[26]

According to another story a miraculous cloud also played a role in the success of the invasion of North Africa by Allied forces in November 1942. During Operation Torch, US and British shipping were vulnerable to airborne attacks by the *Luftwaffe*. Dick Foxhall was a chief petty officer on the British submarine mothership HMS *Maidstone* in the Mediterranean as the landings took place. He described how for ten days he had watched from the deck of the ship as 'an immense cloud' developed in the sky, which seemed to help protect the Allied armada from the attacks of Nazi aircraft.

> It was like the calm seas for days on end at Dunkirk; and with the sea like a car park the Germans could not have missed killing hundreds of men. I was not alone in thinking that Providence set the cloud there.[27]

Belief in divine protection of British sailors and airmen was common not only to shepherds and chief petty officers but also to some of the most senior military figures, such as Hugh Dowding. His belief was shared by some of the most rational scientists who had helped to develop the coastal radar chain that threw an invisible protective curtain around the British Isles. When one morning in March 1941 Fighter Command were notified that unidentified plots had been detected by two radar stations on the south coast, the news caused panic at the highest levels of the Air Ministry.

According to Sir Edward Fennessey, who at the time was responsible for extending the RAF radar chain, the mysterious blips appeared 'as a very large formation of aircraft flying at a low speed from the Cherbourg area at about 80 knots'. Checks were made with the radar research station at Swanage and engineers made various adjustments to the equipment, which they hoped would help to eliminate false plots. After much frantic adjustment, the radar continued to 'see' waves of blips moving from the French coast towards England until after some time they faded out. The speed of the blips gave the impression they might be towed gliders and, fearing an invasion was underway, Fighter Command gave the order for Beaufighters to intercept them. The crews were guided by ground radars towards the blips over the Channel but the pilots could see nothing visually and returned to base, leaving the mystery unsolved.[28] When Sir Edward related this story 60 years afterwards he remained puzzled about the events he had witnessed. He recalled:

> No explanation was ever obtained and because we were busy fighting a war we spent no time investigating this phenomena. So it remains a mystery. After the war, and after a good dinner with friends, I recounted this story and ascribed the phenomena to the souls of British soldiers killed in France over the centuries returning to defend their country. One of the guests wrote a short story based upon my fantasy which was published.[29]

Sir Edward recalled that more of these mysterious blips were picked up by RAF radars after the war ended. In 1947 they were given the name 'angels' or 'ghosts' by Signal Corps personnel, and this term quickly entered military folklore as a catch-all phrase to categorize a range of unidentified blips that became familiar to early radar operators.[30] As technology improved, most were explained as formations of birds and anomalies caused by the weather, but a few remained unaccounted for. These phenomena, detected by radar, became linked with the many sightings of 'flying saucers' or UFOs as the Cold War developed and led to new fears of invasion, not only by Soviet Russia but by creatures from outer space. With the possibility of atomic war a very real prospect, others, such as Lord Dowding who had turned to spiritualism, began to place their faith in intervention by benevolent visitors from other worlds in the future conflict that seemed inevitable. As the Second World War moved into the Cold War, the heavenly messengers that had once brought hope and reassurance to soldiers had become transformed into technological angels tailored for a whole new generation. The Angel of Mons was still very much alive.

CHAPTER TEN

Myth or miracle?

The legend is that place where the credible and the incredible come together.

Bill Nicholaisen, folklorist[1]

Since 1915 masses of biographical and autobiographical material has been published by those who were caught up by the catastrophic events of the First World War. The microcosms provided by these narratives carefully document the everyday experiences of those who fought in the early engagements of the war, but few mention angels or other supernatural or miraculous events. Those that do were influenced by stories and rumours they had read, heard or absorbed months, and years, after the events they described. Fewer still of those writing about the desperate and exhausting first month of the war had the opportunity or forethought to commit their experiences to writing at the time. It is only by walking through the perspective provided by history, lined as it often is with mirrors, that we can hope to throw some light upon the motivations of those who produced the primary historical accounts that have survived to the present day.

The appearance of angels at Mons has been accepted at face value by a number of modern historians who have relied upon dubious secondary sources for their 'facts' and have not sufficiently questioned the reliability of the evidence. As one recent critique of the story put it, many 'seem to have been seduced by the charm of the legend into treating folklore as established fact'.[2] Prime among them is the Oxford historian,

A.J.P. Taylor, who in an oft-repeated passage from his book *The First World War*, wrote that Mons was the only battle of the Great War where 'supernatural intervention was observed, more or less reliably, on the British side'.[3]

Another, John Terraine, has done much to dispel what he defined as the myths of the First World War – for example, the blundering Generals, the roles played by the tanks and cavalry – in his articles and books. In his book *The Smoke and the Fire* (1980) he defined 'myth' in the modern sense of 'a purely fictitious narrative' and examined the Angel of Mons within that context. Ironically, almost all the 'facts' cited by Terraine in his account of the legend were equally fictitious. He believed, wrongly, that the angels 'entered the realm of legend within a fortnight' of the battle and summarily dismissed Arthur Machen's claim that the story he wrote was the 'unwitting origin' of all the angel rumours. Terraine's conclusions were based upon misinterpretations of dates and the context of the documents he was relying upon. For example, he claimed the vision of phantom cavalry seen during the retreat from Le Cateau (Chapter 2) was published in September 1914, within weeks of the officer's experience. In fact it was published more than a year after the publication of Machen's story, in response to a great flurry of speculation about the 'Angel of Mons' in English newspapers.[4]

The opinions of Taylor and Terraine, two highly respected historians, have directly influenced other recent writers and commentators, many of whom have demonstrated a superficial grasp of the nature of the evidence and have come to grief on the slippery rocks of the 'facts'. The end result is not a promising one for those who wish to know 'the truth' behind a story that has puzzled many in the post-war era. Before truth can be established, it is necessary to peel back layers of interpretation and misinterpretation that began in 1915 and which continue to this day. We have to deal not only with ambiguity within the primary texts, but also misinterpretation of those texts themselves by commentators in more recent times. The end result of this exercise is that one comes to understand the complicated process by which myths and legends are created and spread in times of war and become widely believed.

One fact is immediately apparent: The 'Angel of Mons' does not accurately reflect the content of the body of testimony that is encapsulated within the legend. As I have demonstrated, very few of the stories and visions actually took place at the Battle of Mons itself and much of the testimony relates to events during the retreat from Mons and subsequent skirmishes. This suggests there is no single explanation of the whole phenomenon, as we are dealing with a wide variety of different and possibly unrelated experiences. Few of the narratives describe angels in the 'traditional' sense defined in Chapter 2. On the contrary, there are stories of bowmen and phantom cavalry, mysterious clouds, lights and shadowy supernatural presences. It is also clear how few of the accounts can be traced to named individuals, or to records that can be verified as contemporaneous with the events of 1914.

When I began my quest to establish the facts about what happened at Mons, it quickly became apparent that although there were numerous written sources for the legend, most were of questionable reliability. The more questions I asked, and the more accounts I traced to source, the more it became apparent that even seemingly impressive testimony, such as that of Brigadier-General Charteris, was not as authentic as it first appeared. Sources that initially appeared to be first-hand accounts turned out to be second-, third- or even fourth-hand. With the possible exception of Charteris, the stories that I originally believed to date from 1914 were found, on further scrutiny, to have been written down decades after the events they purported to describe, when memories had become distorted and contaminated.

Such problems abound with every single source, and 'contemporary' accounts are often no more reliable than the modern ones. In versions of the Angel of Mons published after the Second World War, stories that are at best apocryphal and at worst outright lies are repeated again and again and are often deliberately embroidered in the retelling.

The earliest and possibly the most objective investigation of the visions reported from the battlefields was published in the *Journal of the Society for Psychical Research*. The wide experience of the SPR in the investigation of alleged supernatural phenomena made their London headquarters a natural focus for enquiries about the Angel of Mons during the summer of 1915. The society sent out questionnaires to individuals who were quoted in newspapers and books as having knowledge or direct experience of the visions. This material was collated by SPR member Helen Salter, who was the daughter of Cambridge scientist Dr Arthur Verrall. In her final report, published in December 1915, Salter said the society had decided that a thorough investigation of the claims was needed because the 'whole history of the case throws an interesting light on the value of human testimony and the growth of rumour'. These matters were of particular interest to the SPR because 'it is upon human testimony that [the society's] conclusions must to a great extent be founded'. Salter's enquiries quickly established that the majority of the rumours circulated during the 'tide of rumour' could be traced to the story attributed to Sarah Marrable (Chapter 5):

> In the main ... the result of our enquiry is negative, at least as regards the question of whether any apparitions were seen on the battlefield, either at Mons or elsewhere. Of first-hand testimony we have received none at all, and of testimony at second-hand none that would justify us in assuming the occurrence of any supernormal phenomenon ... all our efforts to obtain the detailed evidence upon which an enquiry of this kind must be based have proved unavailing.

Summing up, Salter concluded that:

> a. Many of the stories which have been current during the past year concerning 'visions' on the battlefield prove on investigation to be found on mere rumour and cannot be traced to any authoritative source.

b. After we have discounted these rumours, we are left with a small residue of evidence, which seems to indicate that a certain number of men who took part in the retreat from Mons honestly believe themselves to have had at that time supernormal experiences of a remarkable character.[5]

Salter highlighted two accounts from soldiers (described in Chapter 2), which she believed were authentic and the closest to first-hand testimony. First, there was the story of the Lieutenant-Colonel who saw a squadron of phantom cavalry during the retreat from Le Cateau. Second, there was the story told by the Lance Corporal who saw three winged figures hovering above the German lines. She accepted that the grounds for interpreting these two individual experiences as supernormal in origin were 'slight'.

Arthur Machen expressed surprise at the SPR's position. He could not understand how Salter could maintain on the one hand that belief in the angels was founded on 'mere rumour' but then conclude that some soldiers 'believe themselves to have had at that time supernormal experiences of a remarkable character'. To him that was to place the proverbial cart before the horse. Machen was alluding to Occam's Razor, a well-known philosophical principle that has been translated from its original Latin to state that entities must not be multiplied beyond what is necessary to explain a phenomenon. The rule is often interpreted to mean that explanations for unexplained phenomena should first be attempted in terms of what is known. Often this will be the simplest theory that fits the known facts. For Machen, the simplest explanation for the stories that puzzled Salter were hallucinations triggered in the brains of soldiers by exhaustion and sensory deprivation. Experiences of this kind were described by many soldiers during the war (see Chapter 2), and for Machen it was not necessary to resort to the supernatural or the supernormal to account for them.

Throughout the remainder of his life, Machen remained convinced that the testimony that emerged during the war fell well below the standard of evidence that was required to establish that intervention by angels or other supernatural forces really had occurred at Mons. After the war was over, the great mass of witness testimony promised by Phyllis Campbell failed to materialize, but the story would not go away. It had taken on a life of its own. By 1931 when he contributed an essay to *The Great War – I Was There*, Machen had grown weary of what he called 'the confirmatory allegations, quotations, asseverations and anecdotes'. Of the testimony presented by Campbell and Begbie he said:

> It was strong evidence, as I say. Or, rather, it would have been strong evidence but for one circumstance – there was not one word of truth in it. Or, in the stronger phrase of Wemmick, these stories were lies: 'Every one of 'em lies, sir.'[6]

The SPR's inquiry was not bettered until 1993 when Kevin McClure published the results of his research in a booklet, *Visions of Bowmen and Angels*. A social worker by profession, McClure has been investigating reports of strange phenomena since the late 1960s and his specific interests are the links between traditional religious experiences and modern accounts of encounters with supernatural beings. His writings cover a wide range of subjects from visions of the Blessed Virgin Mary and angels to UFOs and alien abductions. Despite his sceptical standpoint on the latter, McClure's examination of the evidence for wartime visions was far from dismissive. He felt unable to reject the stories from 1914–18 outright and he came to agree with the conclusions reached by the SPR. At the end of his study he frankly admitted that: 'I still don't know what happened during the Retreat from Mons: I doubt that I ever will.'

McClure found, in common with everyone else who has studied the evidence in depth, that it was impossible to completely separate the angel stories from Arthur Machen's 'The Bowmen'. He accepted that Machen was an honest man, who genuinely believed that all the stories sprang from his imagination. Despite his protests to the contrary, it is impossible to dismiss the possibility that a degree of synchronicity was indeed involved in his inspiration and writing. As creative writers will testify, the brain can act as a sponge that soaks up images, conversations, colours, sensations and pieces of text, and files them away in a mysterious way. The imagination will then open the drawers of this mental filing cabinet at random, pulling out an idea here, an impression there, a story once heard and, using its unique sleight of hand, will bring them together in the form of a piece of creative work. The processes by which all the different components are woven together are subconscious ones and often a mystery and a revelation to writers themselves. Indeed, some artists will go as far as to state that creativity is often at its best when the subconscious is allowed to do its work without interference from the conscious mind.

As a result, I can understand how McClure came to believe that Machen:

> may have been right, but there do seem to be two separate stories of intervention – the 'Bowmen' and the 'Angels' – though there are certainly later accounts in which both appear, the two forms having apparently been amalgamated ... but the initial formats and characteristics of each story are quite different, and it is hard to see how the one could have emanated from the other. There is no written record of any sort of 'intermediate' version, bridging the two.[7]

Unfortunately the most important source of first-hand evidence – private correspondence between soldiers and their families – has not yielded a single account of supernatural phenomena at the Battle of Mons. As Machen's biographer Mark Valentine pointed out, the best evidence for visions would be first-hand statements from soldiers that could be proved to pre-date the publication of 'The Bowmen'. There are in fact no authentic first-hand accounts at all and no second- or third-hand accounts that can be demonstrated to pre-date the publication of his story. In the absence of direct testimony from the soldiers themselves,

McClure chose the next best option: the diary entry by Brigadier-General John Charteris, apparently dated 5 September 1914, of which he claimed there was 'no hint of re-writing or later addition'. It is with the note from Charteris that McClure opens his account, but he failed to appreciate that even this story is self-confessedly unreliable as contemporary evidence. McClure opts for a midway position that does not trace the origins directly to Machen's pen:

> My own personal view is that there was rather more to it than that, and I concur with the opinion of the SPR in effectively suggesting that the men of the BEF – or a number of them, anyway – were aware of reports of a 'cloud' or of 'angels' before the publication of *The Bowmen* on 29 September 1914.[8]

This position was similar to that taken by Mrs Salter. She also found it difficult to accept a direct link between 'The Bowmen' and the angels, primarily because 'the various versions that have been current would have borne clearer traces of their origin'. The angels version, she argued, bore hardly any resemblance to Machen's story beyond the fact that the central incident in each was 'a supernatural intervention on behalf of the British Army'. Ironically, in that sentence she had provided an answer to her own question.

In his account McClure highlighted the dynamic process by which rumours and legends evolve and change as they are circulated by word of mouth before they first appear in print. The mutation of the bowmen of Mons into angels and later angel warriors was the end product of the long period of oral transmission that occurred during the winter of 1914–15. The method whereby stories mutate and adapt to new circumstances as they spread via word of mouth was not fully understood at the time. Today, with the benefit of hindsight, it is possible both to study this process and to identify the Angel of Mons as a classic example of a contemporary or 'urban' legend.

The first 'urban myth'?

Half a century after the First World War ended, a researcher at the Imperial War Museum attempted to summarize the mass of literature pertaining to the Angel of Mons. After searching dozens of pamphlets and newspaper cuttings, he failed to find a reference to a single British soldier who had testified to the appearance of angels on the battlefield. He then realized that to 'pursue the supporting stories to source is to make a journey into a fog'.

On reaching the end of my own quest to discover the truth behind the legend, I reached a similar impasse. Despite the great mass of testimony and documentary evidence I had collected for this book, no solid evidence for supernatural intervention in the war could be identified. This led me to reject the appearance of angels at Mons as a real historical event, but I realized that it would be unfair to dismiss the whole story as false. As a student of supernatural folklore, all my experience leads me to suspend judgement rather than pronounce that any body of belief or tradition is either 'true' or 'false'. The black-or-white approach is a product of the age in which we live. To the modern mind, there is an overriding desire to know what is true and what is false, to find a neat explanation for everything that cannot be pigeon-holed. But even Arthur Machen, uncompromising on the matter of the Angel of Mons, argued that no one fully understands the workings of the universe or the human mind.[9] To adopt a rigid position of belief or disbelief towards the Angel of Mons is to look no further into the reasons why such stories are told, what function they perform and why people continue to believe in them. Is it therefore possible to explain the Angel of Mons simply as a legend or a myth, an example of faith in supernatural intervention during war that is common to all human societies?

In 2002 a BBC Radio 4 programme went so far as to label the Angel of Mons as 'the first example of an urban myth' and the connotation was implicit: a myth is something that is false. In fact the most pervasive and influential falsehood relating to Mons is that hundreds if not thousands of soldiers who fought in the campaign saw the vision. This claim can be traced to the writings of the nurse, Phyllis Campbell, in 1915 and since then it has been widely repeated in newspapers, magazines and TV programmes to this day. It has proved to be both pervasive and persistent.

Three decades later the pioneering psychologist Carl Jung accepted the popular stories told in the war at face value and developed an elaborate theory to explain them. Jung refers to the Angel of Mons in his 1958 book *Flying Saucers: A Modern Myth of Things Seen in the Skies*. He believed the angels were an example of a 'non-pathological' vision that had some level of reality to the soldiers who saw it because of their heightened emotional state created by the horror of war. These were to Jung the ideal conditions for a collective vision to manifest itself in the subconscious mind. The form the vision took was the result of a projection of the conscious or unconscious desires of the subject. Angels were appropriate symbols for the First World War, while 'flying saucers' – with their circular appearance symbolising wholeness – were a reflection of different fears and hopes that characterized the Cold War. To Jung, the angels at Mons and the post-war UFO phenomenon had much in common and he classified both as 'visionary rumours'. These were:

> rather like a story that is told all over the world, but differs from an ordinary rumour in that it is expressed in the form of visions, or perhaps owed its existence to them in first place and is now kept alive by them.[10]

Jung was describing a phenomenon using psychological terms while at the same time folklorists were beginning to define a different concept using their own methodology.

'Urban myth' is an inaccurate term often used by journalists in a flippant way to explain recurring stories that appear to be apocryphal and are told 'as if true'. A far better descriptive term for this type of story is the 'contemporary legend'. They are also known as 'FOAF-tales', which is an acronym based upon the way narrators attribute the source of the story to a 'friend of a friend'. These story types have been collected by folklorists since the 1940s but were only fully recognized and classified as a specific genre of folklore later in the twentieth century. Contemporary legends are traditional stories told as true and circulated by word of mouth within a wide variety of social groups. Their plots and themes reflect the basic fears and moral judgements of societies and groups which circulate them and they contain both ancient and modern elements.

Contemporary legends are often sinister or frightening, such as those that circulated by email in the aftermath of the 2001 terrorist attacks in the USA. One message referred to an Afghan man who disappeared before the atrocity and warned his wife not to fly on 11 September and not to go to any shopping mall on 31 October. Versions of this story were received by an estimated five million email users around the world, including a friend of my partner who was so worried that he immediately copied it to his friends and acquaintances. In the USA the warning was taken so seriously that it was subject to an inquiry by the FBI who determined 'that the alleged threat is not credible'.[11] Agents traced the message to a young woman who sent the original to a friend on 5 October. She claimed she heard the story from a friend, who in turn heard it from the girl who had received the original warning. Attempts to trace her failed, as did the attempts to find the British soldiers who saw the Angel of Mons.

These modern legends circulate faster today because they have migrated from word of mouth onto the Internet. Despite the change of medium, they retain their traditional features and are given authenticity by the stress they place upon the closeness and reliability of their source: the person who tells them as true. We tend to believe rumours if the informant is someone we know and trust, but the context in which they are told is equally important. We may, for instance, be more inclined to believe a rumour if we hear it from a trusted friend at a time of great stress or anxiety. War or terrorist threat is one good example. Folklorist

Sona Burnstein noted that:

> Conditions of stress or special situations such as war or disaster lend themselves particularly to the exercise of prejudice (sometimes otherwise dormant), the revival of folk belief, or the creation of new myths, or the flight of rumour. A notable characteristic of all these conditions is complete disregard of consistency.[12]

The Angel of Mons is a classic example of a rumour that was widely believed despite its many internal inconsistencies. Remember Miss Marrable who, clergymen assured their congregations, heard about the 'troop of angels' at Mons directly from two officers who saw them? If, however one begins to trace the story back to the original narrators, as Arthur Machen did, the chain becomes ever more extended and the source can rarely be clearly identified. Further authentication is often added to these legends by localization of the setting to a familiar place or a particular, well-known person. When these are checked, one finds the source is actually second-hand and not unique. The same or a similar story has been told in dozens of different localities, by many different people, who all believe it happened to someone they know. In the vast majority of examples there may in fact be no real event as the ultimate source. According to David Buchan:

> Whether or not the stories have a verifiable source, are in the limited literal sense 'true' is immaterial; what matters is that they circulate as true. So pervasive is their acceptance as true that they are sometimes printed as actual occurrences in magazines and newspapers.[13]

The power and longevity of the Angel of Mons can be compared to another contemporary legend, the alleged crash of a 'flying saucer' and its alien crew, at Roswell, New Mexico in July 1947. Many thousands of people today believe this story as true and furthermore, believe the governments of the world have conspired ever since to hide the 'truth' from the public. Folklorist Professor Jan Brunvand categorized the Roswell incident as a typical example of the conspiracies about 'the Secret Truth' in his system for the classification of contemporary legends.[14] In the case of Roswell, most protagonists agree there was an objectively real event that triggered the modern legend, such as the crash of a classified Air Force balloon project or rocket. The nature and origin of that event is the subject of an ongoing debate between believers and sceptics every bit as emotional and ferocious as that between Arthur Machen and the pro-Angel of Mons lobby in 1915.

In the case of the angels, the 'trigger' event is less clear-cut. Soldiers certainly testified to having unusual experiences in the retreat from Mons, but these seem to have been related to a range of recognized psychological and physiological factors related to exhaustion and sleep deprivation. Their accounts were later interpreted by the 'divine interventionists' (UFO believers in the Roswell context) as evidence in support of the idea that angels had protected the British Army. In this case, the original *idea* was undoubtedly inspired by the publication of Arthur Machen's fiction at a time when the British people were desperate for news of a miracle. In the cases of Roswell and Mons, the initial trigger stories were revived at a later date and eventually became legends during the latent process of telling and retelling. In both cases, eyewitnesses came forward years later with new versions or variations of the original narrative. When efforts are made to check these accounts, most are found to be exaggerated or even outright hoaxes.

In both examples, there are two distinct and divergent constituents of the 'myth': the popular legend told as true, accepted and believed by thousands; and the few certain facts. As time passes, so the two parts take on an independent life of their own and continue to grow apart. The few certain facts relating to the events at Mons have been summarized in Chapter 2. None of the official histories of the battle and subsequent retreat describe anything other than desperate fighting and exhausted soldiers. Few of the men who fought at Mons survived the first year of the war and of those that did fewer still testified *at the time* to having witnessed an angelic visitation. Others, such as John Ewings, spoke out decades afterwards, in his case on his 101st birthday. At such long distance, personal testimony is heavily contaminated, not only by the distortions of the memory, but also by exposure to the pervasive mythology that has grown up around the war. Military historians Alan S. Coulson and Michael E. Hanlon, authors of an incisive examination of the legend published on the Internet, decided:

> After reviewing every primary and secondary source we could find on the Battle of Mons, we are left with these facts: There is no documented case, single person or group of people named as actually claiming to have made a sighting of benign heaven-sent agents during either the Battle or the Retreat from Mons.[15]

Their conclusions are supported by comments made by historian Lyn Macdonald, who assures me that:

> in 25 years of research I have never known any soldier refer to this 'phenomenon' either by documentation in my extensive archive nor in the 1500 hours of oral recordings with veterans of the First World War.[16]

To be fair, Macdonald adds a caveat to the effect that this was not a topic she would have pursued with the many hundreds of veterans she had interviewed during her fieldwork. However, when the second-hand stories are examined objectively and in hindsight, their interest lies in the complete absence of any first-hand, authenticated accounts from named witnesses. Three factors stand out from analysis of their content and context:

- The presence of literary invention (the influence of 'The Bowmen');
- The power of propaganda and lies;
- The influence of ancient traditions and folklore.

What emerges from this cauldron of belief and invention is a legend that has little if any connection with real experience. The origins of the Angel of Mons lie not so much in the events of the war of movement that characterized August and September 1914, but rather in the bleak phase of trench warfare that followed. It was within this context that the British appealed for divine intervention to break the unremitting suffering and as a result were primed to accept stories that supported their beliefs despite a complete absence of evidence. As the stories spread, other soldiers reinterpreted a range of unusual experiences on the battlefield within the context provided by the Angel of Mons. War historian Philip Haythornthwaite provided a good example in his account of myths and legends in the *World War One Source Book*:

> An employee of the author's grandfather was totally convinced that he *had* seen the angel; and although before the war he was known as a man over-fond of hard drink, after Mons he became not only a teetotal but a pillar of the community, apparently for no other reason than what he claimed to have experienced on the retreat.[17]

I wrote to Haythornthwaite asking if he had a record of the name of the soldier and his regiment. Given my own experience, I was not surprised to learn that the soldier's identity was unknown and the story was second-hand. The author heard the story from his father who knew the soldier. The circumstances were typically problematic:

> Apparently what he described was less of the physical appearance of a figure in the sky ... but more of a very, very bright light which appeared over the battlefield; and he justified his description of this light by saying, apparently, that it *must* have been an Angel, as nothing else could have stopped the advancing enemy on this particular occasion, as he and his comrades were so utterly exhausted as to be almost incapable of any meaningful resistance.

Haythornthwaite believed this was less a case of the soldier believing that he had seen something unusual in the sky at the time, but more that his account had been influenced by what he had read about the Angel of Mons years later. Whatever the case, the story was, he believed, a product of:

> the dreadful predicament in which he and his comrades had been placed, wonderment at why the enemy paused in an attack that would have defeated them, combined, perhaps, with a remembrance of a natural atmospheric effect of sunlight and clouds; and thus presuming that what he saw *must* have been the Angel that someone else had reported.[18]

The powerful influence of suggestion is present in all the narratives and is underlined by a curious sequel to this particular story. When a question enquiring about the Angel of Mons was published in a local newspaper, Haythornthwaite replied with a rational explanation. Immediately afterwards two people replied to him personally to the effect that he was mistaken because their fathers also claimed to have seen the Angel(s) of Mons. This outcome was an uncanny repetition of the position in which Arthur Machen found himself during the First World War. Haythornthwaite replied to both writers in an attempt to elicit any further information, but none was forthcoming.

The only conclusion we can draw is that people *want to believe in angels*. The elusive nature of direct, first-hand evidence for visions at Mons has led many to suspect that the source of the legend lay not on the Western Front, but in England. In 1915 when the war had reached stalemate, rumours originating from the first months of the conflict became immortalized at home by a stream of newspaper stories, pamphlets and books that presented the legend as fact. People wanted to believe in it, and did not think to question the evidence. The stories of divine or supernatural visions that emerged during the war seemed to follow a pattern. Initially there were stories of dramatic, miraculous intervention in the fighting followed by smaller-scale, individual apparitions as the tide of war turned and the stalemate in the trenches was broken. These changes indicate to me that the stories evolved in response to the changing spiritual needs of both the soldiers and the people at home in Britain. By the end of the war, belief in the Angel of Mons was so pervasive that it had become, as Paul Fussell noted, 'unpatriotic, almost treasonable, to doubt it'. In this case a legend had become a part of the social history of Britain, and thousands of people both in Britain and across the world were led to believe that divine powers had intervened on the Allied side at a decisive point in the first battle, and that the course of the conflict had been changed as a result.

It is appropriate that myths are reinvented at a time of great danger and sacrifice as they have been since the very earliest times. As Trevor Wilson wrote in *The Myriad Faces of War* (1986), the Angel of Mons was ultimately the outcome of 'the craving for certainty that some force, earthly or supernatural, would always be to hand to snatch victory out of defeat'.[19] It is unfortunate that almost a century after the events, the Angel of Mons has been relegated to a historical curiosity, a popular but unfounded belief or 'myth'. This is clearly not the case, as this definition of myth tends to downplay the important role belief in the story played in British society during the 1914–18 war. As we have seen, a myth cannot always be defined as 'true' or 'false' but is more of an active force that helps us all make sense of events that appear to be mysterious or supernatural in origin.

Histories of the First World War tell us much about the political and economic machinations that set Europe on the road to war and the deprivations suffered by soldiers and civilians during the course of the conflict. The myths and legends that underpin history contribute to the motivations for war and ultimately peace, but tend to be overlooked by the modern obsession to explain and account in a rational way for all human actions and decisions. Although there were claims that battlefield visions had been reported by soldiers from other nations, none have had the same impact upon the consciousness of a single nation as the Angel of Mons had on the British. It was particularly significant for the British Empire and its army because of its great military traditions characterized by the bowmen of Agincourt and the special protection of St George.

In 1914, Britain was an imperial nation with a long tradition of success in combat that was sustained by belief in divine intervention. At Mons, the cream of the British Army narrowly escaped defeat at the hands of the Germans during the first month of the war. Many believed it was a miracle, and Arthur Machen's story provided a perfect conduit for the creation and transmission of a reassuring modern legend that was based upon ancient precedents. His literary skills gave the story a resonance and power that would sustain it long beyond his lifetime. It was a legend that had an important and positive function during the war, sustaining hope, boosting patriotic optimism and shoring up faltering faith during the dark days of the Somme, Passchendaele and all the other disastrous battles that almost exterminated a generation of young men. Today the Angel of Mons remains one of the undying icons of that war and lives on as a symbol of the loss of innocence that was the legacy it left upon the British psyche. This legend re-emerged for a brief spell during the national crisis of 1940, at Dunkirk and during the Battle of Britain. Maybe one day the angels will be needed again.

The bowmen

by Arthur Machen

I t was during the Retreat of the Eighty Thousand, and the authority of the censorship is sufficient excuse for not being more explicit. But it was on the most awful day of that awful time, on the day when ruin and disaster came so near that their shadow fell over London far away; and, without any certain news, the hearts of men failed within them and grew faint; as if the agony of their brothers on the battlefield had entered into their souls.

On this dreadful day, then, when three hundred thousand men in arms with all their artillery swelled like a flood against the little English army, there was one point above all other points in our battle line that was for a time in awful danger, not merely of defeat, but of utter annihilation. With the permission of censorship and of the military experts, this corner may, perhaps, be described as a salient, and if this angle were crushed and broken, then the English force as a whole would be shattered, the Allied left would be turned, and Sedan would inevitably follow.

All the morning the German guns had thundered and shrieked against this corner and against the thousand or so men who held it. The men joked at the shells and found funny names for them, and had bets about them and greeted them with scraps of music-hall songs. But the shells came on and burst and tore good Englishmen limb from limb, and tore brother from brother, and as the heat of the day increased, so did the fury of that terrific

Originally published in the London *Evening News*, 29 September 1914. 'The Bowmen' (Copyright Arthur Machen): By courtesy of A.M. Heath & Co. Ltd.

cannonade. There was no help, it seemed. The English artillery was good, but there was not nearly enough of it; it was being steadily battered into scrap iron.

There comes a moment in a storm at sea when people say to one another: 'It is at its worst; it can blow no harder,' and then there is a blast ten times more fierce than any before it. So it was in these British trenches.

There were no stouter hearts in the whole world than the hearts of those men; but even they were appalled as this seven times heated hell of the German cannonade fell upon them and destroyed them. And at this very moment they saw from their trenches that a tremendous host was moving against their lines. Five hundred of the thousand remained, and as far as they could see the German infantry was pressing on against them, column upon column, a grey world of men, ten thousand of them as it appeared afterwards.

There was no hope at all. They shook hands, some of them. One man improvised a new version of the battle song: 'Goodbye, goodbye to Tipperary,' ending with 'And we shan't get there!' And they all went on firing steadily. The officers pointed out that such an opportunity for fancy shooting might never occur again, the Germans dropped line after line, the Tipperary humorist added, 'What price Sidney-street?' and the few machine guns did their best. But everybody knew it was of no use. The dead grey bodies lay in companies and battalions; but others came on and on, and they swarmed and stirred and advanced from beyond and beyond.

'World without end. Amen,' said one of the British soldiers, with some irrelevance as he took aim and fired. And then he remembered a queer vegetarian restaurant in London where he had once or twice eaten queer dishes of cutlets made of lentils and nuts that pretended to be steaks. On all the plates in the restaurant there was printed a figure of St George in blue, with the motto, *Adsit Anglis Sanctus Georgius* – may Saint George be a present help to the English. The soldier happened to know Latin and other useless things, and now as he fired at his man in the grey advancing mass – 300 yards away – he uttered the pious vegetarian motto. He went on firing to the end, and at last Bill on his right had to clout him cheerfully over the head to make him stop, pointing out as he did so that the King's ammunition cost money, and was not lightly to be wasted in drilling funny patterns into dead Germans.

For as the Latin scholar uttered his invocation he felt something between a shudder and an electric shock pass through his body. The roar of the battle died down in his ears to a gentle murmur; instead of it, he says, he heard a great voice and a shout louder than a hundred-peal, crying, 'Array, array, array!'

His heart grew hot as a burning coal, it grew cold as ice within him, as it seemed to him that a tumult of voices answered to his summons. He heard, or seemed to hear thousands shouting: 'St George! St George!'

'Ha! messire, ha! Sweet saint, grant us good deliverence!'

'St George for merry England!'

'Harow! Harow! Monseigneur St George, succour us!'

'Ha! St George! Ha! St George; a long bow and a strong bow.'

'Knight of Heaven, aid us.'

And as the soldier heard these voices he saw before him, beyond the trench, a long line of shapes, with a shining about them. They were like men who drew the bow, and with another shout, their cloud of arrows flew singing and tingling through the air towards the German host.

The other men in the trench were firing all the while. They had no hope; but they aimed just as if they had been shooting at Bisley.

Suddenly one of them lifted up his voice in plain English.

'Gawd help us!' he bellowed to the man next to him, 'but we're blooming marvels! Look at those grey ... gentlemen, look at them! D'ye see them? They're not going down in dozens, nor in 'undreds: it's thousands, it is. Look! Look! There's a regiment gone while I'm talking to ye.'

'Shut it!' the other soldier bellowed, taking aim, 'what are ye talking about?'

But he gulped with astonishment even as he spoke: for, indeed, the grey men were falling by the thousand. The English could hear the gutteral scream of the German officers, the crackle of their revolvers as they shot the reluctant; and still line after line crashed to the earth.

All the while the Latin-bred soldier heard the cry.

'Harow! Harow! monseigneur, dear saint, quick to our aid! St George help us!'

The singing arrows darkened the air; the heathen horde melted from before them.

'More machine guns!' Bill yelled to Tom.

'Don't hear them,' Tom yelled back, 'but thank God anyway; they've got it in the neck.'

In fact, there were ten thousand dead German soldiers left before that salient of the English army, and consequently there was no Sedan. In Germany, a country ruled by scientific principles, the Great General Staff decided that the contemptible English must have employed turpinite shells, as no wounds were discernible on the bodies of the dead German soldiers. But the man what knew what nuts tasted like when they called themselves steak, knew also that St George had brought his Agincourt bowmen to help the English.

Bibliography

A great number of books, pamphlets and limited edition offprints dedicated to the Angel of Mons appeared from 1915–17 but none remain in print today. The books by Machen, Shirley, Begbie and Campbell are the best known and the various editions have become collectors' items in recent years. They are listed below in order of publication:

Ralph Shirley, *The Angel Warriors at Mons*, London: Newspaper Publicity Company, August 1915

Arthur Machen, *The Bowmen and Other Legends of the War*, London: Simpkin, Marshall, Hamilton, Kent & Co., first edition August 1915. Contents: Introduction by Arthur Machen, 'The Bowmen', 'The Soldiers' Rest', 'The Monstrance', 'The Dazzling Light', 'The Bowmen and other Noble Ghosts' (by the Londoner, Oswald Barron), Postcript by Arthur Machen. Second edition published September 1915, with expanded introduction and two new legends of the war: 'The Little Nations' and 'The Men from Troy'.

Harold Begbie, *On the Side of the Angels*, London: Hodder & Stoughton, September 1915. Several further editions including a fifth in 1917.

Phyllis Campbell, *Back of the Front*, London: George Newnes & Co., September 1915.

Of the lesser-known booklets and compendiums few copies survive today and in some cases first editions are extremely rare and can be consulted only at the British Library and the library of the Imperial War Museum in London. These are listed below in chronological order of publication. Some of these publications are listed on the Imperial War Museum's information sheet, *The Angels of Mons*, no. 24, (booklist 1256A, undated).

Thomas W.II. Crosland, *Find the Angels: The Showmen, a Legend of the War*, London: T. Werner Laurie, 1915.

Revd George Bassett, *Guardian Angels: With Special Reference to the Vision of Angels after the Retreat from Mons in August 1914* [a sermon reprinted as a pamphlet], Eastbourne: W.H. Smith & Son, 1915.

Revd William Leathem, *The Comrade in White* [booklet], London: H.R. Allenson, 1915.

Anon, *The Visions of Mons and Ypres: Their Meaning and Purpose* [pamphlet], London: Robert Banks & Son, 1915 (second edition 1916).

John J. Pearson, *The Rationale of the Angel Warriors at Mons* [pamphlet], London: Christian Globe, 1916. Three editions.

I.E. Stilwell Taylor, *Angels, Saints and Bowmen of Mons: An Answer to Mr Arthur Machen and Mr Harold Begbie* [pamphlet], London: Theosophical Publishing Society, 1916.

A Churchwoman, *The Chariots of God* (illustrated by Alfred Pearse), London: A.H. Stockwell, 1915.

R. Thurston Hopkins with A.F. Phillips, *War and the Weird*, London: Simpkin, Marshall & Co., 1916.

Charles Warr, *The Unseen Host: Stories of the Great War*, Paisley: Alexander Gardner, 1916. Ten editions, the last in 1928.

Rosa Stuart, *Dreams and Visions of the War*, London: C. Arthur Pearson Ltd, 1917.

Hereward Carrington, *Psychical Phenomena and the War*, London and New York: T. Werner Laurie, 1919.

There have been few detailed studies of the Angel of Mons outside more general discussions of wartime myths and legends. The first chapter in John Terraine's *The Smoke and the Fire: Myths and Anti-Myths of War 1861–1945* (London: Sidgwick & Jackson, 1980) was one of the first to scrutinise the story. A more accomplished recent example is that by James Hayward in *Myths and Legends of the First World War* (Stroud: Sutton, 2002), chapter 3.

The earliest contemporary investigation of the legend was the article by Mrs W.H. Salter (Helen de G. Verrall), 'An Enquiry Concerning "The Angels at Mons"' published in *Journal of the Society for Psychical Research*, December 1915. The next in-depth study did not arrive until 1982 when the part-work magazine *The Unexplained* published three articles by Melvin Harris. An updated version of Harris's paper, 'The Angels with Newspaper Wings' appeared in *Faunus* 6, the magazine of the Friends of Arthur Machen (2001).

Kevin McClure's self-published pamphlet, *Visions of Bowmen and Angels*, appeared in 1993 and is now available via the Internet at ‹http://www.magonia.demon.co.uk/abwatch/stars/bowmen.html›.

Another fine study, 'The Case of the Elusive Angel of Mons', by military historians Alan S. Coulson and Michael E. Hanlon for the *Legends and Traditions of the Great War* website, is also available online at: ‹http://www.worldwar1.com/heritage/angel.htm›.

The original research that forms the basis for this book began with help from a small research grant from the British Academy. The results were published in the research article, 'Rumours of Angels: A Legend of the First World War' in *Folklore*, vol. 113 (2002).

The First World War

There are a great many general histories of the First World War that mention the Angel of Mons. One of the best known is A.J.P. Taylor, *The First World War: An*

Illustrated History, first published in London by Hamish Hamilton in 1963. I found Martin Gilbert's *First World War* (London: HarperCollins, 1994) the most accessible of the recent detailed accounts of the conflict in the west. Also helpful from the European perspective was Professor Richard Holmes *The Western Front* (London: BBC Publications, 1999).

For the testimony and accounts of ordinary soldiers Lyn Macdonald's series of volumes are unsurpassed. I found *1914: The Days of Hope* (Harmondsworth: Penguin, 1989), *1915: The Death of Innocence* (Harmondsworth: Penguin, 1997) and *Voices and Images of the Great War* (Harmondsworth: Penguin, 1991) particularly useful.

For the social context Paul Fussell's *The Great War in Modern Memory* (London: Oxford University Press, 1975) remains a standard work. For the accounts of nurses I used Vera Brittain, *Testament of Youth: An Autobiographical Study of the Years 1900–1925*, first published 1933 (London: Virago, 1978). Additional material can be found in Enid Bagnold, *Diary without Dates* (London: Virago Press, 1978) and Lyn Macdonald, *The Roses of No Man's Land* (London: Michael Joseph, 1980).

The most comprehensive account of the battle of Mons from a military perspective is the study by David Ascoli, *The Mons Star: The British Expeditionary Force 1914* (London: Harrap, 1981). However, a more accessible account of the military campaign fought by the BEF in Belgium and France in August–September 1914 is that by Professor Richard Holmes in his *Complete War Walks: British Battles from Hastings to Normandy* (London: BBC publications, 2003). Also helpful was Kate Caffrey, *Farewell, Leicester Square* (London: Andre Deutsch, 1980).

Arthur Machen

Until recently much of Arthur Machen's writings were out of print and hard to find. The 'Machen revival' has seen the reissue of much of his back catalogue. At the time of writing his 'legends of the war' await a reprint. A number of autobiographies and studies of Machen were consulted for the writing of this book. These are listed below:

John Gawsworth's unpublished MS, *The Life of Arthur Machen* (*circa* 1930), held by the University of California. I was able to consult this account, by one of Machen's closest friends, thanks to Roger Dobson and the Friends of Arthur Machen.

Adrian Goldstone and Wesley Sweetser, *A Bibliography of Arthur Machen* (Austin: University of Texas Press, 1965).

Aidan Reynolds and William Charlton, *Arthur Machen: A Short Account of His Life and Work* (London: Richards Press, 1963).

Mark Valentine, *Arthur Machen* (Bridgen: Seren Books, 1995).

One recent academic study consulted was Adrian Eckersley's PhD thesis, *The Fiction of Arthur Machen: Fantastic Writing in the Context of Materialism*. Birkbeck College, University of London, 1995.

The Friends of Arthur Machen publish a newsletter, *Machenalia*, and a journal, *Faunus*. For subscription details contact Jeremy Cantwell, 78 Greenwich South Street, Greenwich, London SE10 8UN, or visit the society website at: ‹http://www.machensoc.demon.co.uk›.

Supernatural themes

Unsurpassed in this field of study is Gillian Bennett, *Traditions of Belief: Women, Folklore and the Supernatural Today* (Harmondsworth: Penguin, 1987). A new updated version was published as *Alas, Poor Ghost!: Traditions of Belief in Story and Discourse* (Logan: Utah University Press, 1999).

The literature on religious visions is patchy and objective surveys are few and far between. The most recent popular accounts are: Hilary Evans, *Visions – Apparitions – Alien Visitors* (Wellingborough: Aquarian Press, 1984) and Kevin McClure, *The Evidence for Visions of the Virgin Mary* (Wellingborough: Aquarian Press, 1983), both out of print. For the most recent study of contemporary angel beliefs see Emma Heathcote-James, *Seeing Angels: True Contemporary Accounts of Hundreds of Angelic Experiences* (London: John Blake, 2002), based on her PhD thesis at the University of Birmingham.

For the role of the supernatural in the wartime I consulted: Hilary Evans, *Intrusions: Society and the Paranormal* (London: Routledge & Kegan Paul, 1982); Joe Cooper, *The Case of the Cottingley Fairies* (London: Robert Hale, 1990); and Malcolm Gaskill, *Hellish Nell: Last of Britain's Witches* (London: Fourth Estate, 2001).

Notes and references

Dates given immediately after some book titles denote year of original publication.

Introduction

1 Rosa Stuart, *Dreams and Visions of the War*, London: C. Arthur Pearson, 1917, pp. 62–64.
2 *The Guardian* (London), 25 August 2003.
3 *BBC News Online*, 6 April 2003.
4 Keith Thomas, *Religion and the Decline of Magic* (1971), Harmondsworth: Penguin, 1973, pp. 163–71, 487–90.
5 Don Vaughan, 'Relying on Luck', *The Retired Officer*, November 2002; *Pensacola* (Florida) *News-Journal*, 15 April 2003.
6 The Edward Lovett collection of soldier's charms is preserved by the Department of Exhibits and Firearms at the Imperial War Museum, London. The collection was the result of personal conversations with troops in London during the first three months of the war.
7 E.M.R. Ditmus, 'The Way Legends Grow,' *Folklore*, 85 (1974), 244–53.
8 Msgr James O'Neill, 'The True Story of Patton's Prayer,' *Review of the News*, 6 October 1971.
9 Martin Gilbert, *First World War* (1994), London: HarperCollins, 1995, p. 541.
10 Paul Fussell, *The Great War and Modern Memory*, Oxford: Oxford University Press, 1975, p. 115.
11 *The Concise Oxford Dictionary 9th Edition*, Oxford: Clarendon Press, 1995, p. 900.
12 Alan Dundas (ed.), *The Study of Folklore*, Englewood Cliffs, New Jersey: Prentice-Hall, 1965, p. 292.
13 Fussell, *Great War*, p. 115.
14 Kevin McClure, 'Visions of Comfort and Catastrophe,' in Hilary Evans (ed.), *Frontiers of Reality*, Wellingborough: Aquarian Press, 1989, p. 170.
15 See Alan S. Coulson and Michael Hanlon, 'The Elusive Angel of Mons', *Legends and Traditions of the Great War* online essay, ‹http://www.worldwar1.com/heritage/angel.htm›, p. 4.

16 Quoted in John Keel, *Operation Trojan Horse*, New York: Putnam, 1970, p. 201.

17 *Guardian Review* (London), 12 July 2003.

18 Charles Fort, *The Complete Books of Charles Fort*, London: Constable & Co., 1974, p. 577.

1 The unseen host

1 Richard Jefferies, *Wild Life in a Southern County*, London: Smith Elder, 1879, p. 113, quoted in Steve Roud, *The Penguin Guide to the Superstitions of Britain and Ireland*, London: Penguin, 2003, p. 6.

2 Allison Coudert, 'Angels', in Mircea Eliade (ed.), *The Encyclopedia of Religion*. London: Macmillan, 1987, pp. 282–86.

3 2 Kings 18–19.

4 2 Kings 6 : 8-17.

5 2 Maccabees 10 : 29-31; 11 : 8-12.

6 Harold Temperley, 'On the Supernatural Element in History', *Contemporary Review*, 15 August 1915, 189–90.

7 Joseph F. Blumrich, *The Spaceships of Ezekiel*, New York: Bantam, 1974. Others have interpreted Ezekiel's visions as being inspired by a rare natural phenomena such as the parhelia or mock suns.

8 Christina Hole, *Saints in Folklore*, London: G. Bell & Sons, 1965, pp. 23–24.

9 Hole, *Saints*, pp. 23–24, and *Folklore*, LV, March 1944, p. 48.

10 Revd Sabine Baring-Gould in Edward Hardy (ed.), *Curious Myths of the Middle Ages*, London: Jupiter, 1977, p. 100.

11 Hole, *Saints*, p. 30.

12 Anne Curry, *The Battle of Agincourt: Sources and Interpretations*, Woodbridge: The Boydell Press, 2000, pp. 89–96.

13 Richard Holmes, *Complete War Walks*, London: BBC, 1998, pp. 52–85.

14 R.H.C. Davis, *A History of Medieval Europe* (1957), London: Longman, 1979, pp. 13–14.

15 G.N. Garmonsway (ed.), *The Anglo-Saxon Chronicle*, London: Dent, 1972, p. 55.

16 Jennifer Westwood, *Albion: A Guide to Legendary Britain*, London: Paladin, 1987, p. 267.

17 *The Anglo-Saxon Chronicle*, p. 258.

18 Katherine Briggs, *A Dictionary of British Folk Tales*, London: Routledge, 1971, vol. 1, p. 476–7.

19 *Notes & Queries* series 1, vol. 7 (26 March 1853), p. 304.

20 John Michell and J.M. Rickard, *Phenomena: A Book of Wonders*, London: Thames & Hudson, 1977, p. 67.

21 Field Marshal Earl Roberts of Kandahar, *Forty-One Years in India*, London: Macmillan, 1921, p. 219.
22 Kevin McClure, *The Evidence for Visions of the Virgin Mary*, Wellingborough: Aquarian Press, 1983, pp. 48–57.
23 McClure, *Evidence*, p. 57.
24 Vera Brittain, *Testament of Youth* (1933), London: Virago, 1978, p. 409; Acts 2 : 20.
25 *Light*, 13 October 1917.

2 The Battle of Mons

1 Lyn Macdonald, *1914: The Days of Hope* (1987), Harmondsworth: Penguin, 1989, pp. 81–85.
2 'The Combat known as Lumecon', leaflet published by the Mons Tourist Board, 1996.
3 John F. Lucy, *There's a Devil in the Drum*, London: Faber, 1938, p. 734.
4 Quoted in Richard Holmes, *Complete War Walks*, London: BBC, 1998, p. 250.
5 Yves Bourdon, *Mons: Augustus 1914: Notes on the Mons Battlefield*, City of Mons Tourist Board, 1987.
6 *Daily Mirror* (London), 14 October 1954.
7 *Evening News* (London), 14 October 1915.
8 *Two Worlds* (London), 23 April 1915.
9 Regimental History, Middlesex Regiment, 24 August 1914.
10 Regimental History, 5th Regiment, Northumberland Fusiliers, 24 August 1914.
11 Frank Richards, *Old Soldiers Never Die*, London: Faber, 1964, p. 19.
12 Tim Carew, *Wipers*, London: Hamish Hamilton, 1976, pp. 198–99.
13 Quoted in Macdonald, *1914*, pp. 137–38.
14 Letter published in *This England*, winter 1982.
15 Macdonald, *1914*, p. 139.
16 Interview by Helen Madden, BBC Northern Ireland, 22 May 1980. Broadcast on BBC Radio 4, *The Making of an Urban Myth*, 22 October 2002.
17 Liverpool *Evening Express*, 26 August 1915.
18 Arch Whitehouse, *Epics and Legends of the First World War*, London: Frederick Muller, 1964, pp. 15–21.
19 Holmes, *Complete War Walks*, p. 258.
20 *Evening News*, 14 September 1915.
21 *Evening News*, 11 August 1915.
22 *Daily Mail* (London), 12 August 1915.
23 Harold Begbie, *On the Side of the Angels*, London: Hodder & Stoughton, 1915 (2nd edition), pp. 28–30.

24 *Daily Mail*, 18 August 1915.

25 Brigadier-General John Charteris, *At GHQ*, London: Cassell & Co., 1931, pp. 25–26.

26 Ralph Shirley, *The Angel Warriors at Mons*, London: Newspaper Publicity Company, 1915, p. 10.

27 Shirley, *Angel Warriors*, pp. 10–11.

28 *The Star* (Johannesburg, South Africa), 11 October 1914.

29 Begbie, *On the Side of the Angels*, p. 58.

30 Major-General Sir John Hanbury-Williams, *Emperor Nicholas II as I Knew Him*, London: A.L. Humphreys, 1922, diary entry 24 November 1916.

3 Rumours of war

1 *Daily Dispatch* (Manchester), 7 August 1914; *Daily Mail* (London), 8 August 1914; Hansard (House of Commons), 8 August 1914.

2 *Keighley News* (Keighley, Yorkshire), 15 August 1914.

3 Robert E. Bartholomew and Benjamin Radford, *Hoaxes, Myths and Manias*, Armherst, New York: Prometheus, 2003, pp. 166–74.

4 Hansard (House of Commons), 18 November, 21 November 1912.

5 Douglas Robinson, *The Zeppelin in Combat*, Pennsylvania: Schiffer Publishing, 1994, p. 36.

6 Nigel Watson (ed.), *The Scareship Mystery*, Corby: Domra Publications, 2000.

7 James Hayward, *Myths and Legends of the First World War*, Stroud: Sutton, 2002, pp. 1–30.

8 *Daily Graphic* (London), 23 January 1915.

9 Hansard (House of Commons), 9 February 1915.

10 National Archives reference: AIR 1/565/15/16/89.

11 National Archives reference: AIR 1/720 36/1/6.

12 Michael McDonagh, *In London during the Great War*, London: Eyre & Spottiswoode, 1935, pp. 21–22.

13 *Manchester Guardian*, 31 August 1914.

14 *New York Times*, 6 September 1914.

15 See Nigel Watson and Granville Oldroyd, 'Snow on Their Boots,' in *Fortean Studies* 2 (1999), pp. 189–90.

16 Brigadier-General John Charteris, *At GHQ*, London: Cassell & Co., 1931, p. 38.

17 *Daily News* (London), 7 September 1914 quoting Central News Agency.

18 Hayward, *Myths and Legends of the First World War*, p. 34.

19 *Daily News* (London), *The Star* (London), 14 September 1914.

20 *South Wales Echo* (Cardiff), 14 September 1914.

21 *Manchester Courier, Daily News*, 15 September 1914.

22 Hayward, *Myths*, p. 24.

23 *Cumberland News* (Carlisle, Cumbria), 1 May 1915.

24 R.V. Jones, 'The Natural Philosophy of Flying Saucers', *Physics Bulletin*, 19 (July 1968), pp. 225–26.

25 Hayward, *Myths*, p. 40.

26 Hayward, *Myths*, pp. 41–42.

27 Hayward, *Myths*, pp. 43–44.

28 Bernard Newman, *The Flying Saucer*, London: Victor Gollancz, 1948, p. 10.

29 *Evening News*, 15 September 1914.

30 Lyn Macdonald, *1914: The Days of Hope* (1987), Harmondsworth: Penguin, 1989, p. 206.

31 Philip Gibbs, *Adventures in Journalism*. London: Heinemann 1923, p. 217.

32 Macdonald, *1914*, pp. 206–07.

33 Macdonald, *1914*, pp. 206–07. See also Lyn Macdonald, *Voices and Images of the Great War*, Harmondsworth: Penguin, 1991, p. 25.

34 Hansard (House of Commons), 31 August 1914.

4 The sinister genius

1 Mark Valentine, *Arthur Machen*, Bridgend: Seren Books, 1994, pp. 72–73.

2 Peter Buitenhuis, *The Great War of Words: Literature as Propaganda 1914–18 and after*, London: Batsford, 1989, p. 102.

3 Arthur Machen, *The Bowmen and Other Legends of the War*, London: Simpkin, Marshall & Co., 1915 (1st edition), p. 8.

4 *Evening News*, 20 October 1914.

5 *Daily Mail*, 28 July 1915.

6 *Evening News*, 29 September 1914.

7 John Gawsworth, *The Life of Arthur Machen*, unpublished MS, 1930, University of California.

8 Arthur Machen, 'Drake's Drum', *The Outlook*, vol. XLIII (1919); Arthur Machen, 'Munitions of War', in Cynthia Asquith (ed.), *The Ghost Book*, London: Hutchinson, 1936.

9 *Evening News*, 19 October 1915.

10 Kevin McClure, *Visions of Bowmen and Angels*, self-published, ‹http://www.magonia.demon.co.uk/abwatch/stars/bowmen.html›, pp. 2–3.

11 Machen, *Bowmen*, p. 10.

12 *Light* (London), 10 October 1914.

13 Granville Oldroyd, personal communication, 30 June 2003.

14 James Hayward, *Myths and Legends of the First World War*, Stroud: Sutton, 2002, p. 58.

15 Gawsworth, *Life*, ch. 18.
16 Machen, *Bowmen*, p. 15.
17 Gawsworth, *Life*, ch. 18.

5 The birth of a legend

1 Kevin McClure, *Visions of Bowmen and Angels*, self-published, ‹http://www.magonia.demon.co.uk/abwatch/stars/bowmen.html›, p. 3.
2 Melvin Harris, 'Angels with Newspaper Wings', *Faunus*, 6 (2001), note 7. Sir Thomas Caine (ed.), *King Albert's Book: A Tribute to the Belgian King and People from Representative Men and Women Throughout the World*, London: Daily Telegraph, 1914.
3 Lyn Macdonald, *1914: The Days of Hope* (1987), Harmondsworth: Penguin, 1989, p. 212.
4 Harris, 'Angels' (no page nos.).
5 Brigadier-General John Charteris, *At GHQ*, London: Cassell & Co., 1931, p. 75.
6 *Birkenhead News* (Birkenhead, Cheshire), 27 October 1915.
7 *Light*, 8 May 1915.
8 Alfred Sinnett, 'Meteorites and the World Crisis', *Occult Review*, May 1915, p. 271.
9 Arthur Machen, *The Bowmen and Other Legends of the War*, London: Simpkin, Marshall & Co., 1915 (1st edition), p. 18.
10 *Weekly Dispatch* (London), 18 April 1915; *The Universe*, 30 April 1915.
11 *Light*, 15 May 1915.
12 *Light*, 15 May 1915.
13 Ralph Shirley, 'Notes of the Month', *Occult Review*, July 1915, p. 7.
14 *Hereford Times*, 3 July 1915.
15 Mark Valentine, *Arthur Machen*, Bridgend: Seren Books, 1994, p. 101.
16 *Hereford Times*, 3 April 1915; Anon: 'St George's Day/The Bowmen', *All Saints'* (Clifton) *Parish Magazine*, April 1915, Bristol Record Office.
17 *Bladud* (Bath Society paper), 9 June 1915.
18 Revd M.P. Gillson, 'Vicar's Letter', *All Saints'* (Clifton) *Parish Magazine*, June 1915, Bristol Record Office.
19 Anon, 'The Angelic Guard at Mons', *All Saints'* (Clifton) *Parish Magazine*, June 1915.
20 W.H. Salter, 'An Enquiry Concerning the "Angels at Mons" ', *Journal of the Society for Psychical Research*, December 1915, p. 114.
21 *Evening News*, 16 July 1915.
22 *Church of Ireland Gazette* (Dublin), 30 July 1915.
23 *Evening News*, 30 July 1915.

24   *Occult Review*, July 1915, p. 9.
25   *Occult Review*, July 1915, pp. 7–9.
26   Manfred Hiebl, 'Die Angels of Mons', ‹http://www.manfredhiebl.de/ angelsofmons/htm›. 'There are no reports from any Germans that the vision, angel of bowmen were seen in the sky over Mons.'
27   *Daily Mail*, 21 August 1915.
28   John J. Pearson, *The Rationale of the Angel Warriors at Mons*, 3rd edition, London: Christian Globe, 1916, p. 10.
29   Walter Raleigh, *The War in the Air*, vol. 1, Oxford: Clarendon Press, 1922, p. 343.
30   *Evening News*, 21 June 1915.
31   *Daily Chronicle* (London), 15 June 1915.
32   *Evening News*, 17 June 1915.
33   *Sunderland Echo*, 16 August 1915.
34   Ralph Shirley, *Prophecies and Omens of the Great War*, London: William Rider, 1914, p. 26.
35   *Sunderland Echo*, 16 August 1915.

6 Ministering angels

1   *Sheffield Telegraph*, 23 July 1915.
2   *Occult Review*, July 1915.
3   *Evening News*, 31 July 1915.
4   Phyllis Campbell, 'The Angelic Leaders', *Occult Review*, August 1915, pp. 166–70.
5   Campbell, 'The Angelic Leaders', pp. 166–70.
6   Phyllis Campbell, *Back of the Front*, London: George Newnes, 1915, pp. 113–14.
7   *Sheffield Telegraph*, 3 June 1915.
8   *Evening News*, 3 June 1915.
9   Arthur Machen, *The Bowmen and Other Legends of the War*, London: Simpkin, Marshall & Co., 1915 (1st edition), p. 80.
10   *Evening News*, 18 August 1915.
11   Campbell, 'The Angelic Leaders', pp. 166–70.
12   Harold Begbie, *On the Side of the Angels*, London: Hodder & Stoughton, 1915 (2nd edition), p. 64.
13   *Evening News*, 18 August 1915.
14   Vera Brittain, *Testament of Youth* (1933), London: Virago, 1978, pp. 144–45.
15   Michael Murphy (ed.), *Starrett vs Machen: A Record of Discovery and Correspondence*, St Louis: Autolycus Press, 1977, p. 51.

16 Melvin Harris, 'Where Angels Take a Bow', *The Unexplained*, 1982, p. 2846–50.

17 James Hayward, *Myths and Legends of the First World War*, Stroud: Sutton, 2002, pp. 82–84.

18 Brittain, *Testament*, pp. 415–16.

19 Owen Spencer Watkins, *With French in France and Flanders*, London: Charles H. Kelly, 1915, p. 43.

20 Melvin Harris, 'Ministering Angels', *The Unexplained*, 1982, p. 2895.

21 Quoted in Campbell, *Back*, p. 11.

22 *The Times Literary Supplement*, 28 October 1915.

23 Campbell, *Back*, pp. 31–32.

24 Campbell, *Back*, pp. 116–18.

7 Angels that refuse to die

1 Henry Danielson, *Arthur Machen: A Bibliography*, London: Henry Danielson, 1923, p. 43.

2 Arthur Machen, *Tales of Horror and the Supernatural*, London: John Baker, 1944, pp. 335–52.

3 *Evening News*, 10 August 1915.

4 Harold Begbie, *The Amazing Dreams of Andrew Latter* (1904), edited by Jack Adrian, Ashcroft, British Colombia: Ash Tree Press, 2002.

5 Harold Begbie, *On the Side of the Angels*, London: Hodder & Stoughton, 1915 (2nd edition), p. 9.

6 Begbie, *On the Side*, p. 21.

7 Michael Murphy (ed.), *Starrett vs Machen: A Record of Discovery and Correspondence*, St Louis: Autolycus Press, 1977, p. 51; *Evening News*, 9 September 1915.

8 From 'Arthur Machen: Replies & Notes to Questionnaires of John Gawsworth preparing his authorised "Life of Arthur Machen"' (Autumn 1930), Department of Special Collections Research Library, UCLA. Thanks to Roger Dobson for supplying this reference.

9 W.H. Salter, 'An Enquiry Concerning the "Angels at Mons"', *Journal of the Society for Psychical Research*, December 1915, pp. 111–12.

10 Arthur Machen, *The Bowmen and Other Legends of the War*, London: Simpkin, Marshall & Co., 1915 (1st edition), pp. 24–25.

11 *Daily Mail*, 24 August 1915; 2 September 1915.

12 Machen, *Bowmen*, (2nd edition), p. 39.

13 T.W.H. Crosland, *Find the Angels: The Showmen, A Legend of the War*, London: T. Werner Laurie, 1915, p. 2.

14 *Evening News*, 6 October 1915.

15 'The Angels of Mons', *This England*, winter 1982.
16 Dennis Gifford, *The British Film Catalogue 1895–1985*, London: David & Charles, 1973: entry no. 05857, *The Angels of Mons*.
17 William Dudley, 'The Setting for the Big Picnic', London: Promenade Productions, 1996.
18 A highly colourful version of the Private Cleaver story appears in Tim Healey, 'The Angels of Mons', *Great Mysteries of the 20th Century*, London: Reader's Digest Association, 1996, p. 114; reproduced by Joseph Trainor (ed.), '1914: Angels on the Battlefield', *UFO Roundup*, vol. 7, no. 7 (10 September 2002).
19 *Sunday Times*, 11 March 2001.
20 Victoria Jenkins, 'In Search of Angels', *Cotswold Life*, November 2001, pp. 143–44.
21 David Clarke, 'Angels of the Battlefield', *Fortean Times*, 170 (May 2003), pp. 30–35.
22 *The Sun* (London), 30 April 2001.
23 Posted on the Doidge's Angel weblog, ‹www.doidgesangel.com/blogger.html› 4 May 2001.
24 *The Making of an Urban Myth*, Radio 4, 22 October 2003.
25 Personal communication from Danny Sullivan, November 2002.

8 Phantoms of No Man's Land

1 *Light*, 5 June 1915.
2 Revd W.H. Leathem, *The Comrade in White*, London: H.R. Allenson, 1916, pp. 5–6.
3 Ralph Shirley, 'The White Comrade', *Occult Review*, April 1916, p. 219.
4 Harold Begbie, *On the Side of the Angels*, London: Hodder & Stoughton,1915 (2nd edition), pp. 78–79.
5 *The Two Worlds* (London), 25 June 1915.
6 *Light*, 25 June 1915.
7 Mary Jane Holt, 'The Truth about the 91st Psalm', *The Daily Citizen* (Fayette City, Georgia), 9 March 2003.
8 Kevin McClure, *Visions of Bowmen and Angels*, self-published, ‹http://www.magonia.demon.co.uk/abwatch/stars/bowmen.html›, p. 11.
9 *Weekly Dispatch* (London), 21 March 1915.
10 *Occult Review*, May 1915, 271.
11 See Hilary Evans, *Intrusions: Society and the Paranormal*, London: Routledge, 1982, p. 144.
12 Arthur Conan Doyle, *The British Campaign in France and Flanders*, London: Hodder & Stoughton, 1916.

13 Arthur Conan Doyle, *The Edge of the Unknown*, London: John Murray, 1930.
14 See Malcolm Gaskill, *Hellish Nell: Last of Britain's Witches*, London: Fourth Estate, 2002, pp. 56–58.
15 Richard Holmes, *The Western Front*, London: BBC Publications, 1999, p. 63.
16 *Light*, 24 June 1916.
17 Peter Buitenhuis, *The Great War of Words: Literature as Propaganda 1914–18 and after*, London: Batsford, 1989, pp. 172–73.
18 Personal communication from Mark Valentine, 16 June 2003.
19 Quoted in H.E. Ellis-Davidson (ed.), *Boundaries and Thresholds*, Stroud: The Thimble Press, 1993.
20 Vera Brittain, *Testament of Youth* (1933), London: Virago, 1978, p. 416.
21 Alan S. Coulson and Michael Hanlon, 'The Elusive Angel of Mons', *Legends and Traditions of the Great War* online essay, ‹http://www.worldwar1.com/heritage/angel.htm›, p. 17.
22 Rosa Stuart, *Dreams and Visions of the War*, London: C. Arthur Pearson, 1917, pp. 71–72.
23 Begbie, *On the Side*, pp. 76–77.
24 Stuart, *Dreams*, p. 72–73.
25 *Evening News*, 3 July 1916.
26 Holmes, *Western Front*, p. 127.
27 *Illustrated London News* (London), 22 July 1916.
28 *Grays and Tilbury Gazette* (Grays, Thurrock, Essex), 17 August 1917.
29 *Grays and Tilbury Gazette*, 25 August 1917.
30 *Daily Mail*, 25 August 1917.
31 'The Angels of Mons', *This England*, winter 1982.
32 Captain C.W. Haywood, 'The White Cavalry', *Fate*, May–June 1951.
33 *Household Brigade Magazine*, winter 1942, pp. 136–37.

9 The hidden hand

1 Lord Arthur Ponsonby, *Falsehood in Wartime*, London: Allen & Unwin, 1928.
2 *Daily News and Leader*, 17 February 1930.
3 *Daily News and Leader*, 18 February 1930.
4 *Sunday Times*, 26 January 1997.
5 E.H.G. Barwell, *The Death Ray Man*, London: Hutchinson, 1944, pp. 123–24.
6 National Archives reference: FO 898/6.
7 'Magic at War', Channel 4 *Secret History*, June 2002.
8 James Hayward, *Myths and Legends of the First World War*, Stroud: Sutton, 2002, pp. 80–94; see also James Hayward, *The Bodies on the Beach*, Dereham: CD41 Publishing, 2001.

9 Philip Taylor, 'Propagandists at War: Working for the Secret Propaganda Bureau at Wellington House', *Gun Fire*, 34 (no date), pp. 14–16.

10 The 'crucified Canadian' claim was examined in a Channel 4 *Secret History* documentary of November 2002. See also *Sunday Times*, 1 December 2002; National Archives reference: FO 395/304.

11 John Terraine, *The Smoke and the Fire*, London: Sidgwick & Jackson, 1980, p. 18.

12 Brigadier-General John Charteris, *At GHQ*, London: Cassell & Co., 1931, p. v.

13 Liddell Hart Centre for Military Archives, King's College, London. Archive reference GB0099 KCLMA Charteris: 2/2 (1914–15).

14 *Fortean Times*, 140 (September 2003), 72.

15 National Archives reference: FO 395/147.

16 Hayward, *Myths*, p. 112–26; *The Times*, 22 October 1925; 4 November 1925; *New York Times*, 20 October 1925.

17 *Daily Mail*, 25 January 1940.

18 *Light*, 22 August 1940.

19 *Daily Mirror*, 8 November 1940.

20 *Daily Mail*, 8 November 1940.

21 *Daily Mail*, 12 November 1940; *Daily Mirror*, 15 November 1940.

22 Bob Rickard, 'Photos of the Gods', *Fortean Times*, 36, winter 1982, p. 38.

23 Rickard, 'Photos of the Gods', pp. 32–41.

24 *Psychic News* (London), 19 November 1977.

25 Nigel McCrery, *The Vanished Regiment*, London: Simon & Schuster 1992; reissued in 1999 as *All the King's Men*, London: Pocket Books.

26 *Sunday Dispatch* (London), 2 June 1940.

27 Harold T. Wilkins, *Mysteries Solved and Unsolved*, London: Odhams Press 1959, p. 165.

28 National Archives references: AVIA 7/1070 and AVIA 7/1300.

29 Personal communication from Sir Edward Fennessy, CBE, November 2001.

30 Roy Bullers, 'Angels – Not Always Blessed Creatures', *Newsletter of the RAF Air Defence Radar Museum*, RAF Neatishead, 35 and 36, April–July 2003, pp. 11–13.

10 Myth or miracle?

1 Quoted at the 20th International Perspectives on Contemporary Legend Conference, Sheffield, 24 July 2002.

2 Alan S. Coulson and Michael Hanlon, 'The Elusive Angel of Mons', *Legends and Traditions of the Great War* online essay, ‹http://www.worldwar1.com/heritage/angel.htm›, p. 3.

3 A.J.P. Taylor, *The First World War* (1963), Harmondsworth: Penguin, 1966, p. 29.

4 *The Times Saturday Review*, 11 November 1978.

5 W.H. Salter, 'An Enquiry Concerning the "Angels at Mons" ', *Journal of the Society for Psychical Research*, December 1915, pp. 117–18.

6 Arthur Machen, 'The True Story of the Angels of Mons', in Sir John Hammerton (ed.), *The Great War, I was There*, vol. 2, London: Amalgamated Press, 1938, pp. 86–87.

7 Kevin McClure, *Visions of Bowmen and Angels*, self-published, ‹http://www.magonia.demon.co.uk/abwatch/stars/bowmen.html›, p. 23.

8 McClure, *Visions*, pp. 23–24.

9 Arthur Machen, *The Autobiography of Arthur Machen*, London: Richards Press, 1951, pp. 167–8. Credit: Roger Dobson.

10 Carl Jung, *Flying Saucers* (1964), Princeton: Bollingen Series, 1978, p. 8.

11 FBI National Press Office, Washington DC, 15 October 2001.

12 Sona Burnstein, 'Folklore, Rumour and Prejudice', *Folklore*, 70, 1959, p. 367.

13 David Buchan, 'The Modern Legend', in John Widdowson and A.E. Green (eds.), *Language, Culture and Tradition*, Sheffield: British Sociology Association Conference Proceedings 1978, p. 3.

14 Jan Harold Brunvand, *The Choking Doberman*, New York: W. Norton & Co., 1984, p. 198.

15 Coulson and Hanlon, 'Elusive Angel', p. 17.

16 Personal communication from Lyn Macdonald, 14 November 2000.

17 Philip Haythornthwaite, *The World War One Sourcebook*, London: Cassell, 1992, p. 373.

18 Personal communication from Philip Haythornthwaite, 28 May 2003.

19 Trevor Wilson, *The Myriad Faces of War*, Cambridge: Polity Press, 1986, p. 740.

Index